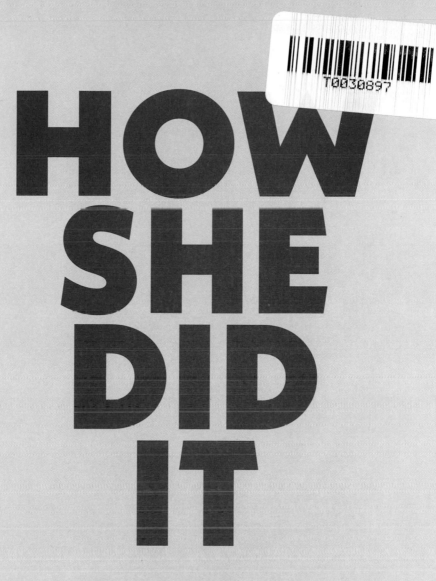

HOW SHE DID IT

A High-Performance Guide for Female Distance Runners
with Stories from the Women Who've Made It

Molly Huddle and Sara Slattery

RODALE

NEW YORK

Library of Congress Cataloging-in-Publication Data
is available upon request.

ISBN 978-0-593-23425-9
Ebook ISBN 978-0-593-23426-6

Printed in the United States of America

Book design by Andrea Lau
Cover design by Caroline Teagle Johnson
Cover photographs: *(front)* © Boston Globe/Getty Images; *(spine)* © John
Mabanglo/AFP/Getty Images; *(back, left to right)* © Mike Hewitt/Getty Images
Sport, © Olivier Morin/AFT/Getty Images, © John Walton/PA Images/Getty Images

Photograph Credits
Lisa Aguilar: page 244
Alamay: page 86
Alphaphoto: page 278
Apex: page 325 (16)
Scott Ash/Now News Group: page 325 (21)
John Dowd: pages 3, 7
Heleana Drossin: page 325 (23)
Margaret Gallagher: page 325 (18)
Getty Images: pages 58, 64, 90, 94
Harry How: page 329
Iowa Tempo Journal: page 328
Paul Martinez/Sar News Chula Vista: page 325 (27)
Kevin Morris: pages 150, 226, 304, 308
The Press Democrat: page 325 (25)
Victor Sailer: pages 107, 114, 154, 158, 177, 186, 194, 200, 212, 232, 238, 252, 258, 266,
270, 274, 282, 286, 290, 294, 324 (2, 3, 4, 5, 6, 7), 325 (24)
Don Sparks: page 51
Cheryl Bridges Flanagan Treworgy: pages 72, 73, 95, 118, 122, 128, 129, 134, 138, 146,
166, 170, 206, 218, 262, 298, 324 (11), 325 (22)
Images provided by subject: pages 324 and 325 (1, 8, 9, 10, 12, 13, 14, 15, 17, 19, 20, 26)

1st Printing

First Edition

To all the sport-loving girls out there,
may they become women empowered by the run

CONTENTS

INTRODUCTION

GREAT RUNS SPARK GREAT IDEAS.

In November 2019, we—Molly Huddle and Sara Slattery—were on just such a run in Scottsdale, Arizona, where Sara lives and Molly trains during the winter. We had a lot to talk about. All fall, a tension had been playing out in our circle, a ripple of conversation moving through the women's endurance sports community after a *New York Times* story revealed the messy underside of one female runner's up-and-down track career.

Nothing in the story surprised us: A talented female runner dominates the field in high school, hits transitional moments (puberty, college, professional life), and suddenly she's knocked off course. The bigger problem is, many such girls in sports don't return. We'd heard it all before. The story sometimes traced dark lines over the notorious arc of a female athlete's development: coercive coaching, hyperfocus on weight, underfueling, chronic injuries, all combined with a lack of acknowledgment or resources for things like mental health challenges. While Mary Cain, the runner profiled in the *Times*, has plenty of road left ahead of her for a comeback, hearing her broadcast her story to the world stirred something in us.

"This is the Foot Locker curse all over again," Molly said. (The Foot Locker Championship is for high school cross-country runners. Over the years, the girls who win the Foot Locker Championship rarely remain at the top of the sport in college and beyond.) "It's so frustrating—our most talented young women constantly getting derailed."

Sara nodded in agreement, thinking of the young women she coaches at Grand Canyon University, and the struggles they come to her with. "It doesn't have to go that way. There are a lot of women who have made it, and a lot of empowering stories to go with them." We wound past a huge saguaro cactus, quiet for a while.

"You know," Sara eventually said, "the success stories are just as important as Mary Cain's cautionary tale. We've all learned a lot over the years. If the women who've made it shared what they know"—the thought hung there as we shuffled single-file through a pair of boulders, kicking up dust—"then the girls coming up would understand the unique issues we face in this sport, and how to navigate them to stay in the game."

Sara turned to Molly in excitement as an idea began to form.

"Well, we know the women who've done it," Sara said. "We've raced alongside them. We could ask them to share their stories as a resource for the next generation."

A slow smile spread across Molly's face. "I would have loved to have that book when I started running—or during the tough times when I was doubting myself . . . or just not sure what lay ahead."

STORIES OF SUCCESS

We finished that run with a mission: We would write a book to show female runners and those around them that stories like Mary Cain's aren't inevitable or insurmountable (a mission Mary is tackling successfully today as well!). You can have a fulfilling relationship with running in your teens, 20s, and for the rest of your life. No matter what your race times are, you can reach your running potential without damaging your physical or mental health. And you can do all this while having a well-rounded life. You just need the right information and role models. That's what you'll find in this book—practical information straight from sports science experts at the top of their fields, and more role models than you'll know what to do with in the form of interviews with the inspiring women who've made it. We hope you'll be able to see yourself in some of these stories.

In our conversations with the experts, we discuss the areas that are most likely to become roadblocks for young runners. There's the balancing act that all runners face—how to run enough to perform well without getting injured—combined with the challenges of a growing body. There are uniquely female physical considerations, especially related to hormonal health. Many athletes have to manage psychological and mental health challenges. And, finally, there's the matter of eating properly in a society that bombards girls and women with unrealistic standards, and in a sport that can send the incorrect message that thinness equals speed. In the first section of this book, you'll get expert advice on how to handle all those issues.

Most of *How She Did It* is made up of stories from top female runners about, well, how they did it. In their own words, dozens of runners from different eras and different countries will tell you about their successes and setbacks, their greatest achievements and biggest disappointments. These legendary champions from yesterday and today were at one point all like you—a runner wanting to do her best. They all went on to have long, satisfying careers. Their stories should give you hope that whatever challenges you face as a runner, you can emerge stronger (and faster!). All of these women have amazing, unique stories to tell. They share their practical tips about training alongside the valuable lessons they've learned throughout life on and off the track.

WHO WE ARE, AND WHAT WE'RE ABOUT

We hope you'll consider us runners who are worth taking advice from, too—so we should probably tell you a little bit about ourselves.

SARA'S STORY

I did lots of sports as a kid—I found that competing brought out a confident side of me that wasn't always there in school or social settings. It came with an instinct that I should never quit.

As a preteen, I was especially drawn to swimming, in which I eventually qualified for the Junior National Championships. In middle school, several of my swimming friends also ran cross-country and track, and talked me into joining them. I was pretty quick to find success, and I won a city championship my first year. In my first high school cross-country season, I qualified for the Foot Locker Nationals. My high school coach, Sabrina Robinson, urged me to set big goals and see what I was truly capable of if I worked hard. Sabrina balanced this push with healthy recommendations, like regular strength training and good nutrition. I ended high school with 10 state titles, the US Junior 3,000-meter title, and a run at the Junior World Cross-Country Championships.

At the University of Colorado, I continued to improve. It turned out that my earlier fears about peaking in high school were unfounded. I had several setbacks in college, including mono, two plantar fascia tears, a posterior tibial tendon rupture, and three femoral stress reactions, but I was surrounded by people who believed in me and supported me. I saw teammates such as future Olympians Jorge Torress, Kara Goucher, and Dathan Ritzenhein come back from setbacks to win NCAA titles. I had a glimpse of future possibilities by watching the success of Colorado-grads-turned-pros like Shayne and Alan Culpepper and Adam Goucher. Seeing them every day made me believe I could achieve my goals. I graduated from Colorado as a four-time NCAA champion, and signed a pro contract with Adidas.

For me, finding a support system after college was tricky. There were only a few distance training groups—a few for marathoners and a few that were more track-focused. It was difficult dealing with contracts and finding a place that was good for me and my husband, Steve, who by then was a professional steeplechaser. I had three different coaches and training systems. There were successes and personal records (PRs)—15:08 for 5K, 31:57 for 10K, an Olympic alternate spot—but more disappointments. Consistency felt impossible. I needed more rest, a support system, consistent coaching, and regular physical therapy and chiropractic to keep me focused and healthy.

In 2016, after having two children, I ran the 10K at the Payton Jordan Invitational and came within 10 seconds of my PR, which qualified me for my fourth Olympic Trials and gave me the Olympic "A" standard of 32:15. I wondered if maybe I hadn't yet peaked.

That season, I became the head men's and women's cross-country coach at Grand Canyon University in Phoenix. I balanced being a new mom, a college coach, and an athlete. My husband, Steve, coached me. I was much more relaxed with my training, putting in consistent hard work but not stressing as much as my pre-kids, not-coaching self. I found myself wishing I had adopted that mentality sooner. I realized all I needed was a coach who believed in me, understood my goals, and supported me in reaching them.

Right after the Payton Jordan 10K, I tore my hamstring. I realized I couldn't balance all three things at the level I wanted to. I decided to focus my energy on being a mother and a coach. Coaching was a new challenge and allowed me to make a bigger impact. There aren't many NCAA Division I women head coaches of both men's and women's programs. I'm excited to be a part of building a program in my hometown, and to be among the new group of women who are leading the sport toward a healthier future.

MOLLY'S STORY

I grew up in upstate New York. I wanted to run after watching my dad run local road races—I thought it was cool that he would train hard and finish near the front. I liked the idea of competing hard at something. I started running with him at a local 5K when I was around 10, but I didn't really train and could barely finish it without walking.

For a long time, my favorite sport was basketball, which I played all through grade school and until my senior year of high school. My school didn't have a girls' cross-country team, so my dad coached me. I qualified for the Foot Locker Nationals my senior year, meeting my first serious athletic goal. After taking the first plane trip of my life to the meet at Disney World, I was so excited to meet fellow running nerds and run shoulder to shoulder with the best girls in the country. I finished fourth at Foot Locker, and then in the spring won two state track titles and set the US high school 2-mile record.

In my first year at Notre Dame, I finished sixth at the NCAA Cross-

Country Championships. *With a few years of improvement, I'll win one day,* I thought, the science major in me running calculations. *Onward and upward from here with precise linear progression!*

Of course, it wasn't a precise linear progression—I experienced setbacks and breakthroughs along the way. I set the American Junior record in my first track 5,000 and often finished second or third at NCAAs. I also broke my foot three times between my junior and senior years of college, didn't get my period until I was 19, didn't manage my time or physical recovery well, didn't know how to juggle my biology major and a three-season athletic regimen, and lived mostly on Pop-Tarts and salads. I was doing OK, but clearly I had a lot to figure out.

During setbacks, I was prone to negativity. *This is it; I won't make it, either,* I'd think. Even when I was able to earn a contract with Saucony after college, those doubts would recur. I was still learning on my feet in those first three professional years. The odds seemed tipped the wrong way. I often thought of that list of talented high schoolers who never made it. The jump between where I was and where I wanted to go still seemed so huge.

Then I found Ray Treacy and his group in Providence, Rhode Island. Gradually, by observing, following, and getting dragged through races and workouts by my training group, I broke bad training habits and learned how to embody my full power as an athlete. Being healthy and training consistently for a few years—that was a big part of it. It was also hugely important to be around women like Olympians Kim Smith and Amy Rudolph every day—seeing how they fueled, how they recovered, how hard they worked out, and how they prepared in the months, weeks, and even minutes before a big race. I realize now how lucky I was to find Ray, who still coaches me, and to find myself surrounded by an instant group of role models.

Although I never did win that NCAA title as a professional, I've won more than twenty-five national titles, held six American records, looked down the starting line of two Olympic finals, run in five World Championships, and placed third at the New York City Marathon. In my late 30s, I still haven't had many seasons without a PR. And the women I'm standing next to on those starting lines? They made it, too. You'll get to hear many of their stories later in this book.

For both of us, running is about so much more than times and finish places. (Not that those aren't important!) The confidence we got from sports has enhanced our lives in every way. It has taught us to take care of our bodies and to value strength, health, and function over what we look like. We also now know how to tackle a challenge. Not everything is as simple as running, but we trust our ability to stick with something difficult and figure it out, because we've done that in sports. And funny enough, we also both met our husbands and made many other amazing relationships through running.

Running has been *such* a rewarding part of our lives. With the help of our friends, doctors, teammates, and role models in this book, we are so excited to help it become just as rewarding for you.

PART 1:
THE EX

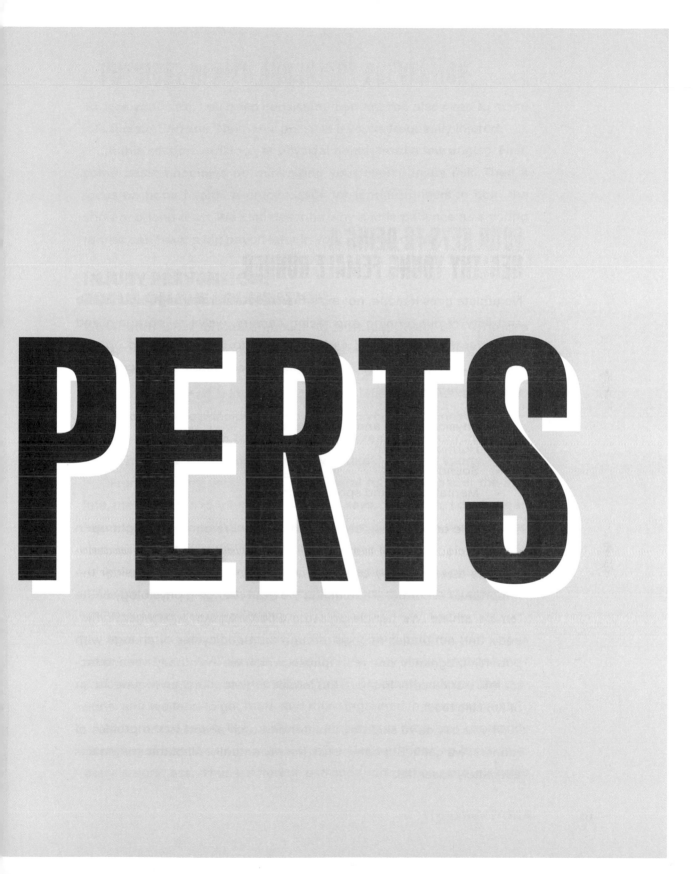
PERTS

and tendons in ways that running doesn't. Don't worry about how good you are at these other activities; just do them. "The ones that you find the most difficult may just be working the most on your weaknesses," John says.

REAL RECOVERY

MOLLY'S TAKE: You've probably heard that the gains from training happen when you're recovering, not when you're running. But what exactly does *recovery* mean?

I learned the answer during my first summer of racing as a pro in Europe. I had thought that as long as I wasn't running, I was recovering. Then I saw how the women in my training group operated. I watched how much energy my training partners budgeted for racing and realized that real rest is turning off your brain and your body for a while each day. I learned I had to save up willpower, mental energy, and physical energy to get the most out of my workouts and races.

In a way, it felt like a sacrifice to give up some things I was interested in. But in a bigger way, it was exciting to go all-in on something and remove all excuses. The result? I set a PR at every distance I raced that summer, even though I was no fitter than I'd been a few weeks earlier in college.

We're not saying to give up everything for your running. But recognize that when you're in your hardest training blocks, or your peak races are coming up, you need to ration your resources. Temporarily set aside things that drain your physical and mental energy. Feel the strength and eagerness grow inside you. You'll enjoy the things you briefly gave up that much more when you return to them.

John recommends focusing on your feet and core as a young runner. Having strength in these areas is so much more important than something like how much you can bench press.

For foot strength, John recommends a few simple exercises, like toe yoga and toe marching, all done barefoot. "Incorporating some strides and drills, especially those done side to side or diagonally, is extra beneficial when done barefoot," John says. "Make it fun—learning how to moonwalk and other similar movements will build some serious foot/ ankle strength."

For core strength, also focus on fundamentals. "Basic exercises like bird dogs and front and side planks, while working to make your movements controlled with crisp angles and sharp lines, may not look cool, but quality movement in the basics is essential," John says.

Most important, stay mindful of your posture. "How you do it is as important as if you do it," John says. Don't hold core exercises for arbitrary amounts of time if you can't maintain good posture. "From time to time, try substituting reps for breaths," John says. "Instead of holding a plank for 30 seconds, try it for five controlled breaths. It's a chance to get better at maintaining and coordinating your posture and breathing as you get tired."

The rest of your strength training as a young runner should also center on basic athletic movements. These include:

- Squats: Sumo, split, goblet varieties
- Pushing: Push-ups, arm presses, leg presses
- Pulling: Rows, pull-ups, hamstring curls

And don't neglect single-leg versions of exercises. "Running is jumping from one foot to the other, so if you're missing balance and single-leg strength, it can be disastrous," John says.

In an overall sense, learn how to listen to your body. "This is undoubtedly a skill, and probably the most important athletic skill you can develop as a young athlete," John says. "It will tell you when you have to change your stride because something's not right, when you're not recovering well, or you're just working too hard on the

> "In an overall sense, learn how to listen to your body. 'This is undoubtedly a skill, and probably the most important athletic skill you can develop as a young athlete.'
> —John Ball

right side. Learning to harness these inputs will teach you to back off when you need to and when it's OK to push it a bit."

BUILDING BONE HEALTH

MOLLY'S TAKE: My mileage doubled between high school and college. The workouts were more regular, and there were no more blow-off days, which I had often filled in high school with Ultimate Frisbee games, a way of working different muscles and letting loose a little. The dramatic changes in volume and intensity led to my first major injuries, a cluster of broken metatarsals during my junior and senior years of college.

I wasn't the only one on the team with stress fractures. There were often as many runners in the waiting room to see the foot doctor as there were football and soccer players. And running is a sport!

I missed a lot of key competitions because of those injuries. But there's an even more important aspect of bone health for young female runners. What you do in your formative years will affect your bone density for the rest of your life. This is really important stuff to get right.

Earlier, John Ball explained why doing a wide range of sports can make you a better runner. There's another key reason not to focus only on running when you're young, according to Adam Tenforde, MD, who ran the 10K at the 2004 Olympic Trials and is now the director of running medicine at the Spaulding National Running Center as well as an assistant professor at Harvard Medical School. Participating in sports that involve jumping and multidirectional movements may lead to stronger and more fracture-resistant bones. Soccer and basketball are great examples. Adam shared several fascinating studies with us, including this one: Women at the 2002 and 2003 national championships who played a ball sport in their youth had a 50 percent reduced risk of developing a stress fracture throughout their running career.*

---

* M. Fredericson, J. Ngo, and K. Cobb, "Effects of Ball Sports on Future Risk of Stress Fracture in Runners," *Clinical Journal of Sport Medicine* 15, no. 3 (May 2005): 136–141. doi: 10.1097/01.jsm.0000165489.68997.60. PMID: 15867555.

Your teen years are also crucial for maximizing bone mineral density. About 25 percent of the bone density you'll have as an adult is acquired in just the four years of your peak puberty growth spurt, according to Trent Stellingwerff, PhD, a senior adviser to the Canadian Sport Institute Pacific and the lead sports science expert for Athletics Canada, the country's track and field governing body. About 90 percent of your peak bone density will be set by age 20.* Building the strongest possible skeleton during these years will benefit you for the rest of your life, however your running journey turns out.

> About 90 percent of your peak bone density will be set by age 20. Building the strongest possible skeleton during these years will benefit you for the rest of your life, however your running journey turns out.

In addition to lots of bone-building activities, diet is really important here. Foods high in calcium and vitamin D are crucial. Adam notes that one study found that every additional cup of milk drunk by young athletes reduced their risk of a future stress fracture by 62 percent![†] Another study found that young athletes with the highest vitamin D intake had the lowest risk of getting a stress fracture.[‡]

See the "Sound Nutrition" section later in this chapter for more on

---

* L. Santos, K. J. Elliott-Sale, and C. Sale, "Exercise and Bone Health Across the Lifespan," *Biogerontology* 18, no. 6 (2017): 931–946. doi: 10.1007/s10522-017 -9732-6.

† J. W. Nieves, K. Melsop, M. Curtis, J. L. Kelsey, L. K. Bachrach, G. Greendale, M. F. Sowers, and K. L. Sainani, "Nutritional Factors That Influence Change in Bone Density and Stress Fracture Risk among Young Female Cross-Country Runners," *PM&R.* 2, no. 8 (August 2010): 740–750. doi: 10.1016/j .pmrj.2010.04.020. PMID: 20709302.

‡ K. R. Sonneville, C. M. Gordon, M. S. Kocher, L. M. Pierce, A. Ramappa, and A. E. Field, "Vitamin D, Calcium, and Dairy Intakes and Stress Fractures Among Female Adolescents," *Archives of Pediatric and Adolescent Medicine* 166, no. 7 (July 2012): 595–600. doi: 10.1001/archpediatrics.2012.5. PMID: 22393172; PMCID: PMC3654657.

eating for bone health. Also see the "Hormonal Health" section to learn more about the links among eating properly, menstruation, and bone health.

WHY AND HOW TO GET ENOUGH SLEEP

Did you know that marathon legends Deena Kastor and Paula Radcliffe would sleep up to 12 hours a day when in heavy training? (Not all at once—they were also champion nappers.) Deena and Paula made sleep a priority because they knew it's key to recovering from the hard work that makes peak performance possible.

According to Randy Wilber, PhD, senior sports physiologist for the US Olympic Committee, research demonstrates the importance of sleep for athletes. In one study, high school athletes who slept five to seven hours a night had injury rates of two to four times those of their teammates who slept eight or nine hours a night.*

Why is sleep so important for athletes? Randy gives two main reasons. First, muscles repair themselves and inflammation goes down. Second, new bone is constructed, and injured bone is repaired. As Randy puts it, "If today's training is when you planted the garden, then tonight's sleep is when the garden grows."

We know it can be difficult to get enough sleep with everything else you have going on. But it's so important! Here are some tips from Randy that will improve not only how much sleep you get but also how restorative it is:

- Stay away from screens (phones, laptops, etc.) for at least an hour before bedtime. The blue light from these devices interferes with your body's natural sleep-wake cycle.
- Take a hot shower just before bedtime. Doing so will stimulate release of the hormone melatonin, which helps to trigger falling asleep.
- Set your bedroom temperature at 60–65°F. A cool environment also causes melatonin to be released.
- Use blackout shades or an eye mask to keep light from reaching your retinas. This also increases melatonin levels.
- Drink organic tart cherry juice as another way to stimulate the release of melatonin.

- Wear silicone earplugs or listen to a soothing white-noise machine to block out external sounds. (Your family or fellow dorm residents might not mean to keep you up, but they can!)
- Use a sleep monitor to track sleep quantity (hours) and sleep quality (deep sleep, REM sleep).

* M. D. Milewski, D. L. Skaggs, G. A. Bishop, J. L. Pace, D. A. Ibrahim, T. A. Wren, and A. Barzdukas, "Chronic Lack of Sleep Is Associated with Increased Sports Injuries in Adolescent Athletes," *Journal of Pediatric Orthopaedics* 34, no. 2 (March 2014): 129–133. doi: 10.1097/BPO.0000000000000151. PMID: 25028798.

PATIENCE DURING PUBERTY

Sara grew up playing T-ball, softball, soccer, and basketball, in addition to dancing, swimming, and running. Molly played soccer and basketball and ran track until her senior year of high school, when she focused solely on running. We certainly didn't plan it this way, but now we know that these backgrounds helped us become better runners in and after college.

The reason? The very top female juniors often don't become the very top women in the open division. Trent Stellingwerff shared with us that almost half of world junior track and field medalists don't even compete past their teens. We mentioned this earlier, but in the United States, there's the well-known "Foot Locker curse." Looking at the first 41 editions of this national high school cross-country championship, only four female winners became NCAA champions, and only two made an Olympic team.

There are lots of reasons female runners don't compete past their teens. But if you like running and really want to reach your potential, it's worth sticking with it. "Female runners mature later in life and improve to a significantly greater extent throughout their 20s, compared to their male counterparts," Trent says.

Trent points out that, aerobically, boys and girls aren't much different before puberty. On average, however, starting at around age 14, girls' aerobic power is 10 to 15 percent lower than that of boys.* Sex hormones (estrogen and testosterone) are probably the largest differentiator between the sexes after puberty, Trent says.

> **Trent recommends that young female runners track their training in minutes rather than miles, because it takes girls about 20 percent longer to run the same mileage as boys.**

Trent makes the intriguing suggestion that because of girls' slower development, their training should account for that—the average high school girl runner isn't just a slower high school boy runner. She's developing at a different rate, so her training shouldn't mimic that of boys her age. Trent recommends that young female runners track their training in minutes rather than miles, because it takes girls about 20 percent longer to run the same mileage as boys. Running 40 miles a week as a high school girl means a lot more time on your feet than it does for a high school boy. Combine that extra stress with a still-developing skeleton, and you could significantly increase your injury risk.

We're really glad that we didn't chase short-term success at the expense of long-term development and health. We hope you don't, either. Be patient during puberty.

II. HORMONAL HEALTH

Girls and women are bombarded with harmful messages about food, exercise, and appearance. Even well-meaning people can give young female runners warped views. It can be extremely difficult to see photos and videos of top runners and not think, "If I want to be as fast as her, I need to look like her."

---

* J. Borms, "The Child and Exercise: An Overview." *Journal of Sports Sciences* 4, no. 1 (1986): 3–20. doi: 10.1080/02640418608732093.

SIZING UP THE COMPETITION

SARA'S TAKE: Regarding body image, I was never concerned about it until I went to the Foot Locker National Cross-Country Championships. That was the first time I noticed I was a lot bigger than most of my competitors. I had broad shoulders and I was a lot taller—5-foot-8—and most of the girls around me still hadn't reached puberty. Getting into running later, I had already gone through puberty at age thirteen.

My high school coach made me focus on being strong and healthy, and to worry more about the training I put in than the way I looked next to everyone else. I know it can be hard, but it's never helpful to compare your body to someone else's. Everyone's bodies serve them in unique ways—focus on your own and how it can serve you.

Messages within the running community can make this situation worse. Maybe you've been told that not getting your period is a sign of top fitness, or that oral contraceptives are the way to manage your irregular menstrual cycles. There's also the runner's "more is better" mentality, which will have you believing if you run a PR at a certain weight and level of mileage, training more and getting even leaner will make you even faster.

These messages have pushed countless young female runners into two common traps: low energy availability (LEA) and relative energy deficiency in sport (RED-S). Both conditions will eventually compromise your health and performance, perhaps with long-term consequences. Let's look at both, and why and how to avoid them.

"LEA results when your body doesn't have energy left to support all the physiological functions needed to maintain optimal health," says Stacy Sims, PhD, a female athlete performance physiologist. LEA can cause undesirable bodily changes, such as endocrine alterations, menstrual irregularities or amenorrhea (not having your period), mental disorders, thyroid suppression, and altered metabolic responses. "When the menstrual cycle becomes irregular or stops, this is a definitive sign that the endocrine system doesn't have enough energy available to function properly," Stacy says.

In terms of performance, Stacy points out that LEA will lead to the opposite of what you might hope to achieve by restricting your caloric intake. "If you compromise your fueling, you reduce your ability to hit the intensities you want and advance your fitness," she says. "If you compromise fueling for recovery, it is as if you didn't do the session at all." Simply put, LEA will keep you from ever reaching your running potential.

In young female runners, LEA often results from bad dietary habits, including excessive calorie counting, skipping meals, bingeing, purging, cutting out entire food groups, or using medications to cause weight loss without medical supervision. LEA can also come about accidentally, by not adjusting your caloric intake when you increase your training, or poor planning that results in going for long stretches without taking in calories.

COMMON SIGNS OF LOW ENERGY AVAILABILITY

- Frequent or repeated illnesses (coughs, colds, skin infections, stomach bugs)
- Recurring injuries that don't get better (e.g., stress fractures)
- Regularly feeling tired, sluggish, as if you're not recovering from training
- Absent or irregular menstrual periods
- Poor concentration, reduced interest, low mood
- Underperforming in training and competition

"LEA is most often not accompanied by weight loss," says Stacy Sims. "The body has amazing tricks to conserve energy for survival and can maintain overall body weight even when there isn't enough energy. One method is shutting down 'non-vital' body systems, such as the menstrual cycle."

Stacy says that educating yourself on how to truly meet your energy needs—not just for running, but for your entire life—is key to preventing LEA. See the "Sound Nutrition" section in this chapter for more information about this.

COMMON SYMPTOMS OF RED-S

- Altered menstrual cycle
- Fatigue, low energy
- Altered mood, poor concentration
- Underperformance, failing to improve
- Recurrent injuries
- Loss of enjoyment from sports
- Low mood

Female runners with prolonged LEA can severely compromise their health and performance. The International Olympic Committee introduced the concept of reduced energy deficiency in sport (RED-S) in 2014 to expand the concept of the female athlete triad (which dealt primarily with the relationships among menstrual dysfunction, bone health, and poor energy intake). RED-S also includes "decreased performance factors, metabolic perturbations, hormone dysfunctions, cardiovascular issues, and psychological issues," Stacy says. (These symptoms can apply to men, too.) LEA is the primary contributor to RED-S.

RED-S may have serious short- and long-term health consequences, Stacy says, including reduced:

- Bone health
- Menstrual cycle function
- Energy metabolism
- Infection resistance
- Protein synthesis

- Cardiovascular health
- Psychological health

If compromised health for the sake of faster times sounds like an acceptable trade-off, think again. RED-S will directly hurt your performance. Poor bone health will increase your risk of stress fractures, which will require weeks or months of time off from running. In addition, "The body will dampen production of hormones in the reproductive system, including estrogen and progesterone in women," Stacy says. "Hormones are important for driving the adaptations to exercise, so any disruption of this system, including that caused by LEA, will reduce the effectiveness of training and hence athletic performance."

Preventing RED-S comes down to regularly avoiding being in a state of LEA. If you struggle to meet your energy needs, consult a sports dietitian to come up with a plan to adequately fuel your running and daily life.

HEALTHY HORMONES

SARA'S TAKE: Hormones play into your health in more ways than puberty and periods.

Fatigue has played a major role in my career. My freshman year of college I came down with mono and relapsed my sophomore year. My coach made sure to add extra rest into my training, but I always wanted to test how far I could push myself. That push-pull dynamic worked until 2009, when I had my first experience with a hormonal imbalance.

It came right as I was changing training groups, moving into a new distance (half marathon), and increasing my output significantly. It was also six months after missing the Olympic team (by one spot!) and a month after having my appendix removed. Suddenly, waking up was a bear. I could sleep 8–10 hours, open my eyes, and feel like I hadn't slept at all. I would do workouts and feel like I had nothing to push with. Normal easy paces felt like I was running all-out.

A sports endocrinologist tested me and determined that my prolactin levels were elevated (the hormone that typically keeps you relaxed during pregnancy). I found out it can be elevated with extra stress in life and training. I later found out that so many female runners struggle with similar issues. It's important to listen to your body, and when you're feeling "off," work with an endocrinologist to see if an imbalance could be at the root of the issue.

III. SOUND NUTRITION

Proper nutrition is key to your health and performance, especially if you want to run well for many years. People know nutrition is important—we're probably asked "What should I eat?" more than "How should I train?" But a lot of runners still make basic mistakes. Those include thinking they need all sorts of special foods and supplements, or that quality doesn't matter as long as they eat enough, or, the worst mistake of all, simply not eating enough to meet their energy needs.

Nutrition is a science, not an opinion. And it's not an obscure science—the basics are easy to grasp and follow.

You can see this in Molly's general nutrition strategy. She focuses on targeting food that fuels distance running rather than eliminating food groups or labeling anything as "off-limits."

At the top of her priority list, she needs a lot of red blood cells (iron and B vitamins), glycogen replenishment (carbohydrates), muscle repair (amino acids and protein), a good immune system (vitamins), solid bones (minerals), and hormonal health (good fats and enough calories). She tries to hit these targets every day and aims for enough variety to ensure getting a wide range of nutrients. This framework has room for squeezing in extra things for enjoyment, convenience, catering to any food sensitivities, and general health.

In high school and college, neither of us was as informed about nutrition as we are now. We've now been fortunate to learn from several experts. One of those experts, Laura Moretti Reece, will be our guide for the rest of this section. Laura is a registered dietitian (RD) and a certified specialist in sports dietetics (CSSD). Look for someone with those qualifications if you're seeking personalized guidance on nutrition.

"Ultimately, fueling with an adequate amount of calories and understanding proper timing and balance of nutrition is what will lead to success," Laura says. Here's an overview of what that means for female runners.

MACRONUTRIENTS AND MICRONUTRIENTS

Before we look at female runners' main nutritional needs, we want to make a really important point: There are no "bad" foods. All foods fit into a balanced, varied diet. Sara loves ice cream, for example, and anyone who follows Molly on Instagram knows she's a doughnut connoisseur. Food is fuel, but it's also one of the main sources of pleasure in life. Labeling foods as "bad" or "off-limits" because you're a runner can start you down the path of harmful eating patterns. So we encourage you to embrace food in all its glorious variety.

Understanding sports nutrition basics will help you plan a diet that makes running rewarding and life fun. This knowledge can keep you from falling prey to misinformation and unfounded claims.

Let's start with the most basic of basics. The three macronutrients that form the basis of a good diet are carbohydrates, proteins, and fats. Each plays a vital role in your health and performance. Laura has prepared the chart on page 25 to help you understand why you need each one, how much of each to consume, and what foods contain them.

MACRONUTRIENT	DAILY NEEDS	ROLE IN SPORTS PERFORMANCE	DIETARY SOURCES
Carbohydrates	Should make up ~45–65% of total calories on a daily basis	Major source of energy for the body in sports, fuels anaerobic activities Supports caloric demands of exercise Crucial for recovery and replenishment of glycogen stores in the body If deficient, the body will break down muscle tissue	Grains: breads, pastas, cereals, oatmeal, quinoa, tortillas, crackers Fruit, fruit juices Starchy vegetables Sports drinks, gels, chews, honey Desserts, candy, soda
Proteins	Needs can range from 1.2–2.0g/kg body weight for athletes (~15–35% of total daily calories)	Muscle tissue building and repair Cell functioning Body functions related to hormones, immune function, and fluid balance Major source of energy (especially branched-chain amino acids: leucine, isoleucine, and valine)	Complete proteins: meat, poultry, fish, eggs, dairy, soy, quinoa Incomplete proteins: beans, grains, nuts, seeds, vegetables, gelatin
Fats	Should make up ~20–35% of total calories on a daily basis • 10% from monounsaturated fats • 10% from polyunsaturated fats • <10% from saturated fat	Endurance training promotes adaptations that enhance the ability of the muscle to utilize fats for energy Can be used in aerobic metabolism for fuel Dietary fats carry fat-soluble vitamins (A, D, E and K) and carotenoids	Nuts, seeds, peanut butter Omega-3-rich fish Avocado, butter Full-fat dairy Olive oil, sunflower oil, canola oil, coconut oil

ENERGY AVAILABILITY

In the "Hormonal Health" section, we looked in detail at the linked issues of low energy availability (LEA) and relative energy deficiency in sport (RED-S). See pages 18–23. Here we just want to reemphasize the importance of simply eating enough, via this great analogy by dietitian Laura Moretti Reece.

"Energy needs are like a bank account," Laura says. "When there is an ample amount of money saved up in the account, one may be more likely to purchase some new running shoes or go grab a bite to eat out with a friend. If the account balance is low, then one may be less able to spend freely and focus more on saving for important 'essential' items.

"The body works similarly. If there is an adequate store of energy, the body will more readily and efficiently burn energy. When the body senses a deficit, it will conserve energy. This conservation of energy leads to a suppression of many systems in the body, leading to negative effects on both health and performance. Athletes who are underfueling experience more injuries and negative performance consequences."

Carbs, proteins, and fats are the macronutrients—your primary sources of calories. Vitamins and minerals make up what are known as micronutrients—essential dietary elements that are needed in much smaller amounts than macronutrients. Of the many micronutrients, Laura identifies iron, calcium, and vitamin D as especially important for female runners. See the chart on page 27 for her helpful guide to what these micronutrients do, how much to aim for, and where to get them from.

NUTRIENTS	AIM FOR	PERFORMANCE EFFECT	TIPS	DIETARY SOURCES
Iron	18mg/day Upper limit: 45mg/day	• Helps to carry oxygen to the muscles • Iron deficiency anemia is common and can decrease performance	Take with vitamin C for optimal effect	• Lentils, kidney beans, chickpeas • Beef • Egg yolks • Whole grains • Spinach • Shrimp • Fortified cereals
Calcium	1,000mg/day Upper limit: 2,500mg/day	• Involved in blood coagulation, nerve function, muscle contraction, weight management, blood pressure regulation • Calcium deficiencies can result in stress fractures or osteoporosis	Do not take at the same time as iron; doing so inhibits absorption	• Cow's milk, cheese, yogurt • Tofu • Kale, bok choy, collards, spinach • Fortified soy milk
Vitamin D	400–600 IU	• Involved in muscle function, immunity, and inflammation response • Reduced risk of stress fracture with optimal levels of 25(OH)D (a form of vitamin D)	Supplementation may be necessary in the winter	• Egg yolk • Mushrooms • Fortified milk, OJ • Fatty fish • Liver

WHAT ABOUT VEGETARIAN AND VEGAN DIETS?

Neither of us are vegetarians, much less vegans. But we understand and respect why others are.

The main concern for a vegetarian or vegan athlete is meeting protein needs. "Most plant-based protein sources"—with the exception of soy—"are considered to be incomplete, since they do not contain all nine essential amino acids, like their animal protein–source counterparts," Laura says. She recommends eating a variety of plant-based protein sources—tofu, beans, nuts, etc.—throughout the day to get all the amino acids you need. If you're a vegetarian rather than a vegan, you can also use dairy foods to meet some of your protein needs.

If you're a vegetarian or vegan, you might find yourself eating a lot of high-fiber foods, such as lentils, beans, and quinoa. Laura warns that these foods, in combination with a lot of high-fiber vegetables, could lead to feeling full before you've eaten enough to meet your energy needs. She also points out that too much fiber can interfere with your running if you have an upset stomach or frequently need to make on-the-run pit stops. Solution? Include lower-fiber versions of carbohydrates like white rice and white bread.

"Vegan diets are found to be low in iron, zinc, calcium, vitamin D, and B vitamins, since these vitamins are commonly found in animal food sources," Laura says. Being deficient in these nutrients can result in low energy levels, poor bone health, or iron-deficiency anemia. Laura strongly recommends working with a registered dietitian if you aim to combine ambitious running with a vegan diet. The dietitian can make sure you're fulfilling all the necessary nutrient requirements, and might recommend supplements to prevent these deficits.

GETTING A HANDLE ON HYDRATION

There are many factors that affect how much fluid you need to drink. Some of the main ones are your size, your body composition, the duration and intensity of your training, and genetics. (You've probably been on group runs where one person finishes drenched while another teammate has barely sweated.) And let's not forget climate—Molly sweats a lot more training in Arizona in the winter than if she were at home in Rhode Island!

But, regardless, you do need to drink. Usually a lot. Muscles are about

70 percent water, and your physical and mental performance can start to suffer when your fluid loss is greater than 2 percent of your body weight. To put that in perspective, if you weigh 120 pounds, a 2 percent loss is 2.4 pounds, or 36 ounces of fluid. That's quite easy to lose during an hour-long run on a warm day.

And while water should be your most frequent fluid, it shouldn't be your only one. "Electrolytes significantly impact our hydration status by replenishing mineral losses through sweat," Laura says. "Consuming adequate electrolytes in the form of sodium, potassium, chloride, and magnesium ensures proper fluid balance and ultimately impacts blood pressure, muscle contraction, and heart contraction."

Here are Laura's guidelines for meeting your fluid needs.

BEFORE TRAINING

- Do not restrict fluids before training or races.
- General guidelines suggest 5–10mL/kg body weight before training.
- Urine should be pale.

DURING TRAINING

- Drink as often as desired, ideally every 15–20 minutes.
- Use sports drinks that contain 6–8% carbohydrates to provide energy to the working muscle and sodium to retain water and increase hydration status.
- In an 8-ounce beverage, try to include 7–9.5 grams of glucose or sugar, 150–180mg of sodium, and 60–75mg of potassium.

AFTER TRAINING

- For each pound of body weight lost during training, 16 to 24 ounces of fluids should be consumed.
- Urine should be clear/pale 2–3 hours after running.
- Drink a protein/carbohydrate recovery drink after longer or harder runs.

PRE- AND POST-RUN FUELING

We all know runners who feel best running on a relatively empty stomach, while their teammates might be able to eat right before practice.

This is an area where you'll need to do some experimenting. It's possible over time to train your gastrointestinal (GI) system to handle more food and drink in the one to three hours before you run.

It's worth making that effort. "Consuming a snack before exercise will fill up glycogen stores—ultimately improving tissue repair and energy recovery, avoiding fatigue, and decreasing risk of injuries," Laura says. The ideal, she says, is taking in 3 to 4 grams of carbohydrate per kilogram of body weight three hours before, and 1 to 2 grams of carbohydrate per kilogram of body weight an hour before.

What does that mean in practical terms? Let's say you weigh around 120 pounds. That's 55 kilograms. Three grams of carbs per kilogram gives you 165 grams (3 x 55). One gram of carbs contains 4 calories, so 165 grams means 660 calories. The math is roughly half that amount for Laura's advice an hour out. Sports drinks can come in handy here, because they might be easier on your stomach. Also, it's not like you need to be this precise before every run. Most people don't need to calculate pre-run fueling for a short recovery run. But for longer and more intense runs, it's worth making sure your fuel stores are topped up.

After longer or harder runs, it's also important to get in some calories in the 30 to 60 minutes after finishing. (Even if your stomach is saying, "No thanks!") There's tons of research showing that consuming a few hundred calories during this time will speed your recovery from hard training. If you were lucky enough to watch the training of the pros whose stories you'll find later in this book, you'd see that they're really dedicated to post-run recovery fueling. This is something Molly has seen real benefit from, especially as she's taken on longer distances. When she refuels within 30 minutes of a hard workout or a longer run, she simply feels better on the next few runs. Molly follows Laura's advice and aims for a carb-to-protein ratio of 3:1 or 4:1. That little bit of protein goes a long way to repairing your tired muscles.

On page 31 are Laura's general recommendations for pre- and post-workout snacks. Experiment to find the foods and timing that work best for you.

PRE-WORKOUT SNACK IDEAS	POST-WORKOUT SNACK IDEAS
• Low-fiber cereal with banana	• Protein shake or homemade smoothie
• Toaster waffle with jam	• Oatmeal, whey protein, banana
• Packet of instant oatmeal with fruit	• Cottage cheese with fruit
• Toast with peanut butter (if tolerated) or jam	• Tuna and crackers
• Apple slices dipped in peanut butter	• Cheese stick and grapes
• Half of a bagel topped with peanut butter and honey	• Pita with hummus
• Small tortilla rolled with sliced turkey and spinach	• Greek yogurt, fruit, granola
• ½ cup trail mix: mixed nuts, dried fruit, cereal, pretzels	• Egg scramble with toast
	• Peanut butter and jelly sandwich with Greek yogurt on the side

IV. MENTAL HEALTH AND SPORTS PSYCHOLOGY

MIND OVER MATTER

MOLLY'S TAKE: One time when I was still playing high school basketball, my mom suggested that my head might be holding me back. She said I threw too many tantrums on the court. Instead of following up an embarrassing, three-point "brick" with a great rebound, I'd stamp my feet and pout, letting my frustration get in the way of a good follow-up play. Mom said I needed to get my head in the game. I shrugged. At the time, I was a firm believer in the power of fitness. I thought, *If you're fitter than anyone else, it doesn't matter what your mind is up to, because your legs will find their way to the podium.* And for a while that was true.

But as the competition got stiffer and the stakes higher, I realized that I really did have to do something about my head. This became undeniably clear at the 2008 Olympic Trials. The pressure was unrelenting. A month before the race, I pulled my calf and had to cross-train for about two weeks.

Then I made a lot of mistakes the week of the race: not preserving my energy amid the hype, not managing my support crew, and not sticking to my normal daily schedule. I felt drained by the time I headed to the track, like I was floating over myself as we headed to the starting line. I could hear specific people in the crowd, instead of being totally focused on the race. I finished ninth in the 10,000, more than a minute and a half behind winner Shalane Flanagan when my PR should have put me in the mix for a top-three finish. Later in the meet, I finished tenth in the 5,000, more than half a lap behind winner Kara Goucher and well off my season's average performance.

When it was over, I promised myself I'd speak to a sports psychologist about how to prepare for events, big and small. And I did—discovering mantras, meditations, body awareness, and even body language to sharpen my competitive edge. Those tools have been key to the improvements I made since the 2008 Trials.

No matter how clear a head you have, you must still contend with societal pressures and signals. These pressures act on us every day without our being fully aware of them. The covers of sports magazines suggest that we should look a certain way. Social media—all the comparing and bragging—can sap even the strongest person's reserves. We need to be prepared from the inside out. In this section we'll look at how to take a zoomed-out perspective to manage the mental challenges of being a female runner.

GETTING BODY AND MIND IN SYNC

Like young Molly, a lot of runners think that their psychological athletic abilities are fixed. That's just how you are, right?

Wrong! As Ro McGettigan, a sports psychologist who represented Ireland in the 2008 Olympic steeplechase, puts it, "Like physical training, mental training is always a work in progress. We can always find areas to improve and refine. Physical and mental energy can be harnessed and maximized and made more efficient." Just as you do specific workouts to build a stronger heart and legs, you can change what goes on inside your head while you're running.

The three questions in this area we most often get from young female runners are about being more confident, getting over failure, and handling racing fear. With Ro's help, we're going to tackle those.

CULTIVATING CONFIDENCE

According to Ro, girls' self-confidence often starts to plummet by age 12, by as much as 30 percent. That can affect all areas of your life, including running.

But running can also help here. As Ro says, "Sports is about risk-taking. It's about failure. It's about going at it again. Even though those are hard things to do, we get used to that." Here are six tips from Ro on how to become a more confident runner and, by extension, a more confident person.

1. CHOOSE HOW YOU DEFINE *CONFIDENCE*

Aiming for perfection and obsessing about the outcome will increase your anxiety levels, and that will drain your confidence. You can't win or set a personal best every day. What's better, Ro says, is to aim to give your best effort mentally and physically. Ro advises telling yourself, "I have what I have, and I have to let go of the rest." That approach boosts confidence because it's under your control.

2. HAVE REALISTIC EXPECTATIONS

Part of the craft of peak performance is knowing your limits and what you're capable of on that day. "If you are reaching so much that you don't actually believe what you're going to try to do, that can kill your confidence," Ro says. "Being realistic isn't being pessimistic." Hitting realistic goals is progress and gives you the confidence to work toward your next goals.

3. BE PREPARED

Anticipating different situations and coming up with a plan for each boosts confidence by lessening fear of the unknown. What if you're in a tight pack and you fall? What if the race starts much faster than usual?

What if your shoelaces come untied? Having a plan for each scenario saves your mental energy. Also accept that you can't anticipate everything that might happen. "The more you're at ease with whatever happens, the more easily you can adapt quickly, and the more energy you can conserve while doing that," Ro says.

4. BE PROCESS-ORIENTED

"Focus your mind on the process of racing," Ro says. "If you get the process right, the outcome will take care of itself." This is great racing advice, period. Breaking the race into a series of tasks—getting a good start, getting in a good position, finding your rhythm in the race, etc.—keeps you in the moment instead of worrying about your time or place. "If we do that, we feel more in control, and that increases confidence," Ro says.

5. JOURNAL AND REFLECT ON YOUR PROGRESS

Even in an all-digital age, it's worth writing down key parts of your running journey. Having a running journal to read and reflect on can be a real confidence-booster. We've both had times where turning to our running logs reminded us of the work we've done and the progress we've made. That helps when the inevitable pre-race thoughts of *Am I really ready?* pop up.

6. SEPARATE YOURSELF FROM THE SPORT

"Remember that you're this person and you happen to do this sport," Ro says. In the profiles later in this book, you'll find lots of examples of pro runners who had to wrestle with this issue when they were injured. Remind yourself that, even without running, you're still a whole person. You choose to run, but running is not synonymous with your identity. "It's a secure place to know and believe that you're whole without this thing," Ro says.

WHAT'S YOUR IZOF?

The graph below shows how your arousal (excitement, anticipation, feeling energized, etc.) and your performance increase in sync—but only to a point. Too much arousal, and your performance starts to decline.

The thing is, what exactly those levels of arousal are, are highly personal. This is what Ro calls your individual zone of optimal function (IZOF). "Your baseline arousal and your optimal peak of what's good for your performance might be very different than my baseline and my level," she says.

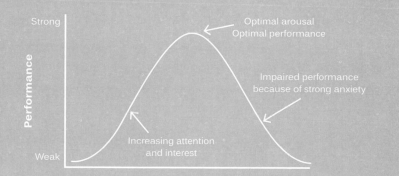

For example, Molly likes to be a little worried about something to be in her optimal zone. That means she's thinking about the race and how it might play out. (See "Be Prepared" on page 33.) Sara also worked through potential race scenarios, but with the goal of reaching race day relaxed. Before her best races, Sara was calm, even joking. Before the NCAA 10,000m, Sara told her teammates that if she won, she would stomp like a buffalo (the University of Colorado mascot) at the finish. She joked that Texas had Hook 'Em Horns and Arkansas had Pig Sooie, so they had to have something, and the Buffalo Stomp it was. And she did! On that day she was a warrior: relaxed, confident, and having fun!

How do you know what your IZOF is?

"Look at your best performances," Ro says. "What was happening around them? What was the lead-up like? Who were you with? What was going on? Those things are like a blueprint for what your optimal performance is."

DEALING WITH FAILURE

As a runner, you're going to have bad days. Sometimes those bad days happen on race day. Every runner we know has lived this reality. We certainly have!

The most important thing to remember after a bad race is that it doesn't define you. As Ro says, "Failing doesn't make you a failure." What Molly does after a bad race, and what Sara tells her runners to do, is to use it as a learning experience. You learn more from disappointment than from victory.

In the immediate aftermath, you're likely to be emotional. That's fine—it's a sign of how much you care. Expressing those immediate emotions can help you to move on to the next, more reflective stage.

"Ask yourself, if you had the opportunity to redo it, what would you do differently?" Ro says. "That is called additive thinking. That is really powerful, because you're always building." Instead of getting stuck on how poorly you ran, or how you let yourself and others down, you can draw out tangible things to work on.

This is especially important if you started out winning a lot of your races. As you move from, say, middle school to high school, then to college, your level of competition is going to get tougher. You're probably not going to win most of your races. That can be difficult if your earlier image of your running self is "I'm a winner" or "I'm the best." As Ro says, learn to fail, and learn how to pick yourself back up and grow from the experience.

COPING WITH PRESSURE

As we said, Ro was an Olympic steeplechaser. She competed on the biggest athletic stage in the world. So she knows what we've all been through when she says, "There's nothing like a race to feel the sheer terror of 'What am I doing? Why am I doing this? I'm going into a fire.'"

You can manage those emotions. Here are Ro's top three tips for handling pre-race pressure.

1. ZOOM OUT, THEN BACK IN

When you need to stop the storm in your head and center yourself, take the big view. The really big view. "Think, *Here I am warming up for this race. I'm in this city*," Ro says. "Then zoom out even more. *Here we are on Earth*. Then zoom out even more. *Here we are floating around in space*."

Thinking like this can give you perspective. It can remind you that your race isn't that big of a deal in the grand scheme of things.

But don't stop there. The goal isn't not to care about your race! Zoom back in. Remind yourself that you're choosing to race. You're the sort of person who does difficult things, and those are always going to produce emotions. "The more you approach it as *I'm choosing to do this*, and acknowledging that participating in sports and getting to know that fear is a choice, the more grounding and empowering it is," Ro says.

2. CHECK IN WITH YOUR GOALS

Whether you write down race goals or just keep them in your head, now's the time to reflect on them. Remind yourself how important this is to you. "Affirm that you love the battles, you love the heat in the kitchen," Ro says. "You're here to express your passion for running and the fitness you've earned and worked hard for."

3. NORMALIZE THE FEELINGS

Acknowledge that pre-race nerves come with the territory. Everyone around you probably has the same feelings. Telling a friend or teammate what you're feeling can release some of the tension, especially if she says she feels the same way. "Being able to discharge a little bit of those feelings and normalizing them can give you more space from them than denying it and telling yourself to calm down," Ro says.

KEEP YOUR HEAD TOGETHER WHILE YOUR BODY HEALS

Being injured stinks. Even if the rational part of your brain tells you that you'll eventually get better, it's easy to spiral into thoughts about how you'll never get back to normal.

When we're injured, we take a two-pronged approach. First, usually with the help of some combination of sports medicine doctors, coaches, friends, and teammates, we figure out what to do physically to get better. What that looks like depends on the type and severity of the injury.

Second, and just as important, we make a mental game plan. It's so easy when you're hurt to slip into a funk. What's much better is to treat your injury the way you do your training when you're healthy—set goals, track your progress, adjust as necessary. "Being injured is not a challenge on the path, it *is* the path, just as much as setting PRs and winning," says Meg Waldron, MS, an All-American track runner at the University of Virginia and now a sports psychologist and coach. "Being injured brings the opportunity to commit to your purpose as a runner, a female, and a human, and develop the mental and emotional resources that are helpful on the path ahead."

As with your training and racing goals, your rehab goals should be healthy and attainable, but also motivating. Specific goals, such as "I'm going to do 15 minutes of rehab work five days a week," are much better than vague goals, like "I'm going to get healthy." Meg says, "By focusing on what you can control—goals, motivation, attitude—it's easier to let go of what you can't and regain that sense of power you had as an active runner."

TALK YOURSELF THROUGH IT

Positive self-talk is the term for the motivating conversations we have with ourselves. You do this all the time when you run—"Keep going," "Just one more mile," "I can do this!," etc. According to Meg, research supports using positive self-talk at least as much when you're hurt to improve feelings of hopefulness and well-being.

Meg recommends asking yourself open-ended questions and focusing on effort instead of results. This approach will help you believe that the dedication and hard work you're putting into rehab is worth the effort. "Asking 'What is going well?' or 'How can I do this differently?' or 'Who can help me?' invites solutions that tap into your innate curiosity to grow and thrive," Meg says. "High-fiving yourself for how hard you are working to do your exercises correctly, instead of focusing on unmet expectations, bolsters feelings of success."

Here are Meg's tips for good goals as an injured runner.

1. Become a top student of your injury. Learn about:

- Why you got injured
- What rehab is going to look like and how long it will take
- What your return to training and racing will look like
- How to avoid getting reinjured

2. With the guidance of your medical team and coach, break down your rehab process into daily and weekly tasks and attainable goals. Don't forget personal needs. This might look like:

- Do three sets of leg extensions with a 5-pound weight daily
- Do your core routine
- Stay hydrated
- Call your best friend
- Watch an inspiring movie

3. Set long-term goals that include numbers so that you can measure your progress, like a goal number of exercise reps or a future race date. This might look like:

- Do squats with 10-pound dumbbells after four weeks
- Run an easy 2 miles at six weeks out
- Race 5K on date X
- Fill your journal with notes by the end of your recovery

GET SOCIAL

When you're hurt, tapping into your social network is a key early step in feeling better. Meg Waldron told us about a study examining differences in coping strategies between elite male and female skiers facing a season-ending injury. The women reported significantly higher satisfaction from connections with friends and other injured athletes than the men did.*

"Research suggests that women are innately primed to 'tend and befriend,'" Meg says. "They want to be there for you, so you might as well ask them. Also, females get a big hit of oxytocin—the happy chemical in the brain associated with hugging—from same-sex social interactions."

* D. Gould, D. Bridges, E. Udry, and L. Beck, "Coping with Season-Ending Injuries," *Sport Psychologist* 11, no. 4 (1997): 379–399. http://journals.humankinetics.com/view/journals /tsp/11/4/article-p379.xml.

Being injured usually means leaning on different mental skills than you do when you're healthy. "Self-compassion and being gentle with your body are valuable strengths to unleash," Meg says. "As we let go of concerns around image or being judged, we are free to focus on getting healthy. Warning signs that you need to process your feelings can look like overdoing PT exercises, excessive negative self-talk, depression, self-harming behaviors, and disordered eating."

To help cultivate self-compassion, journal the thoughts you're having as an injured runner. Find a place to write where you won't be interrupted. Spend a few minutes thinking about how your injury has affected you and your life. Then start writing, guided by these tips from Meg:

- Describe your injury, how it occurred, and how you are feeling about it.
- List ways in which other people might experience similar events.

- Write a paragraph expressing understanding, kindness, and concern for yourself. Taking a step outside the situation often makes it easier to give advice and see the issue more clearly.
- Write a letter as if you were communicating to a close friend in the same situation.
- Describe what happened in an unemotional factual manner. You aren't your injury. Acknowledge the injury without blaming or shaming yourself or others.
- Once you've finished writing, read what you wrote and pay attention to how you feel. Notice any changes in your thoughts or feelings as a result of the writing.
- Make time throughout the weeks to keep writing.

GETTING HELP, NOT HARM, FROM SOCIAL MEDIA

We enjoy connecting with friends, family, and fans on social media. We appreciate the opportunity to inspire others by sharing our successes (and, yes, our setbacks). If social media had existed in its current form when we were young runners, you'd better believe we would have relished the chance to follow runners we admired.

We also have personal experience with social media's darker side. And we recognize that young female runners might not yet have developed the coping strategies that years in the public eye have given us. So we want to devote a little time to how you can get the good stuff from social media while avoiding most of the bad stuff.

First, the good: You've probably noticed that mainstream media sports coverage focuses overwhelmingly on male athletes. The little coverage female athletes get can be about things like appearance rather than accomplishments. So it's great to see female athletes (including us!) take control of the narrative and share and celebrate each other's achievements. We hope you've found some fellow runners to learn from and be motivated by.

You've probably also noticed the not-good. "Women, including athletes, have long experienced pressures to look a particular way and to meet the unrealistic expectations of femininity as presented in mainstream media," says Holly Thorpe, PhD, a professor of sociology at the University of Waikato in New Zealand, who has advised the International Olympic Committee and other sports organizations. "For many women, such limited notions of beauty and femininity have been a source of great anxiety." Feeling bad about your body because you're comparing it to what you see on social media "can lead to depression, low self-esteem, worry, anxiety, or lack of self-confidence," Holly says.

At its worst, this can lead to disordered eating, overtraining, injury, and conditions such as low energy availability (LEA) and relative energy deficiency in sport (RED-S). (See the "Hormonal Health" section, pages 18–23, for more on those conditions.)

And then there are the trolls and harmful comments. Most of them focus on appearance. You might be told that you don't look like a "real woman," or you might get sexualized appreciation. You might also be told that your performances suck.

You don't need any of that. As Holly notes, there are a variety of steps you can take. "Whereas some athletes speak out about the negativity they endure on social media, others adopt different strategies to protect themselves, including not looking at comments, and blocking or reporting abusers and trolls," she says. Do any or all of those steps to keep social media a positive, empowering place for you.

Also, remember that social media isn't real life. Don't give up in-person relationships and sources of support for the sake of a few likes.

PART 2:

THE ATHLET

IN HER OWN WORDS

Now that we've looked at the key areas female runners need to manage to succeed, let's hear directly from dozens of top women runners about their experiences getting to the finish line. Knowing the ingredients for success is one thing. But, just as you need to know the basics of training, the key is putting theory into practice day after day, in different situations and amid different challenges. We talked with many of the best women runners across five decades and from around the world, guided by one main question: How did you do it?

We concentrated most heavily on current and recent American women. But you'll also hear from pioneers who paved the way for today's runners, and international stars whose stories show that we're all more similar than we may think. You'll see how these women found the sport, surrounded themselves with a support system, came through various challenges, and learned to take care of their bodies, among other lessons. Everyone's story has unique components; there are many different paths to the top. But somehow, along all these different paths, a lot of us have come to the same core lessons and values that we hope you can learn from.

We've included the women's personal records (PRs) at various stages of their careers. If you're like us, you live for this stuff! We think it's valuable for young runners to see others' progressions. Maybe you'll find that your high school or college bests aren't far off from those of eventual pros. That can be highly motivating. You can also look at these PRs in an overall sense—even if their times are faster than yours, you can see what amount of improvement is typical from high school to college to post-college.

We know that you'll find lots of valuable takeaways from these women. Our hope is that learning about their journeys will help you have a fulfilling, lifelong relationship with running. Not only can you take these lessons to achieve your highest level of performance, but, more important, healthy, happy running can also show you how to learn to harness the strength of your body and mind in every aspect of your life. That's the ultimate prize we want you to come away with!

WOMEN'S RUNNING TIME LINE

1928

The 800m is the longest of five events added to the Olympic program for women. It's then removed out of (misplaced) fear that running that far will harm women's health.

1960

The 800m is added back into the Olympic program as the longest event for women.

1961

Women are officially banned from road races based on health concerns.

1971

The CIAW is replaced by the Association for Intercollegiate Athletics for Women (AIAW).

1972

Title IX allows for women's sports college scholarships. The 1,500m becomes the longest Olympic race for women. Women are allowed to register for the Boston and New York City Marathons, but as a "separate but equal" event. At New York, women entrants stage a protest at the starting line.

1980

The American College of Sports Medicine (ACSM) declares that women's health won't be harmed by running the marathon. Patti Catalano Dillon signs one of first pro sports contracts for a US woman.

1994

Hellen Chepngeno is the first Kenyan woman to win the World Cross Country Championships.

1996

Fatuma Roba of Ethiopia is the first African woman to win the Olympic Marathon. The women's 5,000m is added to the Olympic program.

2001

The NCAA adds a women's 3,000m steeplechase and eliminates the flat 3,000m race.

2008

The women's 3,000m steeplechase is added to the Olympic program.

Here's a brief overview of key moments in elite women's running. You might be surprised by how long it took women runners to get equal opportunities to participate, let alone thrive!

1966

Cheryl Bridges Flanagan Treworgy (Shalane Flanagan's mother) is the first woman in the United States to receive an athletic scholarship to a public university. She runs cross-country at Indiana State University (see page 72 for her whole story). Roberta Gibb runs the Boston Marathon unofficially.

1967

Kathrine Switzer is issued a bib number for the Boston Marathon after not clearly identifying herself as female. Officials try unsuccessfully to physically remove Switzer from the race once she is identified as a woman entrant.

1969

The Division of Girls and Womens Sports (DGWS) appoints the Commission on Intercollegiate Athletics for Women (CIAW) to assist in conducting intercollegiate competitions (gymnastics/track and field).

1983

The AIAW is replaced by NCAA Women's Sports. The first NCAA Women's Track Championships are held.

1984

Thanks to a charge led by Jacqueline Hansen, the 3,000m and marathon for women are added to the Olympic program. American Joan Benoit Samuelson wins the inaugural women's Olympic Marathon at the Los Angeles Games.

1988

The women's 10,000m is added to the Olympic program.

1991

Kenyan Susan Sirma is the first Black African woman to win an Olympic or world medal with her World Championship bronze in the 3,000m.

2012

Sarah Attar runs the 800m at the Olympics, becoming the first Saudi woman to compete at the Games.

2020

Nearly one-half of International Olympic Committee (IOC) members are women.

2022

The discussion of regulating testosterone in women with differences of sex development (DSD) and trans women in sport is ongoing. In 2020, the 800m runner Caster Semenya lost her appeal to the IOC after they instituted a ruling that women with genetically high testosterone levels must medically suppress them to compete in the 400, 800, and 1,500m events. As a result, we saw other athletes like 800m runner Francine Niyonsaba of Burundi switch to unregulated events like the 10,000m in the Olympics (and finish fifth!).

THE PIONEERS

1960s–1970s

MADELINE MANNING MIMS

Four-time Olympian;
1968 Olympic 800-meter
champion; former 800-meter
world record-holder;
1968 Olympic gold medalist
in 800-meter, 1972 Olympic silver
in 4 x 400, 10-time USA champion
and held national and world
records in 800-meter

DATE OF BIRTH: January 11, 1948
CITIZENSHIP: USA
CURRENT RESIDENCE: Tulsa, OK
COLLEGE: Tennessee State University

PRO PRs:

400 METERS: 00:52.2
800 METERS: 1:57
1,500 METERS: 4:14.04

FAST START

I first got into running by the Presidential Fitness Test that all high school kids had to take. I was very shy at the time and would not have gone out for any sports, but I did very well in the scores. A girl came in another day and beat all my scores. I asked the gym teacher, "Can I take that test over again?" She said, "You can take it as many times as you want." So I took it every day for three weeks straight! When they calculated my scores, they found out that not only was I the most physically fit girl in the school, but nationally, I was one of the top girls. They asked, "Why aren't you in any sports?" I said, "What have you got?!"

Our school had volleyball, basketball, and track for girls. In 1965 I went to my first National Championship after being discovered by the coach for the women's track team, Cleveland Division of Recreation. That's when I realized that this thing was bigger than just school. I ended up becoming the first girl in the world to break 55 seconds in the 440-yard dash. Then I realized I was on the world level. My junior year, I went over to Russia, Poland, and West Germany because they put me on the women's team at age 17.

THE WORK

As hard as I worked out, there were no favorite sessions. What's interesting is this: Usually the workout that you hate the most and is the hardest on you, you eventually come to love.

There was a hill workout that we did, running up, across, and down on a loop, which we repeated like 20 times. It just hurt so bad, it would make me angry! I got to the point where I was determined to master it, and when I could handle 20 of those hills, I knew I was in shape.

Later on, when I was coaching middle school and high school here in Tulsa, I had my kids doing hills and a lot of them hated it, too. But then they saw they were getting stronger and stronger.

When I started, most coaches in America did not know how to train women in the 800. You have to have endurance, which you have to work toward to get through mileage and hills. And then you have to have natural speed.

So it wasn't until later on in my training, when the third coach I worked with started having me do a lot of calisthenics and jumping and weights (not heavy weights but strengthening techniques), and I saw my times starting to get faster. He'd also have me running at race pace during workouts on the track.

I got to the point where I could run 100 meters and tell you my time on each hundred meters. My body would feel it.

Most of the time I was training by myself. My coach was teaching at a school in Broken Arrow, Oklahoma, and I would go over there to run on their track and train there. Sometimes the boys would be out running. So he would have the boys run with me. They hated that—they were like, "We don't want that girl to run with us because she beats us all!"

FIRST AMERICAN WOMAN SUB-2:00

The first time that I had decided to try to break 2:00 in the 800 was at an Olympic Trials. I told the other girls, "The European girls are breaking 2:00. If they can do it, we can do it, especially if we're together."

They didn't want to go out and then die, so I did my thing. I thought, *The Lord has given me a major gift and I'm just waiting for everybody else? I need to go on and try to break this.* And so I did. Whether I ran 1:59 or 2:03, it hurt about the same.

SETBACKS AND COMEBACKS

In 1976 I was on my third Olympic team. Two or three weeks before the Games, I had run a world record for 2,000 meters. So I really expected to win at the Games.

But you know how you have those lethargic races? If you stay in track long enough, you will have those races. You just hope that they don't happen at the Olympic Games! But that's what happened. In my semifinals, I felt lethargic. Going into the last 200, my competitors realized I wasn't picking it up, and then they all just started passing me.

When I came off the track, I was totally confused. One of my teammates came to see me in the warm-up area. She sat down next to me and put her arm around me and she said, "I really don't know what to say, but I just want to let you know that you're the reason that I continue to run. Your way of reaching out to me and helping me in some very dark times of my life has really changed my heart and my faith. Madeline, I love you very much and I appreciate who you are." It was as if the Lord himself came and sat down beside me and put his arm around me. My heart just opened up.

Right after that, a bunch of press with cameras and microphones rushed me. One reporter asked, "Are you still going to run for Jesus, or will you try something else?" (I had written a book and had a gospel album out, both called *Running for Jesus*.) I said, "Whether it's on that track going around in circles or anywhere in life, I will always run for Jesus. He's not a crutch that I've leaned on to make a bargain with." Another guy asked what I meant. I said, "Everything in me that wanted to be great, wanted to be famous, wanted to be world-renowned, wanted a medal, it died. But what I have found out is that the love that I have for my Lord has only become stronger, become deeper. And I truly realized there is nothing that has the ability to separate me from God."

REBOUNDING TO A RECORD

After that race, I thought I was finished. Then I was asked if I would be willing to run in a Russia-versus-USA competition. I had rent to pay, so I went.

The same friend who had comforted me after the Olympic race was in the crowd again. She asked how I was feeling. I said, "I'm just doing this so I can get some money, and because I feel like I haven't done my best race yet." She said, "Remember what you've always said—you're running for Jesus. Just go out there and run for him."

It was like she turned on a light bulb. All of a sudden the nerves started coming, and I decided I was going to make this a tribute for giving me the gift of running. The first-place woman ran 1:56, and I came in second in 1:57.*

MORE THAN RUNNING

I realized my purpose in life through my running. In 1968, I ran against a young lady named Vera Nikolić from Yugoslavia (now Serbia). The year before, she and I had run against each other. During that race, as I was coming to the last 100, getting away from her I felt a sharp pain in my side—because she had taken her elbow and knocked me into the infield. I jumped up and ran her down and out-leaned her at the end and won. She was so angry and upset. She wouldn't allow them to put the silver medal around her neck. When they announced that I was the most outstanding female athlete of the meet, she threw her medal into the crowd and walked off.

We met again in my semifinal that next year at the Mexico City Olympics. She actually walked off the track after 300 meters and tried to commit suicide. Later on, I found out that the dignitaries of her country put a lot of pressure on her because their country hadn't won anything at the Games yet. The Games were almost over and they had told her, "You come back with the gold medal and nothing less." She had a mental breakdown on the track during that race.

Two days later, on my way to race the finals, I see Vera standing outside of her dormitory, really just lifeless. I decided to go to her. I felt like I needed to encourage her in some way, even though she doesn't speak English, and I don't speak her language. I called to her. She didn't answer. I kept calling. Finally, I just shook her by the shoulders and said, "Vera, Vera!" She looked at me with these really dark eyes, very empty. I tried to explain to her that she was young, she can start over again, please don't quit. I was getting no response whatsoever. Finally, I said,

---

* **SARA:** That was her PR at the time, and the American record!

"I don't know if you understand me or not, but God created you, one of the greatest athletes in the world, and that gift belongs to him, not to you. Go back home, get some rest, start all over again, and find Jesus in your life." Tears started rolling out of her eyes, and I embraced her. Then I walked off to get to the Olympic final.

A year later I was in Germany when this guy came up to me and he said, "Miss Manning, I'm Vera's coach." I asked how she was doing, and he started weeping. He finally said, "When we left Mexico City, we took her to a mental institution. I would go every day and I would sit down and talk, but she never answered until a month ago. I was sitting there talking and she interrupted me and said, 'Coach, Madeline came over as she was on her way to her finals.'" He told me, "She realized that you were on your way to the finals and you still came back for her. That's the only thing that started her talking again." I then heard someone calling to me and I turned around and there's Vera running across the field. She said, "I found God!" And I could see life in her eyes.

From that moment on, it hit me: This is not about the Olympic Games—that's icing on the cake. This is not about me winning, or my times or fame or the medal. This is about me being in the right place at the right time with the words of life for someone who's dying. And the reality of my purpose came into full perspective.

Even while you're doing what you're doing, there's a higher purpose.

There's so much more about what you are and who you are and why God has you there.

BEING A ROLE MODEL FOR WOMEN OF COLOR

I was working as a chaplain at one of the world track and field championships years later. A representative from the Kenyan team said to me, "We saw you when you ran in high school and you broke the world record for the 440-yard dash. And then when you won in Mexico, you were so far ahead of your competition. We started looking at each other and saying, 'We'd better check out our women and see what they can do.'

You are a reason why many women of ethnicity run middle-distance and distance. You opened the door for them."

MADELINE'S ADVICE

Learn how to compete against yourself. God has given you a specific gift that may be different from everybody else's. Also, it's important that you fulfill the portion in life that is for you and give back to society.

PATTI CATALANO DILLON

First US woman to break 2:30 in the marathon; three-time runner-up at Boston Marathon; four-time Honolulu Marathon winner; fastest professional Native female runner in history

DATE OF BIRTH: April 6, 1953
CITIZENSHIP: USA
CURRENT RESIDENCE: Windham, CT

PRO PRs:

10K: 32:08
15K: 49:42
MARATHON: 2:27:52

THE FIRST RUN

I was 23. I wanted to lose weight, and I happened upon a book by Ken Cooper called *Aerobics*. I found a chapter called "Jogging." I didn't know what jogging was. The book said to wear your most comfortable pair of shoes. Mine happened to be these knockoff Earth shoes—like walking shoes with a negative heel. I wore Daisy Duke jean shorts and about seven sweatshirts. I got on my bike, rode to a cemetery down the street, and I ran. I ran for an hour. I ran seven miles in an hour for my first run!

Afterward at the Y, when the water hit my face in the shower, I just felt so *good*. I had never had those feelings before. I wept, and I wanted more of it. If I had to run to get that feeling, then I'd run.

GETTING SERIOUS

I fell in with a group of running guys at the local Y not too long afterward. I was not really accepted—I forced myself in. There were five guys and they were all mostly older than me. I could only keep up with them for a mile at first. I was tagging along on runs and I could hear they were talking about "the marathon" and that it was in Boston. I blurted out, "I'm going to do that."

One guy, a cop, looked over at me and he said, "Ha, well, you know, you have to qualify." I asked, "How far is the marathon? What is the marathon?" They just looked at me like I had three heads, but they were very kind. He told me, "Us guys, we have to do 3:00. But the girls, I think they have to do 3:30 or so." I thought, "If he could do it, I can do it." I was tough. I was a worker.

TRAINING FOR THE FIRST BQ

I did one 16-mile run. That day my friend came with me in her boyfriend's car. We drove the loop that I did to measure it, smoking our cigarettes. Afterward, I looked at my thighs and I thought, "Oh my gosh, they did 16 miles!"

Then I took a week off. I did a couple of 10-milers up through the hills, and still the guys would drop me. I think I had one run that I finished with them. I was going to hang on if it killed me.

The Newport Marathon is the race I ran to qualify for Boston. I didn't know what to expect, but I knew from listening to stories that it was going to be hell. I thought, *Well, when death happens, when it starts to hurt, I'm going to run harder. That's all I know.* So the gun goes off, and I don't remember hurting. I don't remember much of the course. I remember finishing and, when I did, the guy announcing the race saying, "And here she comes, Patti Lyons* of Quincy." I thought, *Oh wow, I won.* I ran 2:53:40 that day.

For a while I was a fair-weather runner. I missed running Boston in 1976, '77, and '78 because I got hurt or just didn't want to train during the winter. Then I decided in 1979 I was going to run through the winter and I was going to train. I quit smoking. I was doing push-ups and sit-ups.

I decided I wanted more. The guy who ended up coaching me asked, "What is it that you want?" I said, "I want to be the best I can be."

TRAINING WITH THE GUYS

I would meet all those Boston Marathon guys to run from Bill Rodgers's running store. I had to learn to understand the discipline of training, because I was a wild card. I always took the lead, and there were a few times I got passed doing that, so I had to learn to be patient.

I'm a big practice person. I practiced going out hard and kicking it in. Then I practiced going out easy, working the middle, and bringing it home hard. I even worked on going out really slow, which really helped me win a key race once.

These were fun because the way you ran them was the objective.

I also became strong. I started lifting weights. I could bench and

---

* **MOLLY:** Lyons was Patti's maiden name.

squat quite a lot for a distance runner. I did a lot of sit-ups and push-ups every day, even on race day.

The only thing that I had on my mind was Boston.

SEEKING CONTROL

My personal life off the road was a challenge. I was still struggling in my marriage. I was being told by others what races I could and couldn't run. It was very difficult, especially being one of the first women to have a pro contract. I remember being in the lawyer's office and we're all excited, and he puts the contract in front of me and says, "Oh, by the way, don't get pregnant." That became an issue with me. I wanted kids, but both my husband at the time and this contract didn't.

Also, I couldn't choose my races, I couldn't choose my distance, and I was told not to run cross-country. I was told not to do track. They wanted me to be a road racer only.

LEARNING TO VISUALIZE

I remember being so disappointed that my sponsor didn't want me running the exhibition 10,000m at the 1980 Olympic Trials. They wanted me to do a 15K in Portland the same weekend. I begged to be able to race both of them as a compromise, but I don't think they thought I could win both, so I was sent to the 15K.

I was on the bus heading to the race, and I was livid. One of the other runners is sitting next to me and notices I'm upset. He says, "Well, what are you going to do?" I decided if that I show I'm really fit in this 15K, maybe they'll let me run the 10,000. He told me about visualizations and he said, "If you see it and believe it, it will happen."

I knew Grete Waitz, the best in the world, had run well under 50:00 for 15K. I had run 52:40. I decided to try to break 50:00. I wanted to do something to prove I was fit enough that I could have won both the 15K and the 10,000 that weekend. By the time we got off the bus, I was happy, I was gleeful, because I knew I was going to win and break 50:00.

My coach watched the 10,000 that night, then came to talk to me about my race. He told me not to go hard, just to sit and win. I was deflated. I only slept a few hours that night, then woke up, did a shakeout jog, took a shower, and ate my peaches and oatmeal. Well, the gun goes off and I just couldn't hold it in. I thought, *Girls, I'm not coming back to you.* I won in 49:42.

After that, visualization to me was like a magic pill. Of course, you have to be strong and you have to do the work, but it was fun.

I also learned, when I was in a situation that was very stressful, very wild or anxious, I didn't race as well. When I showed up to a race feeling relaxed and refreshed, I could race well even if I was physically tired. That's where the fun began for me.

EXCEEDING EXPECTATIONS

Don't worry. I worried so much, and I still worry. If you do your homework, you do your studies, you show up and do what you're supposed to do, that's just getting by. But if you do more than is expected of you, you'll carry that through your whole life.

When I started running, it felt like I could breathe for the first time. I had never tried hard at anything my whole life. I never tried to be the best that I could be. When I started to try in running, a different world opened up to me.

That journey of challenging myself afforded me confidence to succeed later in life. I opened up a health food store, despite having never run a business before. I had to be able to go to a bank and ask for a loan; I had to come up with a business plan; I had to do numbers, inventories, and orders. I had to find the store. I had a plan and I did it. All I did was just break it down the way I did when I was running after goals.

THE IMPORTANCE OF HERITAGE

My heritage is Native American. My mother was sold at 11, and that played into her life and my upbringing and why I'm such a hard worker. I did migrant work. My goal is to have an all–Native American Olympic team. I would really like to get an Olympic development training group going for that.

Running is in our history. It's in our ceremonies. It's our rite of passage. But they're struggling right now. They can't even get water, they don't even have food. They need more support. My husband, Danny, and I fostered five Native American kids when we first got married. The depth of trauma from eons ago can carry forward. That's a whole other book, for another day.

"Running is in our history. It's in our ceremonies. It's our rite of passage. But they're struggling right now. They can't even get water, they don't even have food. They need more support."

KATHRINE SWITZER

First woman to run the Boston Marathon as an official registrant (1967); New York City Marathon winner; driving force behind the women's Olympic Marathon

DATE OF BIRTH: January 5, 1947
CITIZENSHIP: USA and New Zealand
CURRENT RESIDENCE: USA and New Zealand

PR:

MARATHON: 2:51:37

EARNING HER OWN CHEERS

I started running when I was 12. I told my dad I wanted to be a high school cheerleader, and he said, "Cheerleaders cheer for other people. You want people to cheer for you!" I was going to go to high school the next autumn and try out for field hockey. My dad figured if I ran a mile a day, I'd be one of the best players on the team. I did not think I could possibly run a mile a day. He said, "Sure you can—help me measure off the yard." I went out and ran seven laps around.

I was absolutely determined because my dad said I'd be a good player, and I was, because I never got tired! I'd never had a stick in my hand before, but I never got tired so I could outrun everybody.

I felt empowered. I felt fearless. I played other sports, but I always ran, sometimes in secret because people thought it was weird. I remember the milkman coming to my mother and saying, "Is everything OK at home? Because I see your little girl out running."

I went to Lynchburg College in Lynchburg, Virginia, and played lacrosse, field hockey, and basketball. One day I was out running after practice and the track coach came over to me and said one of the men had flunked off the team, and could I run a mile? I said, "Sure, I can run three miles." He asked if I would run the mile on the men's team and they could get the points. I said, "Sure." I didn't think anything of it. The guys were fine with it. But this is Lynchburg College in Lynchburg, Virginia: very Southern, very religious, and it really created a sensation for everyone else.

> " I told my dad I wanted to be a high school cheerleader, and he said, 'Cheerleaders cheer for other people. You want people to cheer for you!' "

TRAINING IN SYRACUSE

I transferred to Syracuse University. The men had 25 sports to choose from and the women had nothing. I thought that was really weird, but that didn't matter—I was there to learn to write. I wanted to write sports because I felt there was going to be no sports for me after university, and at least I could run by myself and then I could write about sports and feel like I was close to the action, whatever the sport was.

But I really was full of oats, because I decided I would ask the men's coach if he would let me run on the men's cross-country team. He said that it was against NCAA rules. But he had read about me running at Lynchburg and said, "If you want to come work out with the team, that would be fine." He didn't mean it, because when I closed the office door, I heard him burst out laughing to his colleagues and say, "Well, I guess I got rid of that one."

So I showed up! The men on the team were wonderful to me. So was Arnie Briggs, a volunteer coach who had been a top marathoner and had run the Boston Marathon 15 times. Now he was old and retired and never thought he would run again. He said he had been there 30 years and never seen a woman out there before and sort of took me under his wing because I was slow. I got lost every day on the cross-country course because I was so far behind. Arnie had a bad knee and bad Achilles, but he jogged with me. We trained all through the winter together. He kept telling me Boston Marathon stories on the runs.

One snowy night I said, "Let's just quit talking about it and run it!"

At first he said, a woman can't run it. I said, "Don't be ridiculous. Women have run marathons—Roberta Gibb ran Boston unofficially in 1966." He said, "If any woman could do it, I believe you could do it. But women are really too weak and too fragile." He believed all these myths that my generation grew up with—you're going to get hair on your chest, your uterus is going to fall out, etc. He said, "If you show me in practice that you can do it, though, I'll be the first person to take you."

I got very serious. We kept getting to longer and longer distances. One day, we decided to go for 26 miles. I felt so great that after we hit 26, I said, "Let's keep running for another five miles." The last mile of this 31-mile run, Arnie starts weaving around the road, but we did finish the run. He then passed out. When he came to, he said, "Women have hidden potential in endurance and stamina."

MAKING IT TO THE STARTING LINE

I wasn't at the Boston Marathon to prove anything. I just wanted to run the race. I had to prove to Arnie that I could do it, and I proved it to him with that 31-miler. So when I went to Boston, it was my reward for doing all that work.

I finished in 4:20. After the attack by race director Jock Semple,* I told Arnie, "No matter what, I'm finishing this race." He advised me to slow down then, to make sure we keep it together. The weather was horrible, very cold, the worst weather until 2018, with a headwind and sleet and snow.

LIFE AFTER BOSTON: CREATING OPPORTUNITIES FOR WOMEN

After the first Boston I ran, I was suspended from the athletic federation. It was a huge controversy. Jock Semple maintained that he was totally within his rights to attack me physically. Nowadays I would have to sue him. But I figured he was overworked, he lost it, and I let it go.

What did infuriate me was the next day when he said, "4:20, I could have walked it that fast." So I had a chip on my shoulder and I decided to do two things: create opportunities for women, and train really hard and see if I could become a better athlete. It took me a long time, but in

---

* **MOLLY:** Did you know women weren't allowed to race longer than 800m in those days? It turns out Kathrine had entered the marathon under her initials "K. V. Switzer" because her first name was always misspelled (one "e"!). The race director assumed "K. V." was a man. As Jock drove by on the lead vehicle, he was enraged to see a woman had entered the race without his knowledge, and he jumped off the truck to physically push Kathrine off the road. Her then-boyfriend knocked Semple out of the way and she was able to run on and finish the race. It's crazy to think about anything like this happening today. Talk about running through barriers as a pioneer of the sport!

1975 I popped down to a 2:51 at Boston. I knew then that if I could do it, millions of women could do it, given the opportunity. That gave me the clarity to create the programs I created, like 261 Fearless.

As we campaigned for getting women official entry in the Boston Marathon, Sara Mae Berman, Nina Kuscsik, and I worked very hard within the system. I had to swallow a lot of pride. Sometimes the best way to work with an organization is not to fight it, but to take a leadership role in it. So I took on the responsibility of being the first woman to become chair of women's long-distance running for upstate New York. Together with those women, we lobbied and worked with the system. The guys who were running were on our side, too.

> So I had a chip on my shoulder and I decided to do two things: create opportunities for women, and train really hard and see if I could become a better athlete.

It took five years, but we became official with the Road Runners Club of America and then women were officially allowed into the Boston Marathon. Jock Semple had to welcome us into the race. He said, "If women are going to run in my race, they're going to have to meet the men's qualifying standard." It was 3:30. Pretty tough in those days, but we all could do it. In fact, Nina and Sara were pushing to go under 3:00.

Eight of us showed up to a marathon in terrible, hot conditions that day, and three of us went under 3:30. Jock had to present me with a trophy, which happened to be broken. He was sort of unmanned by it. He was embarrassed and he handed me the trophy and said, "Sorry it's broken. If you send it back, we'll have it repaired. But I've been mad at you for five years and you deserve a broken trophy!"

He became, like so many guys who were so anti-women about things, almost evangelistic. He and I became best friends. I forgave him. I helped him launch his book, and he helped me launch my global women's sports program. People can change, and forgiveness is powerful.

HOW SHE DID IT

ON BEING A PIONEER

I had a bad experience with a woman who tried to drive us off the road once when we were running. I said to Arnie, "Why would I get resistance from other women?" He said, "She's afraid of you, because you're strong and powerful and free. And she's not." I said, "All she has to do is put on her sneakers and go out the door." He said, " You know that, I know that, but she doesn't know that yet." I said, "Well, you know what, I'm going to teach her somehow, and when I'm 40, we're going to be best friends."

I cannot tell you how many women over the years came up to me and said, "I thought you were the craziest person I ever knew. Now running has changed my life." So I just said, "I'm so happy—you pass it on. I want your daughter and your son to be out there doing that. Just pass it on."

That early fear was directed at me because I wasn't "keeping my social place." They thought I was flirting with becoming a man or that I was doing something socially inappropriate, that I was perhaps damaging my biological destiny, and that I was sweating in public. They thought, *Nice girls don't do that*. You think it's incredible to hear that stuff now, but believe me, if you go to some parts of the world that is still there, and much worse.

A group of us were successful in getting the women's marathon into the Olympics. The races that I had organized with an Avon sponsorship from 1977 to 1985 had 27 countries and five continents participating in the program, which helped convince the International Olympic Committee to allow the women's marathon to go into the Olympics because we had the number of countries required.

We had incredible performances. Joan Benoit, Rosa Mota, Ingrid Kristiansen, and Grete Waitz were running fabulous times. We had the medical data. We had runners who were doctors who submitted medical evidence that proved that women's endurance was superior, that the marathon suited them. With the Avon Women's Marathon of 1980, we closed downtown London streets for the first time in history. That event became what is now the London Marathon.

So we got the women's marathon included in the 1984 Olympics. I said, "That's great. We got the women's marathon in the Olympics." But most of the women in the world are still living in a fearful situation because of poverty and ignorance and social and religious restrictions. And they believe myths because they don't know anything else, and they're afraid to step out of that. How are we going to create that opportunity for them and give them the freedom of empowerment?

KATHRINE'S PROGRAMS TODAY

My original bib number of 261 from Boston took on a meaning of being fearless in the face of adversity. I decided to form a nonprofit called 261 Fearless. What we have now is a global series of community clubs. We have a really good training program, trained coaches, and group leaders at a massively good educational program.

It's a two-step process of being empowered by taking that first step and then realizing you can transform your mind and your body by running or walking with a safe community. Somebody holding your hand and taking you out the door and then following it up with an educational program gives empowerment. It launched in 2015, and we're already in 12 countries with 5,000 women. I'm hoping we can now crack that final barrier of getting into isolated places where we couldn't before. You can't, for instance, get on a plane and go to Afghanistan and say, "Hi, I'm here. Let's start a running club." It takes a *lot* of work to start a running club.

GUIDANCE AND LESSONS

I would advise girls that your body is absolutely magnificent and you are going to be thrilled with what it can do. Treat it well, feed it well, sleep, stretch, do all the good core work and everything you need to do and be utterly fascinated by your achievement. It is astonishing, and you can achieve more than you can imagine.

Along the way, you're going to discover so much about yourself. I'm asked why I run. I say, "Running has given me everything." It's given me my career and my health and my exercise, it's given me my religion, it's given me my husband. Most important, every time I run I have a chance to talk with myself and find out things about myself. Let running give you everything—it will.

> **Let running give you everything—it will.**

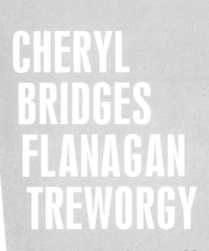

CHERYL BRIDGES FLANAGAN TREWORGY

Former marathon world record-holder; first woman to receive an athletic public university scholarship

DATE OF BIRTH: December 25, 1947

CITIZENSHIP: USA

CURRENT RESIDENCE: Burlington, NC

COLLEGE: Indiana State University

PR:

MARATHON: 2:49:40

SHALANE FLANAGAN

2017 New York City Marathon winner; 2008 Olympic 10,000-meter silver medalist; four-time Olympian; world cross-country bronze medalist

DATE OF BIRTH: July 8, 1981
CITIZENSHIP: USA
CURRENT RESIDENCE: Portland, OR
COLLEGE: University of North Carolina, Chapel Hill

HIGH SCHOOL PRs:

MILE: 4:46
3,200: 10:24

COLLEGE PRs:

1,500: 4:11
3K: 9:00
5K: 15:20

PRO PRs:

5,000 METERS: 14:44
10,000 METERS: 30:22
MARATHON: 2:21:14

THEIR START IN RUNNING

CHERYL: There were no sports for women when I graduated from high school in 1966. Both of my parents were athletes in their day, as much as you could be. My dad was a high jumper and my mom was allowed to play tennis and field hockey, and that was about it. I always wanted to be in sports. I took physical education every semester. I read an article about legendary coach Bill Bowerman. He had gone to Australia and they were walking and jogging in the hills. I thought, *I want to do that*. Nobody was ever on the streets running. They thought you were really, really weird if you were. I would go out after band practice and I would try to run laps on the track. The high school cross-country and track coach saw me and asked me about it, and he invited me to train with the team.

> " Nobody was ever on the streets running. They thought you were really, really weird if you were. "

As a survivor of sexual abuse,* I feel running can have such an impact in a woman's life. It's empowering to be in charge of something that's all yours. No one can take it away from you. Running can be empowering for a female if she is facing abuse in any way, be it drugs, alcohol, physical, sexual, emotional. In so many ways, women are oppressed, and running is empowering. On the run, I used to write letters in my head to the people who I couldn't find a voice to dispute in real time. It would just come flowing. Running is not just good for my physical health, but it empowered me, and to be empowered is threatening to the abuser. I speak about my history with sexual abuse because it's important for us as women to realize that the shame is not ours.

---

* **MOLLY:** Cheryl shared her experience of suffering sexual and verbal abuse at the hands of her stepfather in the book *First Ladies of Running*, by Amby Burfoot (Emmaus, PA: Rodale, 2016). She coped with a disempowering experience by discovering and honing the power of her own body through sports, and tells this story for the many women and girls out there who may be dealing with the same trauma.

Before I began running, I was gaining weight because I was eating out of frustration and as a reaction to abuse, and I was trying to nurture myself with food. I was just fortunate enough at that time to read an article about running that Bill Bowerman put out there. I thought, *I can do that*, and began running laps around the track after school.

SHALANE: Where I grew up, in Boulder, is a unique situation in terms of running. It was a running mecca during that time in the '70s and '80s. Olympic Marathon champion Frank Shorter was living there. There were a ton of runners. So it seemed like that's what you do. I didn't know any better. I grew up in a culture of running. What you see is what you know, and what you tend to want to become, to a degree. So just seeing so many runners around, it seemed natural. It was normal to have a huge pile of shoes by the door and for everyone to go running. My mom literally breastfed me in the back of a running store she worked at, owned by Frank Shorter in Boulder. So running is ingrained in me to a degree.

I tried basketball. I was not very good at it. I played soccer and got into swimming. I swam all the way up through high school, so I never ran indoor track. I didn't really run during the winter because it was just crummy out, so I would ski and swim. I didn't have my first year of year-round running until my freshman year in college.

> "On the run, I used to write letters in my head to the people who I couldn't find a voice to dispute in real life. It would just come flowing. Running is not just good for my physical health, but it empowered me."

ON BEING A PIONEER

CHERYL: When we started out in competitive running, the shame that was thrown at us for doing something different as women was huge. I was shy and lacking self-confidence, so it's kind of funny how going out and running, which was something nobody did at that time—least of all other women and girls—was OK with me. We faced trying to fit in to this acceptable range of what we were supposed to look like as women while being athletes, and what we were supposed to do. We battled trying to meet other people's expectations to make them feel comfortable.

Many of the other women around me faced even more barriers than I did. I kid about this, but I'm truly serious as well, because this was the '60s. It was a sexist time, and what allowed me to do a lot of things was that I had long blond hair.*

I could do a lot of things other females couldn't because I satisfied the question in men's minds that, yes, I was a female. That allowed more doors to be opened to allow me to do what I wanted to do, which was to make myself feel good by running. And that's just the truth of where we were in the '60s.

SHALANE: Yeah, by the way, basically, she's saying she was a babe.

IF IT DOESN'T EXIST . . . MAKE IT

CHERYL: There weren't running bras. There was nothing like that. You had to kind of look through your wardrobe and decide what worked because everything was made for boys. Women didn't do that—nobody knew of anybody who ran. I can remember my grandmother saying, "Those shorts are awfully short." I said, "If I make them any longer, it's hard to lift my legs." There were no pictures to look at. We were so far removed from the rest of the world.

I had three patents on sports bras. I'd grown up sewing. I sewed

---

* **MOLLY:** Sara and I found an old newspaper article about Cheryl—the title was "Pretty Cheryl Tries Running" and it listed her measurements and all. It also said, "Cheryl could be a flight attendant." We were *shocked.*

  SARA: She told us that she's contacted one or two of those old sportswriters since then. They apologized to her and claimed, "We just didn't know how to write about female athletes." Cheryl's take: "They were trying and struggling to make us acceptable in a society that only knew one way to look at women."

most of my clothes when I went off to college. So I came up with this prototype. A leotard company helped produce them. I signed this contract, and they subsequently tried to cheat me out of everything. But they were only selling to leotard companies. Eventually, I opened accounts in department stores and some of the running stores. The bras did really well. They sold the company to somebody else who claimed he didn't know that there was an arrangement with me to get royalties. I have some other prototypes for C and D cups and larger sizes that could still be made.

EARLY RACES

CHERYL: When I first started running, the only teams were city teams. And so I would drive into Indianapolis. Sprinting was all they had, so they tried to make me into a sprinter. Forget about having no speed, I couldn't even come out of the blocks! So I kept moving up. The half mile was as long as they would let you run.

In 1965, I was introduced to cross-country over the summer and it was like, "Oh, man, this is my thing!" It was a mile and a half. It was really hard because I didn't have any background or strength in my legs for that. But it was something I could improve on.

There weren't any other women running when I went to college. That's when I ran with the boys, and that's when I competed against high school boys, with permission. There weren't enough cross-country meets for girls.

Then I went to Indiana State in Terre Haute. My coach talked the school into giving me an athletic scholarship, which was unheard of at the time.*

---

* **MOLLY:** In 1966 Cheryl was awarded the first athletic scholarship for a woman from a public university. It wasn't until 1973, as a result of Title IX, that the University of Miami established proper teams of scholarship spots by awarding 15 scholarships spread across golf, swimming, diving, and tennis. Today women receive one-third of all athletic scholarship dollars in the USA. (Source: https://www2.ed.gov/pubs/TitleIX/part5.html.)

Our team almost won the national track title my senior year. It was the very first women's collegiate nationals in San Marcos, Texas. There were only four of us on our team. We all tripled in events, and tied for second place as a team, which was really amazing. The other teams were mostly from Texas and they had like 24 girls. We all just loved doing it.

TRAINING FOR A MARATHON WORLD RECORD

CHERYL: University of Oregon coach Bill Dellinger was coaching me the summer before I ran a marathon. I wasn't training for a marathon, I was only training for cross-country. I knew at age 23 I probably should retire because nobody else was around that age in the sport. I really wanted to go out on top. So I wrote Bill Dellinger, who was coaching Steve Prefontaine, and I said, "Can you help me out?" He sent schedules through the mail. At first he cranked me up to hundred-mile weeks. I didn't understand that I should back off on the pace if I ran that much, so I was just dying. Seventy-mile weeks were more my speed, where I could actually function and perform well.

SHALANE: In high school I used to write my own workouts. I would look at whatever she was doing back then and make up my workouts based off those. I figured, I'll do a version of whatever Bill said to do!

CHERYL: Bill had never seen me run in person. He had to give me these workouts without ever observing me do them. But he was asking me to do things at the end of a workout that I usually could not do at any point in my life. The beauty of it was that he was simulating a race and then asking me to give it my all. I was training for what it's going to feel like at the end of a race. I ran one of my fastest miles during his training because he always had you dipping back in and getting better at the shorter distances. On Christmas Day 1971, I broke 5:00 in a mile during a workout, which I could never do before.

LONGEVITY AND MAXIMIZING POTENTIAL

SHALANE: I think, to a degree, I overtrained, but I didn't know any better because I didn't really have a group environment for a while. There was a level of fatigue that happened because I didn't get injured a lot. That's a blessing and a curse. I was able to put in so much continuity in my training, but I didn't really get good chunks of breaks in my training. I didn't allow myself that grace period. I think a lot of times we're always just chasing the next carrot, the next goal.

Now I realize, having had knee surgery in the last year and how much rest my body has gotten, I feel a lot better in general! Watching the athletes I coach now, they're really good at taking breaks. I would take little breaks, but I would find a way to somehow sneak in some training—I was obsessed. I just couldn't relax when I knew I needed to. Finally, I was forced to take a longer break with my back injury in 2017 and, after that, during that six months right up to winning the New York City Marathon, I had my best training block. Not because I tried any harder. It's because I had that break. I was able to jump to another level of training just purely based on rest. That stress + rest = growth equation—it truly works.

Toward the end, too, I looked at training as more of a job than a joy. I see in my athletes now, there's a lot of joy in what they do, and they don't seem as stressed. There's low-lying stress, obviously—they're really competitive. But the amount of stress I think I put myself through at times was probably unhealthy and stole some of the joy from what I was doing. I would totally play the "I'm not as talented card" in my head as a reason why I should keep doing training when I was tired.

> "The amount of stress I think I put myself through at times was probably unhealthy and stole some of the joy from what I was doing."

Telling my athletic story, there definitely is a theme in the sense that, when I have had a setback, there have been pivotal moments after which I've had some of my greatest athletic achievements.

For example, I didn't qualify for Foot Locker ever in high school, not even my senior year, when I was predicted to win the race. I was disappointed when there was pressure to win an NCAA cross-country title my sophomore year and I had a really terrible race. I literally stopped and walked! And then, right after college I needed foot surgery. But who would have thought a girl who never went to the Foot Locker Nationals in high school would eventually win two cross-country national titles in college after walking in the race the year before?

Then I make it to the Olympics after having some of those downturns. When I had foot surgery I was told maybe I wouldn't have a running career. However, after that, I set an American record in the indoor 3K and the outdoor 5K. At the Olympics in Beijing, I got food poisoning right before my races, but then I won a medal there. I would say my next big moment was winning the New York City Marathon, which came after I had a really bad fracture in my back. After these setbacks, I've had some of my greatest athletic achievements, and I'm not sure why. I think it makes the athlete reevaluate her commitment and desire to achieve those goals. Sometimes I think those breaks, even though they're not planned and they're hard to take in that moment, can catapult athletes to that next level for some reason. At least for me, what always helped was that reevaluation, and taking that moment to be introspective and reinforce the things that are important to you.

> "Nutrition, strength training, taking care of your body—we didn't do any of that. All we did was run."

I try to tell these things to my athletes who get injured. Those times when you have to take a step back, if you focus on just becoming a great all-around athlete again, there's something about it physiologically that makes you stronger for it. If you can reframe a setback almost as an advantage, even though it doesn't feel like it in the moment, it helps.

CHERYL: Nutrition, strength training, taking care of your body—we didn't do any of that. All we did was run. And if that wasn't enough, you ran more. We didn't do any weight training. I can't remember how old I was when I finally started doing sit-ups and push-ups. We didn't know about nutrition.

The only thing we ever did as far as even getting into a training room was if you sprained an ankle, and they gave you ice. And this was news! I was a demonstrator at a Health, Physical Education, Recreation, and Dance national meeting in Illinois, where they came out with the method of using a frozen Dixie cup of water to ice their injury. Nobody had ever done that before. I mean, it's crazy how far we've come.

POINTS OF PRIDE

SHALANE: For the most part, I was fairly consistent. I wasn't an athlete who wavered in my desire to do well, and I was consistently self-motivated over a long period of time. It's really hard to come to each day with the same level of intention and focus. I did that for a long time, and it wasn't easy. I think that's what I'm most proud of.

Medaling at the World Cross Country Championships is actually my proudest accomplishment. That was probably the hardest I've ever run. It's probably the best race I've ever run.

CHERYL: I have mixed emotions on my world record in the marathon. I didn't train for that race. I just happened to be running it that day. It wasn't a goal. My goals that I had set out for myself—I never really achieved those. But what I think is more important is, I satisfied a need that I had. That was the most important thing to me, to be able to keep figuring out a way to do what I wanted to do.

My best performance was probably when I finished fourth at the 1969 World Cross Country Championships. It was a really hilly course in Scotland. I was one second behind Val Robinson from New Zealand; otherwise the USA would have swept it. Maureen Dickson got second and Doris Brown got first and I got fourth.

FUN ON THE RUN

CHERYL: It's funny now, but it wasn't back then. When I got to college in Terre Haute, Indiana, my coach was trying to find me some races that were close. He asked if I could run in the boys' high school meets. It finally came back that the answer was yes, but there was a caveat: I had to wait until three seconds after the gun was shot before I could take off because he didn't want me to get in the way. I thought it was funny, because what am I going to do, tackle somebody? So I would wait three seconds. But I got sweet revenge. I never got worse than third that year. I was catching the guys up ahead the whole way.

SUPPORT IN THE SPORT

CHERYL: Once people saw how hard I was working, everybody jumped on board to form a support system. It's not like I was trying to show off or anything. I had to prove myself and I had to stay true to that. I was still a novelty. But I think there was respect from the guys I worked out with and at races, and that respect was my support system. They would stand up for me. If the rabid dog came out after us on a long run, they would all kind of try to shield me. I think they saw that I wasn't looking for anything special, that all I wanted to do was get better as well.

> **I think all of us women's running pioneers were always encouraged by the male runners. It was those who weren't knowledgeable about what we were doing who were upset that we were breaking the norm.**

Once somebody knew you and knew your goals and saw your work ethic, pretty much everybody was supportive. There were a few exceptions, like one morning in San Luis Obispo I was running early in the morning and nobody was out. There was a policeman who saw me cross the street in the middle of the block, which was against the rules there. He pulled me over for jaywalking! But I think all of us women's running pioneers were always encouraged by the male runners. It was those who weren't knowledgeable about what we were doing who were upset that we were breaking the norm.

SHALANE: Compared to my mom, I had so many advantages and so much support financially. I had resources, I had the therapists, the doctors. I really feel like I had every advantage. But one thing I think that made the biggest difference is having a husband who is willing to basically give up whatever he was pursuing at the time and go all-in on my career. That made the biggest difference for me. I had that consistent support system. So when I didn't have training partners, he was my training partner at various times. He was my coach at various times because, early in my career, my coach lived in Florida. My husband's all-in support allowed me to really embrace what I was doing. That was vital.

RUNS IN THE FAMILY

CHERYL: It's really hard to describe what it has been like watching Shalane's career. Shalaney, she's my daughter. But when I look at what she's been able to do, it's almost like she's somebody I don't know. I'm out there in awe and admiration! It's hard not to be proud. It's hard not to brag. It's hard not to test people to see if they know her. It really is hard to explain how you feel about that. You know it. You love your kids so much.

I love being around people talking about her and just kind of sidling up, trying to hear the conversation. It just blows me away. I think back to how excited I got when she did go with us to that first cross-country race as a kid. It was Junior Olympics—we were going for her sister, Maggie. I said, "Shalane, well, you're in the car. Just go and run." So Maggie did not advance to Nationals, but Shalane did! The next season Shalane decides she's going to run cross. The fact that she loved the same thing I love—it's a special connection at such a different level.

SHALANE: It's a unique bond that you have with your parents if you both love running or have anything in common like that. It enhances that overall relationship because there's a common-

> *It was Junior Olympics—we were going for her sister, Maggie. I said, 'Shalane, well, you're in the car. Just go and run.' So Maggie did not advance to Nationals, but Shalane did!*

ality and the opportunity to seek advice in that capacity through your parents. I think it brings something really unique to a parent-child relationship when you can share something that you both genuinely love.

In high school I asked my mom for advice because I lacked a really strong coaching figure. I wrote up a lot of my own training, and then I'd ask my parents to look at it and we'd talk about it during dinner. When I got to college and then as a pro, I put full trust in my coaches to make decisions. But I'm sure I bounced around ideas or maybe things that I was just stressed about. I tried to trust my own intuition a lot and then have faith in my coach. Obviously, my parents were sounding boards quite a bit, but I think I also respected the fact that I had a relationship with my coach and that he and I needed to work on things and to make decisions.

But I think the coolest part is when I would go to World Cross, both my parents competed in that race, so they know how hard that is. When I ran my guts out and I was ninth, they're like, "We know it's the hardest thing you've ever done. We're so proud of you." They know what it feels like. They can watch and feel the lactic acid, they can feel the deliriousness. They can feel the sickness in their stomach. They can relate to all of that.

> "It's a unique bond that you have with your parents if you both love running."

THE
1980s

JOETTA CLARK DIGGS

Four-time Olympian, 1988–2000; broke 2:00 for 800 meters every year but one between 1985 and 2000

DATE OF BIRTH: August 1, 1962
CITIZENSHIP: USA
CURRENT RESIDENCE: PA

HIGH SCHOOL PR:

800 METERS: 2:03

COLLEGE PR:

800 METERS: 2:01

PRO PR:

800 METERS: 1:57

JOETTA'S JOURNEY

My father wanted us to run.* He thought distance running built character and there were not any Black Americans running distance or middle distance at that time. His notion was that Black people could do anything anybody else could do. At 12 years old, I ran cross-country and the 1,500 and 800. In high school, I went undefeated at the 800.

There were times where I would be out running and stopped on the street by the police asking where I'm going. My dad wasn't this famous guy at the time.† When I would tell him and my mother, the late Jetta M. Clark, about it, they would have conversations with the officers, telling them that we live in this community and to leave their kids alone. My community knew who I was and they'd tell them the same thing.

PUSHING THROUGH DOUBTS

At the 1988 Olympics, it was known that the drug situation was rampant. It was exciting to make my first team, but then when I got knocked out in the first round of the 800, it was devastating. I wanted to give up on the sport because I didn't know where this was going to go. I was going to grad school for a while and had to face the question: Do I continue to train or do I go get a job? Do I give it one more year or do I just cancel everything at that age?

I hung in there one more year. When the Berlin Wall came down in 1989, that affected the sport.‡ Now my times made me one of the best in the world. Although I still had another job, I went on to run for many years.

---

* **MOLLY:** Joetta and her younger sister, Hazel Clark (page 138), are part of the "First Family of Track and Field." Their sister-in-law, Jearl Miles Clark, was a World Championship medalist in the 400m and an Olympic Trials 800m champion, and also an American record-holder.

† **SARA:** In 1989, Joetta's dad, the legendary educator Joe Clark, would become the subject of the movie *Lean on Me*, starring Morgan Freeman.

‡ **SARA:** After the fall of the Berlin Wall, state-sponsored doping in sports became less rampant.

When you're at your breaking point, that's when you have to dig in and really analyze everything. I had to ask: Am I leaving because I got my feelings hurt or am I leaving because I'm done? During those tough times, there is a good process to follow. You have to analyze, initiate, organize, and follow through. By that I mean, analyze the situation, initiate an action plan, organize it, and then follow through with it. It's a good way not to let our emotions get in the way of what we're doing.

THE REST OF THE STORY

I see a lot of high school kids training really hard, doing collegiate and open-level kind of training, and they may have coaches with coaching degrees. We just didn't know about that kind of training when I was in high school.

I would tell those athletes it is important to rest. You have to rest and you have to know when it's OK to do that. Athletes may think, "I'm being a wimp. I'm not giving it my all." Really, when your body is ready to perform well, with all the training that has gone on, you could even take five days off and feel fresh. Especially when you get to the point where you've done such consistent training over the years, you're going to be OK.

I've run well after a few days off because my body was rested, and my mind was rested. But a lot of times coaches and athletes don't want to take a break, or maybe they get one day off. No one has a quote endorsing rest. We push "No pain, no gain" or "Go hard or go home." Well, I say, "You've got to rest to be your best" or "Rest, and then take the test."

> " No one has a quote endorsing rest. We push 'No pain, no gain' or 'Go hard or go home.' Well, I say, 'You've got to rest to be your best' or 'Rest, and then take the test.' "

LONGEVITY IN THE SPORT

I remained healthy and was lucky to have a body that adapted. We didn't really cross-train back then. I didn't do pool workouts, we didn't have AlterG treadmills, I wasn't getting massages. I guess my body was able to endure that type of training. That's a God-given, genetic piece of it.

Mentally, I enjoyed it. It was fun. I'd be doing well, but even when I wasn't, and I was finishing in the back, I still would go run overseas and enjoy it. When I did hit my stride, around 1991 onward, I remembered the pain of the struggle that I felt earlier. So I didn't take it for granted. I appreciated every moment.

WISDOM FROM A WINNER

Take your time and grow and learn and develop. Maximize your own talent, and then go from there. Don't compare yourself to anybody else.

Whatever training someone tells you they did or posts about, that doesn't mean a thing. That's what they did. You may not need that type of training. Appreciate your own talent and work your own talent.

Also, be able to communicate with coaches. Say, "I want to do this" or "I don't want to do this." You may want to run the mile, but your coach may have you in the 400, for example. Talk that out.

For high schoolers, your parents have to be your advocates. You just can't send your kid off to the coaches. If issues arise, the parent can see what's going on first and address it. Whether it's being tired or something is wrong with their health or emotionally, the parent will see that first.

Appreciate and understand why you're doing it. Is your goal to be a champion, a conference champion, part of a team? Whatever it is, know your reasons.

JOAN BENOIT SAMUELSON

First women's Olympic Marathon champion (1984); two-time Boston Marathon winner; former US marathon record-holder

DATE OF BIRTH: May 16, 1957

CITIZENSHIP: USA

CURRENT RESIDENCE: ME

COLLEGE: Bowdoin College and North Carolina State for two years (1977–1978)

PRO PRs:

10,000 METERS: 32:07

HALF MARATHON: 1:08:34

MARATHON: 2:21:21

STARTING OUT

I love to ski and I had ambitions of making it to the Olympics in ski racing. I broke my leg my sophomore year in high school, when I was also playing field hockey and basketball. I started to run to get back in shape. I found the accessibility and affordability of the sport much more enticing than the expensive ski racing and waiting for the snow and traveling to the mountains, etc.

There wasn't an organized track team for women my first two years. I was a sophomore in high school in 1972 when Title IX was passed, so my career and the opportunities that Title IX provided are parallel to each other. I kept challenging myself with longer and longer distances.

PROUD MOMENTS

I'm proud of the longevity of my career—and being able to enjoy my career for as many years as I have. And also, being able to enjoy the sport with our children. I'm proud of the way I have rallied in most situations, even when the chips were down or the odds were not good. I mean, a lot of people didn't think I'd be able to come back from knee surgery 17 days before the Olympic Trials in '84.* [She won the women's Olympic Marathon.] I just knew there wasn't anybody out there training as hard as I was. I didn't lose sight of that.†

I've managed flare-ups and the aging process and trying to balance a career with community service and public appearances and raising children. I've been able to strike a pretty decent balance and live a full life, I think that's why I'm able to enjoy the longevity that I have.

---

* **MOLLY:** In historic fashion, Joan won that first women's Olympic Marathon in front of a home crowd in Los Angeles. The year before, she had set the world record in the event. It was a special moment for women's distance running in the United States!

† **SARA:** Also, it is incredible that she was able to go into the Trials and race a marathon 17 days after surgery!

THE FIRST WOMEN'S OLYMPIC MARATHON CHAMP

The first time the marathon was an Olympic event was in 1984. I knew we were on home ground, so to speak, here in the States, and I knew I'd have a lot of support out there. Nike had put up a bigger-than-life wall mural* on a building not too far from the LA Coliseum in Watts. I had seen that mural the previous fall because I'd run a half marathon in San Diego. It's actually what kept me going through the trials and tribulations of the knee issue before the Olympic Trials, because I knew Nike was counting on me and they put a lot of faith in me to do that.

A lot of people had written me off and chose to do cover stories on other athletes due to my injuries. *Life* magazine had planned to do a big spread, but after the injury they instead put a little insert of me in a rocking chair in a nightgown sipping a mug of tea.

That just added fuel to my fire. When people count me out, it really motivates me. Viewing it as going in as an underdog without expectations is a much easier way to go than being on the top. I think the fact that I came back for the Trials so close to the arthroscopic surgery should have sent a message out to all my competitors that I wanted to get to LA for a reason.

I think most young people have dreams of becoming an Olympic or world champion. I wasn't any different from those kids. I had early dreams of making it into the Olympics as a ski racer. At the time, I was devastated. The silver lining was that I broke my leg and started to run as a form of rehab. When people are injured and lose faith or lose heart, I just tell them my biggest frustrations and my biggest injuries have been the best motivators and the most meaningful lessons I've learned.

---

* **MOLLY:** The mural was a giant Joan! Having just set the world record in Boston in 1983, they believed she could do big things at the next year's Games.

ON STARTING A MAJOR ROAD RACE

When I came into the finishing tunnel in LA in '84, I asked myself if I was capable of carrying the mantle that went with the first woman to win an Olympic marathon. I didn't have a lot of time to think about it, but I said to myself, *I'll figure it out*. I made my friends and family promise me afterward that I would give back to a sport and a community that had given so much to me during my training and career.

The first year of the Beach to Beacon 10K was 1998. I always thought I'd trained on some of the most beautiful roads in the country. I had the opportunity to meet a banker who wanted me to do some work with the bank, and as I was leaving his office I noticed a picture of him finishing the New York City Marathon. I spun on my heels and said, "Excuse me. Do you run marathons?" And he said, "Oh, yeah, I've run five or six New York City Marathons." I said, "Well, I have an idea for you! I want to start a race, and we can call it the People's Beach to Beacon 10K, because it's for all the people."* Our sport is special because you can put the best runners in the world side by side with recreational, everyday runners.†

---

* **MOLLY:** The Beach to Beacon 10K was on my racing bucket list for years, and it was so beautiful to run it in person! Joan is chair of the race today, and her event brings pros to her hometown (Cape Elizabeth, Maine), inspires young runners, brings the community together, and provides a cash donation to a deserving charity in Maine each year. It makes Joan's legacy even more golden!

† **SARA:** The whole community is involved. Families in the community house the elite athletes and there is a big lobster dinner afterward with the elite athletes, sponsors, and families involved. Everyone there loves Joanie!

LIZ McCOLGAN

1991 World Championship 10,000-meter gold medalist; 1988 Olympic 10,000-meter silver medalist; winner of New York City, London, and Tokyo Marathons; three-time Olympian

DATE OF BIRTH: May 24, 1964
CITIZENSHIP: UK
CURRENT RESIDENCE: Doha, Qatar
COLLEGE: University of Alabama

HIGH SCHOOL PR:

800 METERS: 2:07

PRO PRs:

5,000 METERS: 14:59
10,000 METERS: 30:57
HALF MARATHON: 1:07:11
MARATHON: 2:26:52

EILISH McCOLGAN

Two-time Olympian

DATE OF BIRTH: November 25, 1990
CITIZENSHIP: UK
CURRENT RESIDENCE: London, UK
COLLEGE: University of Dundee

HIGH SCHOOL PRs:

800 METERS: 2:12
1,500 METERS: 4:27

COLLEGE PRs:

1,500 METERS: 4:13
3,000-METER
STEEPLECHASE: 9:48
5,000 METERS: 15:44

PRO PRs:

1,500 METERS: 4:00
3,000 METERS: 8:31
3,000-METER
STEEPLECHASE: 9:35
5,000 METERS: 14:28
10,000 METERS: 30:58

LIZ'S STEADY START

LIZ: I started running when I was 11. We came from a fairly poor background, so we never got an awful lot of opportunities to do sports. I was always one of those kids who rushed about like mad everyplace and loved sports, any kind of sport.

My PE teacher was a marathon runner. Instead of doing hockey or netball [a sport similar to basketball] in class, he put us in cross-country runs. Whereas all the other kids would stop and walk, I'd run the whole course. I wasn't that good, but I never gave up. I always ran the full way. So he advised me to join a local club.

I was never the best. I qualified for Scottish School championships— I'd be maybe fourth or fifth on our team of 10 girls. It was a very competitive age group—we had girls like Yvonne Murray, who went on to win an Olympic bronze medal, and we had girls who would run European juniors and things like that. I was never a standout, but I'd say I was the most hardworking.

I got the opportunity to go on scholarship to the United States when I was 17. I went to school in Idaho for a year, and ran some National Junior records there. Then I was recruited by the University of Alabama, and went there for three years and won NCAA indoors. I was still pretty unknown back home in the UK. I came back home after winning the NCAA title and won my first British title, which was in the 10,000. That qualified me for the Commonwealth Games in 1986. That was my first championship. That was the first time that I realized that I was pretty good at the longer stuff. The 10,000 came pretty easily to me. The workload suited me. Around the age of 19 to 20, it became quite clear to me that I really wanted to make a career out of running. But it took me that length of time to excel at it and to be comfortable with it and to start to win races and have people taking note.

THE BIRTH OF GLOBAL 5Ks AND 10Ks

LIZ: I was at a disadvantage because I was a true 10,000-meter runner, and we could only run 3,000 and 1,500 most of my career.* It was quite restrictive on how good I could be. I wasn't winning medals at championships before the 10,000 because it was just too short for me. I still ran 4:01 for 1,500 but it was 64-laps the whole way, strength rather than speed. When the 10,000 became a possibility for me, it was brilliant. Then I went on to the marathon. But it came along at the right time for the development of women's sports, and for me it opened up a whole different level of athletics.

HAVING PRO RUNNER PARENTS

EILISH: I suppose because my parents were both runners, people may think I was forced into it, or I just came out the womb with trainers on and was forced down to the track.† My parents almost shied away from me doing athletics. My mom says all the time she always wanted the decision to go into sports to be my decision.

To be honest, I don't really remember much about my mom racing. I never saw a race. She didn't have medals around the house and never forced me to sit and watch videotapes of her running back then. It was really only when I turned maybe 15, 16, that journalists used to throw the same questions at me: "Have you watched your mom's races? Have you seen your mom's medals?"

It was a similar progression to my mom's running with regard to how a teacher at school put me into a local cross-country race, probably because of the McColgan name. I just loved it. I also was never the

---

* **SARA:** The first Olympic 10,000 was in 1988; the first Olympic 5,000 was in 1996.

† **MOLLY:** Eilish's father, Peter, ran the steeplechase at the 1991 World Championships.

best kid running. I wasn't breaking records, but finished in the top four or five. I just loved everything about it. I came from playing a lot of team sports, like netball and field hockey. As much as I love those, I felt like I could never control everyone. When you're in a team sport, there's so much more going on. I liked the individuality of running.

In primary school, someone had scouted me to go along to the local running club. As a kid you feel like this is a big deal. In reality, they take the top 10 kids and just ask everyone, but I felt so special that someone had asked me to come to the club. I remember asking my mom and dad to take me, and they were a bit hesitant at first. I begged and begged. My mum said to me, "Look, if you stay here a certain amount of months, and if you enjoy it and try all the events at first, when you find something you enjoy, then I'll coach you." That's the way it naturally progressed. I was doing high jump, long jump, hurdles. I think my first Scottish medal came in the javelin, when I was under 13. I naturally enjoyed those longer distances more than I did the others. I was about 15 or 16 when I started to focus on that and my mom started coaching me.

PACING YOUR DEVELOPMENT

LIZ: Training Eilish, I was very aware of pushy parents. When I went to the track for training on my own as a youngster, I used to see all these girls getting pressured from the parents and crying and not wanting to do reps. It really struck a chord with me. I said if I had children I didn't want them to do something that they didn't enjoy, and I've kept that ethos all along. There's no point in training a kid the way you'd train an adult. If you're really serious about it when you're 18 and you're still in the sport, then it's time to get excited about it. My job was to get Eilish to 18 healthy and enjoying the sport. Then the more serious training started.

> "I said if I had children I didn't want them to do something that they didn't enjoy, and I've kept that ethos all along. There's no point in training a kid the way you'd train an adult.

It was very difficult because I remember her being 15 and 16 when we would go away to compete on junior national teams. She would speak to other girls who were out running 10 miles a day and she'd come back and say, "I'm not training hard enough. I need to do this because this girl does this." But when you look back now, Eilish is probably one of very few girls who actually made it right through from 12 years old to the senior national teams.

EILISH: I definitely agree with what my mum has said. I remember being angry sometimes, coming home from competitions after finishing sixth or seventh. Some of these girls would be breaking records and setting championship best times. At 15 years old, when you're 20 to 30 seconds behind these top girls, you tend to think, "I'm never going to get there" or "I'm just not good enough," because that's just the way you think when you're young. You may not yet have a concept of how everyone's bodies develop at different rates. Everyone progresses at different rates.

It's not until you get to the age of maybe 20 that you realize that's where things level out. People have stopped growing, people have stopped developing. You become stronger as a female athlete as well. You know exactly what you want to do—your mind-set changes as well. So I'd say, as a kid, I found it really challenging to be almost held back. But now when I look back, it was one of the best things that happened to me, because what happens in the juniors is almost irrelevant if you want to make it as a senior athlete. You don't have to be breaking all the records or winning all the races as a junior to become an Olympic athlete.

> "At 15 years old, when you're 20 to 30 seconds behind these top girls, you tend to think, 'I'm never going to get there' or 'I'm just not good enough,' because that's just the way you think when you're young. You may not yet have a concept of how everyone's bodies develop at different rates. Everyone progresses at different rates."

OVERCOMING INJURIES

EILISH: I came into the sport as a steeplechase runner. I ran it because my flat times weren't good enough to make teams. I remember how, as a junior, they were really struggling to fill the steeplechase spots because nobody wanted to do it. Nobody wants to jump in the water! I was about 17 years old and said, "Put me in it. I'll try to get a point for the team," and I won the race. My first national team was as a steeplechaser, and it just progressed in that way. I made the Olympic Games at that event and thought, "This is what I'm going to do."

I eventually had two serious injuries while steepling in 2011. I broke my navicular bone in my foot and shattered all the bones around it as well. So I had five screws on a metal plate—they had to re-create the middle of my foot. From 2011 when I broke it to 2014, I was still in quite a lot of pain through the foot. I never got the flexibility back, and it was just painful running all the time. I used to run twice a day before this, but because of the pain, I just couldn't do it. It was difficult for my mum as a coach because she's thinking you need to be doing this certain amount of training to get to a high level.

So we changed things. Instead of running every evening, I would cross-train. I would do 40 minutes in the evening, easy. I qualified for the Olympic Games again doing it like that. I wasn't in the best shape ever, but I was good enough to make the team, and then we got back into normal training again, around 2013, 2014. I had a fair share of injuries even throughout those years—some stress fractures in my shin, a hamstring injury—all sorts of stuff.

The final straw came in 2015. I broke my ankle and spent nine months in a boot and it just didn't heal. I had to have surgery, another two screws in that one foot. The same thing happened when I started back running. I was in more pain than even when I first fractured it. That is really when the cross-training was crucial. I started running in the morning, building up my running week after week as I could tolerate the pain, and in the evenings cross-training anywhere from 30 minutes to an hour. (I've never gone over an hour of cross-training. My priority is always the running.)

Less than a year later, I qualified for the Olympic Games in the 5,000. I ran 15:09 off just cross-training in the evenings and running less than 40 miles a week. I couldn't believe it. That was probably the first indication to me and my mom that we found something that seems to work for me. Yes, it's low mileage, but I still have two really good-quality track sections throughout the week. Those were the priority. If I'm able to hit paces on the track that I need to be hitting, then that's what's going to help my fitness forward when it comes to racing, and everything around that is supplementary.

My mileage has obviously gone up now because I am looking toward the 10,000 and eventually the half marathon and eventually, further down the line, the marathon. I'm aiming for 60 miles a week, hopefully 70 as we get into next year. But cross-training will always be a huge part of my program because I've found it really beneficial. I think it helped me recovery-wise, and I incurred fewer injuries, for sure. I'm very grateful that I can still continue to run the flat events and do something that I love.

LIZ: I really didn't pick up a lot of injuries for a while. My only bad injury that I picked up was later in my career, when I was getting a numbness in my foot from a back issue, so they made an orthotic for my shoe. I went for a 5-mile run with one orthotic in my shoe, and tore something in my knee. I had to go in for surgery. Unfortunately for me, when I went in for surgery, I got an infection and I was left with a knee that I couldn't bend and I couldn't straighten. I was out for six months and I had all sorts of physical therapy.

After that, I went to Florida because it's warm. I hoped it would help my muscles loosen up. When I was out there, I met Gerard Hartmann,*

---

* **SARA:** Gerard Hartmann was one of the most world-renowned physical therapists at the time. He worked with Bob Kennedy, Sonia O'Sullivan, Paula Radcliffe, and even rock star Bono. When you are dealing with running injuries, it is important to find a doctor and physical therapist you trust and one who is knowledgeable.

a physical therapist. He was working for me for like four to six hours a day because I just couldn't straighten my leg. We worked together for about seven months straight. I went from not being able to do anything other than jogging—I could barely sprint, and when I did turn around a corner it was just a nightmare—to eventually getting back. It took me two years.

FUN ON THE RUN

LIZ: I was in great shape for the London Marathon. Before the race I was in Hyde Park. I'm running around thinking I'm the bee's knees and getting ready for my big race on Sunday. As I was running about 6:00 per mile, out of nowhere came this guy running with a backpack on and a pair of flip-flops. He passes me like there's no tomorrow. I started chasing him. For about five miles this guy ran side by side with me, and then he just bolted off to run to work. I can't believe he ran as fast as he did in all that. And I was fit—I won the marathon that year. It was an eye-opener to what people are capable of doing!

EILISH: I was preparing for the Olympic Games in Rio, and mine was one of the last events on the schedule, so the whole Great Britain team were already in Brazil, and half the team had already competed. I was still in France until the last minute.

I was in the gym and had been cross-training. I sat down to text my mom splits from my final session. The Olympics were on TV in the gym, and this French guy came by and said, "If texting was an Olympic sport, you'd be in Brazil right now! That's unfortunate for you." I just looked up and thought, *How cheeky—you have no idea!* I should have said, "Actually, I am an Olympian, and I'm going tomorrow," but I thought he'd just think I was a psychopath.

A DREAM JOB

EILISH: It's been rewarding to do something that I love. As a kid, I never believed I would be able to be an Olympic athlete. I didn't go to bed dreaming of winning Olympic gold or dreaming of becoming a professional athlete. It's always been something I've enjoyed doing. like a hobby. I never, ever believed it could be a job or my profession. I am so grateful that I have the opportunity to continue doing something that I love every single day.

Another rewarding part is the people you meet along the way. Joining the running club as a kid was one of the best things I ever did. The friends that I made at the club molded me into the person I am today. I think that's one of the most rewarding parts of the sport—being able to meet other people who have the same passion and the same drive as you.

LIZ: When I was young, I wasn't given a lot of opportunities and I was very unconfident. But athletics gives you an education, and it gives everybody the same opportunity to excel. You can decide how you push yourself, where you're going to go with it, and what enjoyment and level you want to get out of it.

I'm just grateful that I was given the opportunity to get into the sport. When I started, there was no way that you would ever have thought you could make a living out of athletics because women just didn't. Then it developed in such a fast way over the years. It's been so rewarding how the sport educated me and grounded me in a way that I've gathered a lot of information on endurance running, and I've been lucky that I've been able to share that with a lot of people.

And I love coaching. I love watching Eilish, because, obviously, I'm her mother, and it's great to see that development. You're always learning, and you always learn from new people. That's what's great about the sport, too.

McCOLGAN WISDOM

EILISH: Focus on yourself. I know how easy it is to get sucked into what other people are doing. When I was younger and had been around young girls who were training so hard and doing all these long runs and doubles, I would think, *Should I be doing that?* It makes you start questioning your own training. Same thing with regard to eating well and fueling. You may see some girls who aren't doing that correctly. It would make me ask myself, *Am I doing this wrong? Is it me?*

The most important thing is to be strong in your own decisions and also to have the right people around you. If you know you have a good, supportive family member and a good coach, then that's half the battle. It's important to focus on yourself rather than other people because you can't change what they do.

> **Enjoy your running first and foremost. You don't need to be doing anything outstanding as a youngster. You just need to be consistent.**

LIZ: Enjoy your running first and foremost. You don't need to be doing anything outstanding as a youngster. You just need to be consistent. You just need to turn up and tick boxes. If you keep yourself healthy and keep the love for what you're doing, when you get to age 18 and 19, then you can step up and take it to whatever level you feel you want to do.

But when you're young, it's all about just being fit and healthy and enjoying doing what you do. You don't ever want to get a fear of racing. You want to enjoy every race. Every race is a learning experience, even if it's good or bad. There's always something that you can take from a race to make it better.

SOCIAL MEDIA AND TODAY'S ATHLETES

EILISH: It's nice to be able to connect with the next generation. Paula Radcliffe was the one on the TV all the time when I was getting into the sport. If I could message Paula, or ask Kelly Holmes a question, that would have been amazing as a kid. Now because of social media, you do have the opportunity to do that. Every single day I get messages from young girls who are 12 or 13. I encourage them to keep healthy, keep fit, to have body positivity. There are so many positive things that can come from sports.

> **It's nice to be able to connect with the next generation.**

I am very well aware of the negatives of social media, but I think the positives far outweigh all the negativity. The negativity is on other people. I'm almost 30, so I'm strong enough to be able to take the negativity, remove it, and carry on with my life. But I think if you're a teenager, it's probably very difficult to remove that negativity. I think it's probably something that weighs on your mind.

With regard to comparison, I think that's there in young girls. Do they look at supermodels or people on TV or certainly even athletes being lean and skinny and just associate that with thinking that person doesn't eat or that person eats only some vegetables? They may create a story by looking at a picture without knowing that the athlete—if they're at the Olympic Games and they're running fast times—is fueling correctly. They're strong, they're doing things correctly, and they're looking after their bodies to get to that high level, certainly if they can do it year after year.

The older you get, the easier it is to recognize that. But it's very difficult for youngsters to make that connection. I think it is important that we as athletes get that message across that, yes, we're skinny. I'm always going to be skinny. I was skinny when I was 12 years old. I'm going to be skinny when I'm 42 years old. That's just my body shape. But it's important to get the message across about how I look after myself and do it in a positive way. I'm fueling this body correctly because it needs to handle the amount of training that I'm doing.

THE
1990s

LYNN JENNINGS

Three-time Olympian; 1992 Olympic 10,000-meter bronze medalist; three-time World Cross Country champion

DATE OF BIRTH: July 1, 1960
CITIZENSHIP: USA
CURRENT RESIDENCE: Portland, ME
COLLEGE: Princeton University

HIGH SCHOOL PRs:

1,500 METERS: 4:18
MILE: 4:39
2 MILES: 10:10

COLLEGE PR:

3,000 METERS: 9:01

PRO PRs:

MILE: 4:24
3,000 METERS: 8:40
5,000 METERS: 15:07
10,000 METERS: 31:10

STARTING WITH THE BOYS

Like a lot of kids who grew up in the country, I didn't have a lot of organized things going on. The town of Harvard, Massachusetts, at the time was—and still is—rural, but sort of in a sophisticated, near-Boston way. The only option when I hit ninth grade was girls' field hockey or boys' cross-country. The school was small, with about 45 to 50 kids per class.

There had never been a girl who went out for cross-country. I tried girls' field hockey and lasted a day. The sticks hitting the shins and the skirts dissuaded me, so I showed up for the boys' cross-country team. It didn't occur to anybody that I shouldn't be allowed to run. And so I did.

At first, I was slower than all the boys, although I had always been naturally fast. But I was not a trained runner. So I would go home after school, get my dog Otis, bring him back to school, and run with him in practice.

That very first season as a ninth grader, I finished, if not last, close to last in every race. I would be the only girl on an entire bus of soccer boys and cross-country boys and the male coaches. I always sat in the front row with a book. It was intimidating and isolating. I felt very different, like an outsider. It's not that anyone was discouraging me from running—but the minute I'd get off the bus and we were doing a warm-up on the course, I'd hear, "They've got a girl on their team." I would just pretend I never heard that.

> " Now the doors are wide open and women are running through them and not looking back. It's fantastic. "

In the end, one of the lifelong lessons I got from that experience was that a lot of things that happen to us end up having value in often completely unintended ways. I didn't figure into the team scoring. I was free to create my own racing strategy and plan, and I was desperate to never finish last. I would keep my eyes up and ahead and I would find some poor, hapless boy to run down over the last part of the race so I wouldn't finish last. I became adept at forcing myself to focus on that.

Those skills were exactly how I raced cross-country the rest of my career. I kept my eyes up and ahead, and I would run down anybody in front of me. I also learned to embrace and cultivate who I was becoming that first season. I was becoming a runner. I trained over the summer, came back as a 10th grader, and was number one on the boys team! That first season was incredibly formative and it really shaped who I was. I was a really tough track runner, but I was absolutely passionate and completely wedded to being a great cross-country runner.

ON RUNNING THE FIRST WOMEN'S OLYMPIC 5,000 AND 10,000

My parents took me to the 1976 Olympics in Montreal when I was 15. The longest a woman could run was the 1,500 meters.

Toward the end of my career, in 1996, the 5,000 was added to the Games, and I dropped down to run it because I was like, "Been there, done that with the 10K. I'm going to try this." I also ran the 10K the first year it was in the Olympics [1988]. It's insane to think that's how long and slow the progress has been. Now the doors are wide open and women are running through them and not looking back. It's fantastic.

COLLEGE SETBACKS

I had a fairly tumultuous five years that was essentially the by-product of having been wildly successful as a high school athlete and living a pretty elite kind of life as a teenager, then getting to Princeton and being overwhelmed by umpteen things.

In a way, my running disappeared when I was at Princeton, which was four years, plus I was asked to leave for a year. I kind of got it together my senior year. Happily, there was no internet at that time, so I didn't have people wondering where I was and saying, "Whatever happened to Lynn Jennings?"—at least not in a public way.

I graduated in 1983 and the Olympic Trials were in '84. I thought, *I'll train for the Trials and just go despite not being at the top level.* That was the first year of the marathon, with Joanie [Benoit Samuelson] winning. It was also the first year the women's 3,000 was added. I promptly finished last in one of my heats of the 3,000.

I hadn't really been training. I'd been living alone. I'd just been sort of playing at running. I crossed the finish line, absolutely humiliated. I could hear the track announcer calling my finish. "Here comes former national junior 1,500-meter champion Lynn Jennings," which was something I had accomplished five years earlier.

I went home to my parents and I said, "I quit. I'm done." There was something about my maturity level and my ability to figure out how to get where I wanted to go, along with dealing with being on a women's team for the first time at Princeton, dealing with the academics, dealing with the social stuff at Princeton—it was way above my pay grade coming from a smaller town. It all just stymied me.

The summer of 1984, my parents hired me to paint their house. So I spent the summer going up and down a ladder and occasionally sneaking inside to catch glimpses of the Olympics on my parents' tiny bedroom TV. I still remember standing there in my paint-splattered clothes, holding my paintbrush, watching Joanie win her gold medal and thinking back to how I used to just routinely beat Joan when we raced in high school. She was three years older, but we ran for the same Liberty Athletic Club. I remember thinking, *Why is Joanie winning a gold medal at the Olympics and why am I standing here painting my parents' house?* It just was enough of a kick in the butt to get me going.

But I was lost. I didn't have anyone to train with. That fall, I started training seriously again. I slowly gained momentum when I was around 21, 22, 23 years of age. I really emerged when I was 25. At that point, I was going to take my career and run with it and not let anything stand in my way after that big hump I had to get over earlier. The college years can be extremely difficult to get through. I was not exempt from that.

ON NOT RACING IN TRAINING

Early in my career I had exercise physiology work done by Jack Daniels. He knew I trained alone and would tell me, "Lynn, do your work every day. You're going to train at one level, but you're going to race at a much higher level. You go into the beyond for racing. So your training doesn't need to be hammerhead incredible every day."

The athletes who push so hard every day are, almost by definition, insecure. They overtrain. I pretty much saved my most brilliant running for racing. I think overtraining is one trap that a lot of athletes fall into because of doubts. We all have doubts—that's part of being an athlete. But overtraining is just an absolute career killer. We know too many bodies on the side of the road that were overtrained, and they don't exist anymore as athletes.

LESSONS IN LONGEVITY

I think I was fortunate that I had a body that was suited to running from a biomechanical standpoint. I lost extremely little time to injury and illness. I really did not struggle with injuries. I think that I attribute it to training with determination and great intensity, but never crossing the line into destructive body training.

If something was tweaky or pinched or squeaky, I backed off. I knew that if I ran over 100 miles a week, I was going to start to squeak. So I didn't do that. My most effective mileage was in the 70 to 90 range.

I also mixed it up. I ran indoors, outdoors, cross-country, roads. That was what kept me sparky, doing all these different kinds of seasons. I think that that spoke to my body's ability to be resilient. A lot of it was just that I picked my parents well, but I also took great care not to overtrain and did all the right things, like eating and sleeping well.

PROUD MOMENTS

I'm proud of the Olympic medal, of course, because that's such a singular thing. I'm proud of the world cross-country titles, definitely. I'm also

> It takes a real magic trick to make it through the quadrennial and to have everything work out so that on the day, you not only show up with the correct fitness, but with the correct mental state, and that you race in a way to bring home the medal, and that you do it today and not yesterday or the day before or tomorrow.

proud of my mile PR of 4:24. I remember feeling like I wasn't legitimate until I could run a decent mile.

But I'm proudest of the Olympic bronze, because the Olympics are every four years. It takes a real magic trick to make it through the quadrennial and to have everything work out so that on the day, you not only show up with the correct fitness, but with the correct mental state, and that you race in a way to bring home the medal, and that you do it today and not yesterday or the day before or tomorrow. A lot of it is a lottery.

Being an Olympian has a specialness. I see it as a subconscious beacon—it reminds me of who I am and how to stay true to myself. Having the medal, it's like a North Star. It reminds me of how I was training every day, and how I would tell myself to just do what I can today. Tomorrow will come, and I'll do it again tomorrow. That process is something to treasure in oneself, the ability to be able to do that.

THE POWER OF ONE

I took a certain amount of pride in training alone. However, I enjoyed it very much when I was out in San Luis Obispo training in the group.* If I had had the ability to go back and do something differently, perhaps I might have thrived in a group training environment.

But I'm also extremely solitary and introverted in a way, so I'm unsure if it would have been a complete asset for me. I'm not sure I know

---

* **MOLLY:** Brooks Johnson had a group there that Lynn ran with during a training camp for two winters. Lynn's coach, John Babington, sent her workouts, and Brooks oversaw them for the three-month warm-weather stints.

full well the value of having really seamless training partners. I think that can extend a career and make runners better. It may not necessarily be good for every runner, but I would have liked to have tried it more. In the end, I think I used training alone as a way to make myself feel more powerful. I go out the door every day on my own and I use that as a spur for myself. My fierceness came from some of those things.

LYNN'S ADVICE FOR YOUNG RUNNERS

Love your body. See it as this incredible tool and possession that you own, and treat it with the utmost respect. If you disrespect your body and don't treat it well, it's going to be a much harder road for you. I'd say that comes first and foremost.

> **Love your body. See it as this incredible tool and possession that you own, and treat it with the utmost respect.**

The one thing about sports that is so fascinating is it's not what you look like; it's what you do. I absorbed that. My whole running career was what I did, not what I looked like. It helped me stay true to myself.

I was not afraid to fail. I was willing to go after huge goals and try again and again, over and over. Resiliency was one of my calling cards. That's life in a nutshell.

SONIA O'SULLIVAN

1995 World Championship 5,000-meter gold medalist; 2000 Olympic 5,000-meter silver medalist; two-time World Cross Country champion; four-time Olympian; five-time NCAA champion

DATE OF BIRTH: November 28, 1969
CITIZENSHIP: Ireland
CURRENT RESIDENCE: Cobh, Ireland/ Teddington, UK/Melbourne, Australia
COLLEGE: Villanova University

HIGH SCHOOL PRs:

800 METERS: 2:05
1,500 METERS: 4:35
3,000 METERS: 9:01

COLLEGE PRs:

1,500 METERS: 4:05
MILE: 4:33
3,000 METERS: 8:52
5,000 METERS: 15:17

PRO PRs:

1,500 METERS: 3:58
MILE: 4:17
3,000 METERS: 8:21
5,000 METERS: 14:41
10,000 METERS: 30:47
HALF MARATHON: 1:07:19

BEGINNINGS

I began running with my local club in Ireland, Ballymore Cobh AC. I also participated in school athletics competitions. I realized that when you win just one race and enjoy that feeling of competing, then you become more motivated to keep training harder and training more often to be better. You continue to set annual targets and goals for yourself through time and make specific race targets that bring you to new levels.

COLLEGE YEARS: PROMISE SHOWS THROUGH INJURIES

I had a number of injuries just as I was starting at Villanova University, so it wasn't the smoothest start to my college career. I was mentally motivated to compete and be a part of the team, but my body let me down throughout the first two years with numerous stress fractures. Even so, I still had at least one positive result each year that gave me hope that one day I would run faster than I did as a junior and be able to compete at college and then also on the Irish team at the European and World Championships and Olympics.

I was on and off running throughout my freshman and sophomore years. I think I was just too keen to get back to running every time. As I had maintained fitness in the pool and gym aerobically, I was fit to run, but often did too much too soon. It took me a while to work out a slower return to training and competition.

In my junior year, during the indoor season, I did a lot of training outdoors by myself, running around grass fields and on soft surfaces. I believed the hard indoor track was not good for me, so I asked my coach, Marty Stern, if I could do fartlek sessions outside by myself, and he agreed. I did pre-race sessions of things like 200s with the team that season, and I was able to win the 3,000 at the Big East and Regionals and qualify for Nationals, where I finished third. This was a big breakthrough for me after two years of injury and lack of any momentum in training and racing.

PRIDE IN PERSISTENCE

My first coach, Sean Kennedy, always told me that great athletes always come back from disappointments. The 1996 Olympics was my most difficult time as an athlete. I was unable to finish the 5,000, even though I was world champion the year previously and one of the favorites going into the Olympics.

It took time, but eventually I got myself back to win the World Cross Country Championships in 1998. I am proud that I was able to persist and compete again and renew my confidence as an athlete.

SECRETS TO SUCCESS

I think the Olympics can seem greater than they are. Many athletes will train harder in an Olympic year and try to do everything they can. In reality, if you can be the best in the world one year, not much changes in a year. You just have to train at the same level and in a more relaxed way, rather than looking to force a gain from every session.

Success in distance running is achieved through the accumulation of blocks of training, topped off with some races in preparation for the main race that you are aiming for each year. It's not rocket science. I have heard many coaches say there are no secret sessions required to be the best in the world.

> "Be patient and take time to build up strength and endurance. This is the foundation required to compete on a high level year after year."

SEEING THE WORLD

The most rewarding thing for me has been the opportunity to travel the world and experience different cultures and share the journey with athletes from all over the world. Everywhere I have run has a special memory. Those memories mean even more now when I get the chance to revisit these places and explore more. When competing, what you see can often be limited to airport, hotel, and track!

LESSONS FROM A LEGEND

Be patient and take time to build up strength and endurance. This is the foundation required to compete on a high level year after year. Don't try to achieve everything at once and take all the stepping-stones along the way. If you try to skip steps, the foundation will be weak and more likely you will struggle to finish out the season each year. Be flexible and listen to your body. A few days' rest and checking on any discomfort may save you from longer time spent on the sidelines.

AMY RUDOLPH

Two-time Olympian; two-time NCAA champion

DATE OF BIRTH: September 18, 1973
CITIZENSHIP: USA
CURRENT RESIDENCE: Ames, IA
COLLEGE: Providence College

HIGH SCHOOL PRs:

1,500 METERS: 4:23
1,600 METERS: 4:55
MILE: 4:52
3,200 METERS: 10:54

PRO PRs:

1,500 METERS: 4:06
3,000 METERS: 8:39
5,000 METERS: 14:56
10,000 METERS: 31:18

A LIFELONG LOVE

I ran my first race when I was six at a local track meet. I ran the 50-yard dash, and I won. I just loved running as a kid. I loved the whole process. I had a lot of energy, and it was a good release. Even now, if there's some big decision that needs to be made, I find running is a really great outlet to process things.

FINDING HER SWEET SPOT

I was fortunate that I didn't have that many injuries in running. I suffered more from anemia and worked to keep my ferritin high. So, for me, it was more learning to manage my body and what it could handle.

Often, I would see what other athletes were doing and think, *If I could just do a little bit more, I'd be able to compete with them.* That comparison is a normal thought process, but it's not necessarily the right one. I had to learn the hard way what my sweet spot was with mileage. I had to tweak the workouts to get better and manage my diet and iron.

A SUDDEN 5,000-METER STAR

I actually was a miler in college. My senior year, I got hurt right around the time of the NCAA indoor meet. I had won the title as a junior and came back for outdoor NCAAs and got beat there. So my coach, Ray Treacy, and I sat down at the end of the season. He said, "I think you are close to maxing out at 1,500 meters, and I think you should move up to the 5K. It is going to be a new event at the Olympics. This is a really good opportunity to just get your feet wet and go to the Trials and see what it's all about. You can see where you stack up and use it as an experience to tap into in four years when you're stronger and more mature."

We went there and I actually made the team and was like, "Oh crap, here we go!" The final at the Trials was only the third time I had run the event. Ray advised me to go to Europe and get in a fast 5,000 to practice some race tactics. We went to Stockholm, and it was just one of those special nights. Everything clicked, and I felt like I could have run forever.

That was when I broke the American record. It's crazy—I actually never ran faster than that 14:56. I knew there were points in my career I could have; I just didn't get the opportunity.

LESS IS MORE

One of the biggest lessons I learned is "less is more." It's hard to find where that line of "too much" is and to know not to cross it in training in order to get the most out of yourself.

If I had to go back and do anything over, it would probably have been 2000. I made the Olympic team by default. Someone decided to run a different event, so I moved up from fourth to third. I was on a mission to prove that I deserved that spot on the team and I was going to do something really special at the Games. I was in the best shape in my life going into it. I pushed a little bit too far over that line and got sick at the Olympic Village. You don't ever get that opportunity back.

> "Your body is your biggest asset, your biggest tool. If you learn how to read it and listen to it, it's going to tell you what you need. It's really your best compass."

I should have been a little more relaxed leading into the Games. Your body is your biggest asset, your biggest tool. If you learn how to read it and listen to it, it's going to tell you what you need. It's really your best compass.

When you want success so badly, it's so easy to try to skip steps along the way and then you don't actually enjoy it. All the things that the sport is giving you—whether it's a personal best or state titles or national championships or just the friendships that you forge—absorb it and enjoy the process and everything that is involved in the process.

Don't try to force it. Realize that it's one day at a time. It's about the body of work, not just that one workout or that one race. It's about everything you can accomplish. I've had some athletes who had big goals and dreams and, for whatever reason, it just wasn't in the cards for them. You never know when it can be taken away. Take time to take it all in and look around you and be thankful for the opportunity. Enjoy the process!

THE EARLY
2000s—2010

AMY YODER BEGLEY

Two-time NCAA champion; 2008 Olympian; sixth in the 10,000 meters at the 2009 World Championships

DATE OF BIRTH: January 11, 1978
CITIZENSHIP: USA
CURRENT RESIDENCE: Atlanta, GA
COLLEGE: University of Arkansas

COLLEGE PRs:

1,500 METERS: 4:12
MILE: 4:41
3,000 METERS: 9:17
5,000 METERS: 15:45
10,000 METERS: 33:02

PRO PRs:

3,000 METERS: 8:53
5,000 METERS: 14:56
10,000 METERS: 31:13

HOW SHE STARTED

I went to road races starting when I was 10, because I would see a woman, her name was Julie Manger, running around the local park. She took me and my dad under her wing and told us about road races around our area. In middle school I didn't have a girls' team. At first I ran with the boys. I loved running on the boys' team. But there were times where my coach had to really fight for me to count because I wasn't in the top five and they didn't want me to count because I was running in the boys' race.

By the time I was an eighth-grader, we had a girls' team. By the time I got to high school I thought that was kind of boring, only racing the women. I grew up doing all of the cross-country and the club stuff. It was really fun going all over the country to race. A few women I raced way back then I also raced all throughout my career, like Kara Goucher and Carrie Tollefson.

DIETARY DISCOVERY

Gluten intolerance is the thing that was probably the worst challenge for me as an athlete. But also trying to find a place to train and people to train with was very hard. At the time there weren't many options. When I graduated, you could go to Team Minnesota for women or Hansons for men. There weren't the options that there are now. As a result, I moved around a lot.

Every time I'd get a new injury or a new illness, I'd head to a new place, with a new doctor, who didn't have my entire health history. In college, I was diagnosed with thyroid issues, and then just progressed from there with stress fractures and definite GI issues. Every time, I would get diagnosed with something new and it was never fully resolved. Finally getting diagnosed with celiac disease and going off wheat and just having my body fully recover was so helpful. I was amenorrheic for over five years, even though we tried everything and I gained 20 pounds to ensure I wasn't underweight. We tried every birth control method under the sun, but I never got my period back.

When I removed gluten from my diet, then I got my period back. Within two or three weeks, I felt different. I didn't realize how much swelling and water retention it caused. It took a while for the GI issues to get better. I would have to go to the bathroom every 30 minutes during training runs or workouts. My bone and stress injuries went away after I was diagnosed as well. I wouldn't get dehydrated so badly, which was really nice.

It was a slow process. About 18 months after I got a diagnosis, I made the Olympic team. It was probably a little over a year before I felt like my body had really turned the corner. My recovery was better, my iron levels were finally staying up. The biggest improvement was because I was able to absorb the nutrients in my food.

Not until 2009 did things really start clicking, and I really felt like I could recover, and race the way I wanted. That was the start of figuring out my potential.

DISRESPECT FOR AN OLYMPIAN

It angered me that people said that making the 2008 Olympic team was a fluke. Alberto [Salazar, Amy's coach] told me that I got lucky to make the team.* So all of 2009, I was motivated by thinking, *I'll prove that I can compete on the world stage.* Getting sixth at the World Championships was my way of really showing I belonged. I could be here, I should be here, I can compete with the best in the world.

---

* **SARA:** I'm not sure if Alberto was saying this to motivate Amy or if he really believed that she was lucky to make the team. Yes, there is luck involved in being fit, healthy, and ready on the day of the Trials to make the team. However, Amy had always been a top-level athlete and had trained hard for two years with her teammate Kara Goucher, who also made the team. She had to gain confidence with her teammate doing well and believed she could do it, too. It has to be difficult to hear that from your coach, one of the people you trust the most.

I've always responded that way when I was told I couldn't achieve a goal.

LOOKS AREN'T EVERYTHING

Alberto and I always argued about my weight. He always thought I should weigh less. We agreed that I would work with a nutritionist. We did bone-density scans and she made meal plans for me to follow. I had a couple of checkups a week with her. She had my back and went to bat for me with the coach.

Using a specialist who is grounded in science and understands the demands of your sport is critical. The person needs to be strong enough to stand up to the coach and to set healthy goals for you.

For example, regarding recovery, it's about the timing of eating and what you eat. It's about working with the coach to see what this day is going to look like. Is it a long-run day, a hard-interval day, etc.? Those are all different, depending on what you need for recovery and calories. Work with someone who's knowledgeable and also has a support system that you can lean on who's not always going to say, "Well, coach said that you should do it." Your parents or husband or a best friend can help you there.

When coaches put more emphasis on what the athlete looks like as opposed to what their workouts are—I don't even know how we got to that point in our sport.

I had my husband, Andrew, and my parents the whole time. Every time I wanted to quit, they would tell me, "Give it one more year." Finding that support system outside of the coach is important because the power dynamic can be hard. You need something outside to keep you grounded and see the bigger picture, because you can get sucked in really, really deep sometimes. It's really hard when you trust someone so much. You're putting faith in them to help bring you to a certain level, and then not having them have that same faith in you is really difficult.

Alberto was still talking about my size to his athletes nine years after

I left. He was still talking about me and my "big butt" and all these other terrible things.* At first, I was just angry and upset. Andrew says, in a way, I should be flattered, because I left an impression, even years later. He didn't think I could run well, and by doing so, I proved all of his theories wrong.

SIGNIFICANT (OTHER) CHALLENGES

As a pro coach right now, when I recruit, I ask athletes, "Is there a significant other who's going to affect your decision on where you're going?" Most of the men say, "No, I don't care what she does" or "No, but I have one." The women will say, "Well, my boyfriend might get into law school, so I'll go to one of the three places that he gets into." Or "My boyfriend is going to go work on Wall Street" or "My partner is going to go to get a master's."

Usually nothing is going to top their partner's influence. Transitioning from college to professional running is not an easy or smooth process. In college, athletes have all their training and recovery needs covered. If an athlete follows their significant other to a place that doesn't have a team or support system, they are going to have a harder transition.

FUNDAMENTALS FIRST

If I could go back to when I was younger, I would pay more attention to things like form drills and speed drills. I would work on more of the

---

* **MOLLY:** Alberto was served with a four-year ban from the sport by US Anti-Doping Agency (USADA) in 2019 and also faced a Safe Sport violation in 2020 for allegations of misconduct as a coach. His treatment of Mary Cain (see page 1) was an elevated example of a dynamic we see too often in women's and girls' sports. She came to him as a prodigy athlete when she was a teenager and he became preoccupied with her weight, pressuring her to push her body to an unhealthy level that led to injury. He also dismissed her mental health struggles. This kind of unbalanced power dynamic, a win-at-all-costs approach, and a misunderstanding of the female athlete's body have caused many women and girls to leave the sport early. Mary's story was one of many things that motivated us to put this book together.

fundamentals instead of just mileage and workouts. I would also try a wider variety of distances. If you can run different events throughout high school and college, you're going to be better off than just specializing.

REWARDS OF RUNNING

Learning the history of women's running has been rewarding. When I got done running, I didn't know what I wanted to do. So I did this project and interviewed 50 women for the Road Runners Club of America. Listening to all these women talk about how they got started running and the barriers they had to go through made me realize that I wanted to continue to help the next generation with running and getting there. My goal with coaching has always been to help women make that transition from college to the pros, but to do it in a better, faster way than I did. What I am enjoying the most is that now I can use all the things that I learned throughout my career to continue to help people.

ANN GAFFIGAN

2004 Olympic Trials steeplechase champion

DATE OF BIRTH: October 5, 1981
CITIZENSHIP: USA
CURRENT RESIDENCE: Kansas City, KS
COLLEGE: University of Nebraska

HIGH SCHOOL PR:

1,600 METERS: 4:55
3,200 METERS: 10:27

COLLEGE PRs:

800 METERS: 2:11
MILE: 4:43
STEEPLECHASE: 10:17

PRO PRs:

800 METERS: 2:13
1,500 METERS: 4:21
MILE: 4:43
3,000-METER STEEPLECHASE: 9:39

LISA AGUILERA

Two-time US steeplechase champion; former US steeplechase record-holder; NCAA steeplechase champion

DATE OF BIRTH: November 30, 1979
CITIZENSHIP: USA
CURRENT RESIDENCE: Scottsdale, AZ
COLLEGE: Arizona State University

HIGH SCHOOL PRs:

800 METERS: 2:14
1,500 METERS: 4:42

COLLEGE PRs:

1,500 METERS: 4:19
3,000-METER STEEPLECHASE: 9:58

PRO PRs:

800 METERS: 2:08
1,500 METERS: 4:16
3,000-METER STEEPLECHASE: 9:24

* **MOLLY:** Ann Gaffigan and Lisa Aguilera are two pioneer athletes in the women's steeple. Ann won the exhibition of the women's steeplechase at the 2004 Olympic Trials and earned the American record. Ann also ran the website steeplechics.com, a resource for women steeplechasers with history of the steeple, basic knowledge of the steeple, and upcoming races. Lisa Aguilera was one of the first American women steeplechasers and held the American record (9:28.75) in 2007.

THE FIRST HURDLES

LISA: The athletic director at Centennial High School [in Arizona] came to my middle school and talked to us about track and cross-country. I had been in gymnastics from third grade up until then. And so I said to my parents, "Yeah, I'll do it, but I'm still doing gymnastics." But then everyone on my gym team quit, and so I started really investing in cross-country. I ran with my dad all summer.

I did 300m hurdles in high school. The hurdles really helped me gain proper form for steeplechase in college.

A RELUCTANT RUNNER

ANN: I learned that I was fast in gym class, because we did the mile every year and I beat every boy in my grade. At some point I was beating every boy in the school, and I was in a K–8 school. I knew I was fast. But I loved soccer. I thought I was going to be a soccer player.

Junior high was the first time we had a track team. It was multiple Catholic schools that came together. I actually hated running at first, but my parents encouraged me to stick with it. I just couldn't wait to get to high school and play soccer and not have to do track. I ended up doing it anyway and got really good. Then I couldn't quit. I honestly did not like running for a while, and felt like I was just supposed to do it. I got better at track than soccer, though. I was more highly recruited for track than soccer, too. I held on to hope that I could do both sports at Nebraska, but when the time came, it was clear I was going to do track.

The summer before I started college, my dad took me to Mizzou at the Big 12 Championships, and we went up and we sat with my new coach at Nebraska, Jay Dirksen, in the stands. He said, "Ann, I want you to run the steeple. It's gonna be a brand-new event for women next year in the NCAA. With you being a soccer player and having a multi-sport background, I want you to try it." I was super excited because with steeple I wouldn't have to just run—it sounded more exciting. It isn't so monotonous.

One of the reasons I struggled to love running was I just felt like I didn't fit in. I fit in with soccer players. I didn't feel like I fit in with runners. I wasn't ever skinny enough. I wasn't quiet and polite enough. I fit in more with steeple. The other girls who ran it looked more like me.

We would show up at a race, and there would be two other women in the event. It was bonding. I remember the first steeple I did. It was in Arizona. We hadn't been on the water jump yet because it was too cold in Nebraska to do it—the water would freeze. I remember warming up at the pit and having never jumped over it before, I said to this other girl, "Have you done a pit before?" She said no. And she said, "It's fine. We can always just hold on to the barrier and climb over it if we have to."

A STEEPLE PIONEER

ANN: I didn't expect to win the 2004 Olympic Trials. I kept thinking that, by the time I'm at that level, the event will be in the Olympics. Winning the Trials and not having a team to be on was the first time in my life that I had not been able to do something because I was a girl.* I'd always been able to do anything boys had. It stunned me. I mean, the marathon was added for women in 1984, and that's a more grueling event.

The reason that steeple took so long to become an Olympic event has mostly to do with the water pit. The standard water pit is 12 feet long and the barriers are 36 inches high for the men. And so to make a women's event, obviously you lower the barriers just like they do the hurdles. Along with that you naturally would shorten the pit, because you can't jump as high or as far if you're starting from a lower height.

But while most barriers are adjustable, most water jumps are not.

> "One of the reasons I hated running was I just felt like I didn't fit in. I fit in with soccer players. I didn't feel like I fit in with runners. I wasn't ever skinny enough. I wasn't quiet and polite enough. I fit in more with steeple. The other girls who ran it looked more like me."

---

* **SARA:** Steeple was not an Olympic event for women until 2008.

The pit was just the pit. My freshman year, every race was a different pit length. The American record, before I broke it, was on a 10-foot pit. Finally, women just said, "We'll do the 12-foot pit, just put us in the meet, please!"

As professionals, we had to figure out which meets were going to actually hold a steeple race, and then we would all talk to each other and go to that meet because otherwise nobody would be there. We had to organize everything together.

OVERCOMING TRAINING BARRIERS

LISA: My coach would have someone run without going over hurdles in lane 1. I would run in lane 2 over hurdles so we could still run together. We did kilometer repeats, 800-meter repeats, longer anaerobic stuff. Everything was at goal, race pace, and was very consistent on the time we were supposed to run.

We never practiced water jump, because the water jump is where everyone would injure their Achilles. We practiced technique, just going over the water jump. Sometimes we would focus on it a little more if we were trying to get somebody to be able to jump out farther in the pit. We would put it in front of the long-jump pit and jump into it—that way they weren't doing a whole bunch on a hard surface. We never did a bunch of reps over the water.

LAYING THE GROUNDWORK FOR TODAY'S TOP STEEPLERS

ANN: Seeing the success that the US women are having in the steeplechase at the world level has me beaming with pride, as if I birthed them myself. One really cool thing about having the Steeple Chics website*

---

* **MOLLY:** The Steeple Chics website has all the basics of the steeple—including how many laps, where the starting line is, and the specifics of the barriers and water jumps.

was connecting with other athletes. It's so awesome when I get an email from the parent of a daughter who wants to try the steeple and has questions.* I love watching the competition get better every year, the American record continue to get broken, and more women committing to the event. It used to be the event people would ditch for the more glamorous events once they got really good at it. Not anymore.

Seeing the success that the US women are having today at the world level, I'm just beaming with pride.

---

* **MOLLY:** Ann even gave advice and encouragement to a young Emma Coburn and her dad through the Steeple Chics website when she was first getting into the event!

JEN RHINES

Three-time Olympian; five-time NCAA champion

DATE OF BIRTH: July 1, 1974
CITIZENSHIP: USA
CURRENT RESIDENCE: San Diego, CA
COLLEGE: Villanova University

HIGH SCHOOL PRs:

1,500 METERS: 4:31
3,000 METERS: 9:56
5K CROSS-COUNTRY: 17:56

COLLEGE PRs:

800 METERS: 2:11
1,500 METERS: 4:22
MILE: 4:40
3,000 METERS: 9:06
5,000 METERS: 15:41

PRO PRs:

1,500 METERS: 4:05
MILE: 4:33
3,000 METERS: 8:35
5,000 METERS: 14:54
10,000 METERS: 31:17
MARATHON: 2:29:32

THE MENTAL SHIFT THAT CHANGED EVERYTHING

My freshman year in college was a huge transition for me. Oddly, I got to Villanova and everything just went perfectly for the first month. But I was going to parties all the time, and for some reason my classes weren't that hard. I wasn't doing much work. I ran my PR and I was third for the team at the first meet of the year, and the next meet I was fourth and still ran pretty well. But I got worse each race during cross-country. We still won NCAAs, although I didn't score for the team. However, it still didn't sink in that I wasn't being responsible.

My low point really came at the indoor Big East Championships. I don't know what place I came in, but basically I got lapped twice by my teammate in the 5K. At that point, I also no longer made our traveling team to go to races since I was going to have zero chance to qualify for Nationals. Over spring break, I was one of the few people on the team who wasn't still competing. That was when I realized, *I have to mature and be a lot more organized and need to start taking responsibility for myself.*

I didn't get the results I wanted right away. But I went from running 18:35 for 5K indoors to running 17:12 outdoors. When I was in college there was a provisional and automatic qualifying list for NCAAs. My goal was to just make that list, to hit the provisional time, which I ended up missing by a few seconds. Although I missed the goal, I could see these little improvements and it kept me really motivated to keep going over the summer.

One of our alumni, Sonia O'Sullivan, sat me down and wrote me a training program for the summer. I followed that to a T. I started thinking about how much I want to contribute to the team. My teammate came in second at NCAA cross-country individually when she was a sopho-more. I made it my goal to do that, too, and started visualizing that all summer. When I came back to school, I actually did make that big jump. We won another NCAA team title, and I came in second! In outdoor track I won my first 5K title. So within 13 to 14 months, I made this transition by making better decisions and being more mature, which led me from getting lapped twice at conferences to winning an NCAA title.

It wasn't like I went home and ran 90 or 100 miles a week. It was really more like a mental commitment to come back ready to contribute to the team.

HEALTHY FOOD HABITS

In high school, I was really into running and enjoyed it. But when I was that age, it wasn't 100 percent of my life. At the Foot Locker High School Cross-Country Championships, I was one of the bigger athletes there, and I was aware of that, but it didn't bother me. I thought, *I did really well to get here, but if I want to be more serious and train harder later, there's gonna be time for that.* A lot of my friends were not runners. So there was never a big emphasis on food or restricting food in my social group in high school.

Over the years, especially as a pro, having cycles throughout the year was really important. I definitely had phases during the year, like when we were in Mammoth Lakes [California] altitude training in the fall, where I didn't really pay attention to what I was eating. We'd go to the brewery every Sunday for happy hour.

I think cycling your season allows your body to recover. I don't think there were many times I was running an energy deficiency. It would be a couple of weeks at the end of the season when you're kind of under stress and at a championship, and that stress adds to getting super lean. But that would be a short cycle and then that's over, and you're taking a break and starting the whole thing over again. I think I had the foundation when I was a teenager and was able to carry that forward all the way through my career.

I had a lot of women to chase who were good role models. When I finished college, Amy Rudolph had just set the American record and made the Olympic team right out of school. Deena Kastor had also started running phenomenally well. They were doing what I wanted to do. So when I got to know them better and traveled with them in Europe, it was the best thing ever for me. They were both people I really looked up to, and they were both completely comfortable with food. Having people around you who already have that attitude helps so much.

JEN'S TWO CENTS

One of the things I learned over the years is to give yourself more credit for your accomplishments, instead of always focusing on what you haven't done. That sets a foundation for a good racing mind-set. It's easy to be distracted by that no matter what level you are at. For example, if I was racing Molly Huddle,* I could think, *She's an American record-holder and I haven't done that*, instead of thinking, *I've made three Olympic teams, and maybe this is my day!*

I also would have let go of my mistakes faster. Even though I'm very logical and rational, I was still really hard on myself. As I got older and was still competing, I stopped wasting time being angry and down on myself for a couple weeks after making mistakes in a race or bombing out. It took me a while to realize how much time and mental energy is wasted.

> " Give yourself more credit for your accomplishments, instead of always focusing on what you haven't done. "

When I was younger, I was also stubborn about admitting mistakes. As an older athlete, I realize that there's no point in wasting time with that, either. Be honest with yourself—the faster you know, the faster you're going to correct it and move on.

Have belief in yourself and understand that you decide what you're capable of; no one else can tell you what you can or can't do. I think that really sets the foundation for success. If a young girl has that strong belief, they can handle whatever's thrown at them.

---

* **MOLLY:** Haha—thanks, Jen! But seriously, this is good advice on framing things in a way that serves you and empowers you. I tend to be overly pragmatic, too, and it can bring doubts to the forefront of my racing brain. Be realistic, but also choose to focus on the facts that support your success!

HAZEL CLARK

Three-time Olympian; three-time NCAA champion

DATE OF BIRTH: October 30, 1977
CITIZENSHIP: USA
CURRENT RESIDENCE: Bermuda
COLLEGE: University of Florida

HIGH SCHOOL PR:

800 METERS: 2:05

COLLEGE PR:

800 METERS: 2:00

PRO PRs:

400 METERS: 00:53.69
800 METERS: 1:57
1,500 METERS: 4:16

GROWING UP IN THE FIRST FAMILY OF TRACK AND FIELD

I got into running at around 16 years old. Before that, I avoided running at all costs because my older sister [Joetta Clark Diggs] was a four-time Olympian, my brother [J.J. Clark] was a really high-level track athlete, and my sister-in-law [Jearl Miles Clark] was an Olympic medalist. They were all full-scholarship athletes in college. I didn't want to take on the pressure of following in their footsteps, so I tried every other sport. I did tennis, figure skating, soccer, field hockey, lacrosse, gymnastics, equestrian, cross-country skiing, and basketball! I tried everything trying to find something besides track.

One time when I was figure skating I fell and busted my chin open. I was unconscious. When I woke up my dad said, "You're sticking to running."*

My dad took me to the track for my first race, and I remember trying to find every way out of it. He told me, "You're going to run this race and you're going to win." Meanwhile, I didn't have a coach, and I never practiced. He said, "You're a Clark. Give it your all. You got it. I know what it looks like." I still did not want to do the race, but I had no choice.

The race starts and I take off. I'm in the lead and I'm thinking, *He's right. I'm the bomb athlete! I'm killing these girls.* Everyone was way behind me. I got to the bell lap and, one by one, every person in the race started passing me. I was almost walking at the end. I could hear the people in the stand saying things like, "Oh, poor thing, you can do it!" They were giving me the slow clap as I came in last.

My dad said, "That's all right. Next time you're going to win, you're going to be awesome. You just learned a lesson. You need to practice and have a coach and work hard." I guess he was trying to teach me that I have talent, but I needed to work hard.

---

* **SARA:** Hazel's dad is Dr. Joe Clark—the legendary principal at Eastside High School in Paterson, New Jersey. Morgan Freeman played him in the movie *Lean on Me*.

Within a year of starting track, I was number one in the nation. So it really happened quickly once I got serious about it.

I can't imagine what it would have been like if I'd started running even earlier, because I felt really tired and burned out at a certain point. To sustain being very good in college and then to have a professional career, I was on fumes at a certain point, and I started at 16, so for the kids who started earlier and were serious earlier, it would be even harder.

I think trying other sports and things, and not being good at it but seeing the season through, teaches you things.

DEALING WITH ANXIETY

My challenge was mental, and it lasted my entire career, from my first race to my last. It was the same challenge. I never did get over it.

I felt pressure and stress that I realize now was performance anxiety, but no one stopped to help me because I was winning. The assumption is that nothing is wrong. I remember sitting in the dark and shaking and sweating and feeling anxious to the point where I could barely eat. I felt like I dreaded running before races. Even when I won, I always felt relieved that I didn't lose instead of that happiness that I won.

It held me back when I could have performed a lot better. I was running tight. I was running anxious.

> I felt pressure and stress that I realize now was performance anxiety, but no one stopped to help me because I was winning.

I was afraid to admit to people that I was scared because I felt, *If I'm supposed to be a champion and I'm so anxious that I'm considering not even going through with a race, then that's weak.*

I wasn't very friendly to my competitors. I regret that, because I'm actually a girls' girl. But I couldn't even talk to them or look at them or forge friendships because I was so stuck in this anxiety around racing.

I remember going into the 2000 Olympic Trials and seeing all the articles, "The Clark Sisters: Can They Sweep the 800? Can They Make History?" That was my first Olympic Trials, which is enough stress already. Add to that how we have a chance to make history and I'm the unknown factor. I'm 21 years old. I have never made a team. Joetta and Jearl have made multiple teams, so I think, *If anyone's going to be left home, it's me*. It was negative thinking, but that's how I felt. The Clark family standard was a lot of added pressure. I just kept thinking, *What if I don't do this and I'm the one to let my family down?**

ON THE FAMILY TRAINING GROUP

My brother, J.J., did a good job of not treating me too differently.[†] He understood my background and my quirks a lot more than someone else would. He's an amazing coach. It could be challenging training and running with my sister and sister-in-law. It's hard to carve out your own identity. He did a good job with all of us. He's got three people in the final at the Olympic Trials, all trying to make the team, trying to give us different strategies and give focus to all of us. I don't think I would be where I got without him. He really protected me and my body so that I could have a professional career.

Because he was my brother, when I first got to college I was playing games, I was testing him. I was showing up to practice late after going out with my friends at night. In the morning he would come to my dorm honking the horn, screaming out my name. I was so embarrassed. I tried him at first, but he acted crazy, and that stopped that!

---

* **SARA:** The women's 800 meters produced a rare family affair at the 2000 Olympic Trials. Hazel Clark finished first in 1:58.97, Jearl Miles Clark took second in 1:59.12, and Joetta Clark Diggs slipped into third by a hundredth of a second in 1:59.49.

[†] In addition to being Hazel's brother, J.J. Clark is a renowned middle distance/distance coach and the Team USA women's 2008 assistant coach. He currently coaches at Stanford University.

ON BEING INFLUENCED BY HER FATHER

I think my dad probably had the talent and the running genes, but he was not a runner because his life didn't allow him to be one. He grew up with no parents, struggling, having to work a job instead of playing sports. When my oldest sister, Joetta, started running, my dad made her run distance because he felt that Black people were always told they were sprinters. He wanted us to bust that stereotype and do distance running, and he felt it also made us disciplined.

SOURCES OF SUPPORT

My college teammates were a great source of support for me. They knew I was struggling with the anxiety. Although they weren't psychologists and they didn't know what to do in that sense, they were friends and sources of support. For example, if I felt too weak to go to the restaurant, they would eat room service in the room with me and try to make it as normal as possible and always pump me up, saying, "You can do this." Sometimes they even had to physically push me to the starting line.

It was hard leaving that supportive group in college, because, as a professional, I didn't have that. I was really on my own. I had my sister and sister-in-law, but they were also my competitors. I didn't want to be the baby by saying, "I'm struggling." I'm not even sure they were aware of how much I was struggling.

LESSONS IN SPORT

What I would have done differently is change how I looked at running. From the very beginning, I saw running as a burden. I thought, *Why do I have to be a part of this family with all these maniacs who run so fast? Why do I have to be a Clark?* instead of viewing the situation as *Awesome! I'm at the table with these awesome women who are Olympic finalists. My sister-in-law has an Olympic gold medal. My brother is a world-class coach. Let me soak in this knowledge and just be the best I can be.*

I was so weighed down by the burden of trying to live up to expectations. I would remove that mind-set and try to focus on what was positive.

I would also be honest with myself and others around me so I could get support. I'd tell them I'm struggling with this because I think someone talking to me about it or speaking with a sports psychologist would have made such a huge difference for me.

PROUDEST MOMENTS

I'm most proud of two things. I'm proud that I was even able to perform at the level I did with the type of anxiety I was facing, because, when I look back, there were some times where people don't know how close I was to literally not even lining up. I was that overwhelmed. To get out there and win the Olympic Trials and be an Olympic finalist, I'm proud of that because I was struggling with something that was painful and really heavy.

Also, I'm proud of the way I came back after a really tough year in 2004. I had a navicular stress fracture that came and went throughout my career over and over again, so I dealt with that in 2004. I made that Olympic team but then I actually got badly burned in an accident at the Olympics.* All these really horrible things happened in 2004.

After all that, in 2005 I came back and ran 1:57 and I was ranked my highest place, sixth in the world.

> " Your motivator can't only be to make your parents proud, or to make a coach or someone else happy. It really has to be about you. You have to find the thing that gets you up, makes you push to the next level, and makes you happy. You've got to run happy. "

DO IT FOR YOURSELF

Your "why" has to be something meaningful to you. Your motivator can't only be to make your parents proud, or to make a coach or someone

---

* **MOLLY:** Hazel was getting her hair braided in the Olympic Village when boiling water was accidentally spilled all down her back. The injury prevented her from training, and she wasn't able to make it out of the first round.

else happy. It really has to be about you. You have to find the thing that gets you up, makes you push to the next level, and makes you happy.

I love running now more than when it was a professional career because I'm doing it on my own terms. Some parts of it are always going to be hard—you may have to run in the cold, or run so hard you throw up. That's part of getting better. But overall, you've got to run happy and you've got to find out a "why" that is really positive and meaningful to you.

Success really is failure turned inside out. Most of the time, my biggest failures were followed by my biggest successes. Before the 2000 Olympic Trials, which I won, I came in last in the 1,500. You have to be resilient and have short-term memory as a champion. If things didn't go your way, take the good out of that and turn it into something positive for the next race.

> "Running has shaped every facet of my life and has given me every gift of my life, from my job today as the director of sports business development in Bermuda, to my best friends from school, and even my husband."

MORE THAN MEDALS

The most rewarding part of it all has been the people I met and the experiences I've had traveling the world. Being an athlete, an Olympian, shaped me as a woman. It made me tough. It made me resilient and taught me to be a winner in life. It's given me a platform to help change the lives of young people, and that makes me feel really good. Running has shaped every facet of my life and has given me every gift of my life, from my job today as the director of sports business development in Bermuda, to my best friends from school, and even my husband.

KARA GOUCHER

Two-time Olympian; 2007 World Championship 10,000-meter silver medalist; podium finishes at Boston and New York City Marathons

DATE OF BIRTH: July 9, 1978
CITIZENSHIP: USA
CURRENT RESIDENCE: Boulder, CO
COLLEGE: University of Colorado

HIGH SCHOOL PRs:

1,600 METERS: 5:00
3,200 METERS: 10:48
5K CROSS-COUNTRY: 17:51

COLLEGE PRs:

1,500 METERS: 4:12
3,000 METERS: 8:54
5,000 METERS: 15:28

PRO PRs:

1,500 METERS: 4:05
3,000 METERS: 8:34
5,000 METERS: 14:55
10,000 METERS: 30:55
HALF MARATHON: 1:06:57
MARATHON: 2:24:52

INJURIES AND SETBACKS

I had a lot of injuries and nine surgeries in my career. Coming back from those injuries posed huge challenges. Sometimes my layoff was just a few weeks, and sometimes it was months. I really tried to focus on myself as more than a runner during those times. I tried to strengthen my body in different ways, tried to spend more time with family and friends, and tried to really dive into other interests in my life that were normally put on the back burner.

POINTS OF PRIDE

I think my season in 2006, which finally set me up to achieve some of the big goals I had set for myself, was the best. I'm probably proudest of competing at so many different disciplines over the years, winning a silver at the World Championships, running 1:06:57 for a half marathon, and making two Olympic teams.

> "Looking back, I would have celebrated my victories along the way more. I was always hungry for what was next, and never really took a moment to pause and appreciate what I had accomplished."

HINDSIGHT IS 20/20

Looking back, I would have celebrated my victories along the way more. I was always hungry for what was next, and never really took a moment to pause and appreciate what I had accomplished. I wish I had acknowledged my success along the way.

In the prime of my career, my support system was not very healthy. While I had a very loving and supportive husband and family, my coach [Alberto Salazar] and the rest of the team staff were way too involved and controlling in my life. It was a very demanding and controlling situation, and I would never wish it on anyone else.

RACING RADCLIFFE

Probably my most interesting race was when I raced Paula Radcliffe in the half marathon in 2007. My plan was to race with her as long as possible, but halfway through I started getting competitive with her and started trying to drop her. I opened up a lead on her, but then started to die and was so worried that she was going to go zooming past me. So many people kept cheering "Go Paula!" as I ran by because they thought I was her. It was an amazing experience.*

MOTHERHOOD

My motherhood story is a long story, but it was very difficult. The system is not built for mothers. I really relied on others to help me out, but I also had to really stand up for myself and demand more from races and sponsors. For me, it was a great balance, as it gave my life more meaning. Running was an escape for me and something I could do for myself, but motherhood put my running in perspective.

A LESSON FOR LONGEVITY IN THE SPORT

I thought it was very hard to maintain a healthy body image. There are so many thin women with perfect bodies, and it definitely would get in my head that I was too big. I tried to remind myself that everyone is different. I may be taller and not as thin, but I am strong. I had to learn to really focus on my own self and what my body could do for me and not how it looked compared to others'.

My advice to girls is to be patient and kind to your body. If you treat yourself with love and kindness, you can be in the sport for a long time. Try to not rush your progress—a little each year really adds up. Take what you get, fuel yourself well, and be kind. Over years and years, you will improve and be able to enjoy the whole journey.

---

* **SARA:** Kara ended up beating Paula that day and running faster than any other American in that distance (1:06:57). However, it did not count as a record because it was a point-to-point course.

DEENA KASTOR

Three-time Olympian; 2004 Olympic Marathon bronze medalist; US record-holder in open and masters marathon; winner of London and Chicago Marathons

DATE OF BIRTH: February 14, 1973
CITIZENSHIP: USA
CURRENT RESIDENCE: Mammoth Lakes, CA
COLLEGE: University of Arkansas

HIGH SCHOOL PR:

3,200 METERS: 10:29

COLLEGE PRs:

5K: 15:52.80
10K: 34:15

PRO PRs:

5,000 METERS: 14:51
10,000 METERS: 30:50
HALF MARATHON: 1:07:34
MARATHON: 2:19:36

HOW SHE STARTED

I got into running at age 11 after failing or being totally bored with other sports. I tried many—soccer, softball, ice skating. It wasn't until I went to my first youth track practice where we ran on trail connectors to the Santa Monica Mountains that I fell in love with running. There was so much freedom, socializing with teammates, momentum, and control in the running experience.

EARLY CHALLENGES

I think I've been pretty fortunate as a female athlete, since so many heroic women fought before me. Wilma Rudolph, Bobbi Gibb, Kathrine Switzer, and Joan Benoit Samuelson come to mind.

The most challenges I had were in college. Despite having a full ride to the University of Arkansas, which I should have seen as an enormous privilege, I felt the burden of performing and was very hard on myself. The pressure was too great for my maturity level, and I had a hard time mentally and emotionally.

It wasn't until I became a professional runner that I realized my perspective hindered me so much, and I was able to take great control over being able to drive myself physically and mentally toward the height of my dreams.

> " If we choose not to be defined by the challenge and instead define ourselves in spite of it, we are really exercising the greatest gift of resiliency. "

The burden of my thinking wreaked havoc on me my entire five-year collegiate career. But, in reality, it was a conscious mental shift that changed everything. That shift happened within seconds inside the wrestling of my mind.

Good races always follow setbacks or disappointments because that is the time we self-reflect and refocus. If we choose not to be defined by the challenge and instead define ourselves in spite of it, we are really exercising the greatest gift of resiliency.

MASTERING THE MENTAL GAME

A race that pops to mind is unassumingly getting seventh place at the 2015 Chicago Marathon. I was past my prime as an athlete, but going for the American masters record. My buildup seemed like such a disaster compared to my others, I almost didn't get on the flight to Chicago because I questioned if I should even race.

My husband shared with me that despite the excuses I was listing, I still got in an amazing amount of work. We were both right, but only one story was going to support my attempt at that record, so I dropped the excuses and committed to memory the reasons I should succeed. The race itself was laden with challenges: missing a water bottle, getting tripped, bonking with 5 miles to go. Every time an excuse emerged or a reason to throw in the towel presented itself, I dug down, knowing that the accumulation of positive choices was the only way forward.

I reached my goal that day and was amazed at the process. I had a million excuses to give up along the way, and would have justified those excuses to this very day. Instead, I was persistent in my focus of thought, driving forward and committed to the process every step of the way. Those thoughts and steps added up to my proudest moment in sport, and its most valuable lesson in fortitude of thought.

THE COMPANY YOU KEEP

The thing I'm most proud of is the choice I've made to surround myself with good people. I'm thoughtful about my inner circle: choosing the best agent, the greatest coaches, working with the finest athletes, alongside the most generous and caring husband and friends. I choose them as well. I'd do anything for them, and they are understanding of my alternative lifestyle as an athlete. They have characteristics I deeply admire, like being compassionate, über-fun, and generous. I cherish all the relationships I have, what I offer to those relationships, and what I receive from engaging in them. It's richly rewarding to have that type of abundance in my life, even with the time and nurturing it takes.

My mom, dad, and sister have been my greatest supporters since I started running competitively at age 11. They traveled, encouraged, consoled, and celebrated a lot with me over the years. *Fortunate* or *grateful* aren't strong enough words to express how I feel having been so supported. I've often encouraged people who are pursuing a sport or passion without family support to find that support through friendships, mentors, or other trusted adults. Our loved ones can't be everything to us all the time, so accept what the various relationships in our lives have to offer without expectation and search for others to enrich other areas of your life.

> Think of a purpose while tying up your laces, and running will provide whatever it is you need.

I wouldn't do anything differently because, despite struggle and disappointment, I truly believe those moments mold us to be better, to do better. If we use harder moments in our lives to self-reflect and grow, we are never defeated.

SET YOURSELF UP FOR SUCCESS

There are so many runners who have the passion to run, but the passion to succeed must be greater. Long-term success requires equal attention to consuming a boatload of good nutrition and getting a tremendous amount of sleep in order to recover.

RUNNING'S RICH REWARDS

Running offers anything all the time. I have used the sport to focus my attention and passion, but also get in my running shoes to problem-solve or think through a to-do list. Think of a purpose while tying up your laces, and running will provide whatever it is you need.

JO PAVEY

Five-time Olympian; 2007 World Championship 10,000-meter bronze medalist; 2014 Commonwealth Games gold medalist

BORN: September 20, 1973
CITIZENSHIP: UK
CURRENT RESIDENCE: Devon, UK

HIGH SCHOOL PR:

1,500 METERS: 4:27

PRO PRs:

1,500 METERS: 4:01
3,000 METERS: 8:31
5,000 METERS: 14:39
10,000 METERS: 30:53

OVERCOMING CHALLENGES

After some pleasing performances as a schoolgirl, I struggled with injuries for around six years. I never gave up, but I was stuck in a stop-start cycle where I'd run for a few weeks or months but then kept having to stop due to injury. My husband [Gavin] and I decided to take a career break and go backpacking around the world. We had the secret ambition to train hard while we were traveling to see if I could improve enough to make the senior athletics team. We ran in so many beautiful and inspiring locations, and on our return I made my first World Championships, which was in Athens in 1997.

After making that team, I badly injured my knee and ended up having surgery. The surgery was badly done, and it cost me two and a half years out of the sport. It felt like my career might be over when it had only just begun. I was told by specialists that I'd never run again and that my only chance would be to have further surgery.

But I was determined to try to make it back, as I really wanted to fulfill my childhood dream of going to an Olympic Games. I started to go for jogs. My knee was very painful and continually swelled up a lot. But I knew I had to persevere and hope it would eventually settle down, as time was running out for getting fit enough to run in the Olympic Trials. I combined running with hours of aqua jogging and did nearly all my running on good-quality grass. I then gradually introduced going to the track once a week. I made the team for the 2000 Games and it felt like my dream had come true. Never would I have thought then that I would have been lucky enough to go to five Olympic Games!*

JO'S ADVICE

Enjoy your athletics! Always keep that in the forefront of your mind. When I was 14 years old, I enjoyed it so much—working toward goals

---

* **MOLLY:** Jo is one of the best runners in British history, having made five Olympic teams from 2000 to 2016!

and making lots of friends. But I also felt a lot of pressure that I felt was put on me. A lot of this was probably coming from myself. Looking back, I feel that I should have put it in perspective and thought of sport at that level more as a stepping-stone to a senior career. If I had my time again, I would change my approach as a young athlete and follow a more long-term development plan. Then I might have been able to avoid the years of injury problems I experienced as a younger athlete.

> **"If I had my time again, I would change my approach as a young athlete and follow a more long-term development plan. Then I might have been able to avoid the years of injury problems I experienced as a younger athlete."**

To have long-term success, listen to your body, build your training up gradually, and don't attempt high mileage and long sessions too early. Try to be sensible and flexible with your training plan. Do what you can do that is safe and helps you to stay injury-free, rather than blindly following a program that you feel you should do. It's all about prioritizing the important aspects of training, rather than focusing on high volume.

I would also say be kind to yourself. Growing and developing can take a lot of your energy, and sometimes you may struggle to run the times that you were hoping to run. This is totally natural, so give yourself time to get stronger. It's also tough when you've got exams and other pressures, so be kind to yourself and enjoy it, as you've got years ahead of you.

PAULA RADCLIFFE

Four-time Olympian; 2005 World Championship marathon winner; former marathon world record-holder; two-time World Cross Country champion; three-time London and three-time New York City Marathon winner

DATE OF BIRTH: December 17, 1973
CITIZENSHIP: UK
CURRENT RESIDENCE: Monte Carlo, Monaco
COLLEGE: Loughborough University

HIGH SCHOOL PR:

3,000 METERS: 9:25

PRO PRs:

3,000 METERS: 8:22
5,000 METERS: 14:29
10,000 METERS: 30:01
MARATHON: 2:15:25

ON YOUR MARK

My dad was a runner. As soon as I was old enough (age nine), my friend and I joined the local athletic club.

The system in the UK is club-based, and you only run a little bit with schools—two or three competitions a year. The rest of your training and racing is all through the club. So the club coaches I met when I was 11 carried on coaching me throughout my career. I was exceptionally lucky with my coaches from the beginning, and with my parents—the way they looked out for me but gave me independence as well. It was always my sport, and it was always my choice.

UNIVERSITY DAYS

I went to Loughborough University, which was the top university for sports in the country. I came back on weekends to train with the club, and then my coach would drive up on a Wednesday. It worked out really well—he would drive up, take back my dirty laundry, and my mom would have it washed and ready to take back!

I was welcome to jump into the sessions at Loughborough. There would be, say, mile repeats, and there would be five rows of people waiting to get started! It was definitely advantageous to be able to dip in and out of that, and be running with the guys. I was like the little sister tagging along on runs. It opened my eyes to a different level of training, and it also meant I had company and safety when I was out running.

SUPPORT AND SETBACKS

One of the reasons that I always look back on my support team with such gratitude is because, from the beginning, they said, "You have to have your qualifications, you have to have your university degree, because you're always one injury away from being finished." I was always really glad I did that.

In terms of the big, big career setbacks, it would be the 2004 Olympics.*

But in terms of my overall career, I would go back to 1994, when I had the original stress fracture in my left foot that I've had to manage my whole career. At the time the scans weren't good enough. They put it in plaster for three weeks, I'd run again, plaster for three weeks, run again, and it just kept breaking down. In the end, it took nine months. It never really healed. It was managed all the way through my career.

I clearly remember going to my dad in tears because a physical therapist said, "You're not going to be able to run again on this." When you're 19, 20, that's not what you want to hear. My dad said, "Millions of people go through life and they don't run." I said, "Yeah, but I'm not millions of people. I have to get it better."

The disappointment of dropping out of the marathon at the Athens Olympics was huge, because it was the Olympics and I was the favorite going in. My body just completely gave out on me. I was really scared because I didn't know why—at that point I'd never hit the wall. I didn't even know what that felt like. I didn't know that's what that was. And I didn't know why my body wouldn't just keep running, wouldn't be able to keep one foot in front of the other.

I think I coped as well as I could have, but it probably contributed to trying to get into too good shape for the 2008 Olympic Marathon and then not being able to handle my foot breaking down just before. The London Olympics in 2012 was similar because it gets to that point where you feel like the Olympics is almost too big of a deal.

---

* **MOLLY:** In 2004, Paula had to drop out of the Olympic Marathon because of stomach trouble. It was upsetting because she seemed poised to win her first Olympic medal, already having set the world record and won some majors. Looking for redemption in 2008, she was disappointed again when injury slowed her to a 23rd-place finish. In 2012 she was selected for her fifth Olympic team but had to pull out due to injury. It shows how difficult it is to be ready on one special day every four years to earn an Olympic medal. You can be the world record-holder, but still your body, heart, mind, and even some stars must align.

NEW YORK CITY: LAND OF COMEBACKS

New York City was always my big comeback city, and it started in 2004.

After Athens, I went to get all the medical checks done—a colonoscopy and everything because I had severe GI issues there. I had to go on a special diet for a while. We went to Flagstaff, Arizona, and I said, "If I feel like it, I'm going to run, if I don't feel like it, I'm not going to run."

Things gradually started to get better. About two and a half weeks out from the New York City Marathon, I came back from a long run and thought, *Could I get into the New York City Marathon field this late?*

I didn't really think about the fact that the British media thought it was a really stupid thing to do. I was just focused on that I was healthy. Maybe not 100 percent fit, but I just wanted to get out and enjoy racing again.

I was able to win that year. Though I wasn't in amazing shape, I actually didn't end up running too much different time-wise to what I ran in 2007 or 2008.* In 2007, it was a different kind of comeback—coming back from something great, because I'd had my first baby, Isla, in January.

TRAINING WITH A BABY

I didn't train for the first five or six weeks of my first pregnancy because I was recovering from neuroma surgery, but I was cross-training. Then, I was able to run all the way through. I got some really good advice about the main things, like stay hydrated, support your sacral area, and don't let your temperature get too high. I trained twice a day up until the middle of the second trimester, and then I started running in the morning or whenever it was comfortable and then just jogging or biking a little bit

---

* **MOLLY:** Paula has won the New York City Marathon a lot of times! She won in 2007, and it was cool to watch in person from the stands the day after I'd been a spectator at the US Olympic Marathon Trials, run in Central Park, as baby Isla greeted her at the finish. She also won in 2008, which I got to see as I was there to cheer on my training partner, Kim Smith.

in the afternoons. She dropped around about eight months, and then I could only run every other day, sometimes every third day, because she was bouncing on my bladder and just too painful afterward. But you get slower and slower through the final trimester. After she was born, it was probably about 10 days before I was able to start back slowly jogging.

I think the biggest physiological changes are adapting to the running and breastfeeding, and that your hips are still settling back into position. They said it will take nine months for them to go back exactly to where they were. And I was like, no, I'll do it quicker! But it probably was nine months in the end.

It was more complicated with the second baby. I was a little bit older, and after I had Raphael, I developed hyperthyroidism. I wasn't able to run well at all. I was way too skinny. It felt like I was eating all the time, but I was just tired all the time. I was really struggling to hit times in training. When they found out what it was, they said with postpartum hyperthyroidism, there's nothing you can do. You just have to keep all your mineral and vitamin levels as high as you can and it'll just settle on its own. Luckily, it settled about two weeks before the Berlin Marathon that year.

PROUD MOMENTS

I started out in cross-country when I was a little kid. That was my favorite. To finally win the World Cross Country title in 2001 was a really, really big thing, because I had been second, third, fourth, fifth, always getting outsprinted and not quite strong enough. In 2001, it was not quite a sprint finish, because it was really muddy and a gale was blowing in our faces. But I did win in the home stretch. That was something that I'm really proud of.

Running my 3,000-meter PR of 8:22 was massive for me, too, because I imagined what I could do in the 10,000 and the 5,000, but I don't think I ever thought I could run that fast for 3,000. I remember coming down the home stretch and seeing the clock say 8:00 low as I was coming in and thinking, *That can't be right.*

Obviously, the world records in the marathon were proud moments. But my first marathon was just as magical because I felt like finally I'd found the event where I was the most at home, and there were different ways I could run it.

STANDING UP FOR YOURSELF

Believe in yourself, value yourself, decide on and set your goals for what you want to do. Respect yourself enough to know if something doesn't feel right, it's probably not right, so you need to speak up. That's across life, not just in sports, but I think in sports it's maybe exaggerated a little bit because we are that much more aware of our bodies and how we treat them.

PERIODS AND PERFORMANCE

When I just started university, I was getting two or three periods a year. During the time when I was really studying hard and training hard, I would skip it. Then if I had some time off, it would just come back. When that stress load adds up too much, that's when you start to miss them or they get delayed. You have to manage that stress and not take too much energy from the bucket without putting more in. If you've got a lot going on as a stress in some other area, you have to drop the training a little bit until it balances.

When I was young, around 1993, British Athletics tried to insist that I go on the pill. My next race was the trial race for the World Championships. I got my period that day unexpectedly, and I completely freaked out. Thank goodness we had an older runner on the team, Alison Wyeth. She gave me a tampon and told me it would be OK.

I felt like being put on the birth control hormones ruined my year. My physician said that

> " You have to manage that stress and not take too much energy from the bucket without putting more in. If you've got a lot going on as a stress in some other area, you have to drop the training a little bit until it balances. "

because my estrogen level was fine I didn't need to mess around with taking the pill or anything like that. After that, the most I would do was use a really low-dose pill, a long way out from the competitions for the few times I was going to get my period on race day to try to move it away. It didn't always work. I got it the day I set the world record in Chicago.

THE LASTING IMPACT

If I hadn't been a runner, I don't think I would be the person that I am. It does shape you through all of those experiences. You get to meet so many interesting people, so you're not set in one mind-set. The running community is one of the most open-minded, accepting communities.

You also learn to become a stronger person. I'm a far more confident person than I would have been if I hadn't been involved in running when I was at school. Also, the fact that we're more aware of our bodies is a big reward.

KIM SMITH

Three-time Olympian; four-time NCAA champion; New Zealand records from 3,000 meters to the marathon

DATE OF BIRTH: November 19, 1981
CITIZENSHIP: New Zealand
CURRENT RESIDENCE: Attleboro, MA
COLLEGE: Providence College

HIGH SCHOOL PRs:

800 METERS: 2:14
1,500 METERS: 4:39

COLLEGE PRs:

3,000 METERS: 8:49
5,000 METERS: 15:09

PRO PRs:

3,000 METERS: 8:35
5,000 METERS: 14:39
10,000 METERS: 30:35
HALF MARATHON: 1:07:11
MARATHON: 2:25:21

WEIGHTY ISSUES

You see a lot of college and high school athletes and you know that there is a problem there. I've always been very small, so I guess part of it is being genetically determined that I can eat whatever I want. But you see it year after year with college and high school athletes. It might work in the short term to lose weight, but it's definitely not good in the long term.

Fueling is very important for staying injury-free, especially with bone injuries. You don't want to get in that cycle of getting injured. Young girls need to learn to fuel and not be restrictive—after running, before running. That was an important part of my running.

I never thought about my weight or thought about my diet much. It was about eating enough. I like to eat, so it was never a problem. Amy Rudolph was always a good role model. She used to get a loaf of bread at LaSalle Bakery and basically eat the loaf in one day. That's probably harder for young girls who are around runners with disordered eating. That's why it gets onto college teams and spreads.

AN EARLY HEALTH SCARE

I was at home in New Zealand. It was spring of 2005, right after my last college season and I was going to run at the Commonwealth Games, and I partially tore my Achilles. So I wasn't running at the time, which, I think, contributed to it. I was on a birth control pill that has been taken off the market. It was known for causing blood clots.

I was getting ready to fly back to the United States. I just stopped being able to breathe properly, so then it was found out that I had large blood clots in both my lungs. I went to the hospital for about a week, and then they cleared me to run after the heart damage healed. I had some "moderate" heart damage after it, so they had to monitor that to make sure that it was at "mild" before I could start running. They said I could go try and run, but they weren't really sure if I would be able to run at the level I could before.

I was back racing that summer. I pushed things pretty hard, and I got back to running pretty quickly. My first race back was a small meet in Europe. I ran 8:50-something for 3,000 meters. It was a surprise for me to run that fast.

The doctors think I probably have a genetic blood-clotting disorder, though they can't find what it is, which is why I have to be on blood thinners for the rest of my life now.

PERFORMING UNDER PRESSURE

I would say, with injuries in running, not trying to run through them is a big one for me, because I was really bad at doing that and I realize now it just does not work to run through injuries. Getting more physical therapy treatment and things like that are what I would go back and do.

My last college race was the NCAA cross-country championships. I'd won the indoor 3,000 and 5,000 and the outdoor 5,000 the school year before. So there was definitely a lot of pressure on the cross-country championship. Everyone expected me to win and that it wasn't going to be hard for me. I felt this massive amount of pressure that year. I felt like anything but winning would have been a massive failure. Every race, I had a feeling of just wanting that season to be over already, which is kind of sad because it was fun, too. But there was so much pressure.* I just wanted it to be over and done with.

I probably felt less pressure at the Olympics and bigger races. I was less nervous because ob-

> "I felt this massive amount of pressure that year. I felt like anything but winning would have been a massive failure. Every race, I had a feeling of just wanting that season to be over already, which is kind of sad because it was fun, too."

---

* **SARA:** Kim handled the pressure by running away from everyone in the field and winning by 18 seconds.

viously I wasn't a favorite. That one race sticks out in my mind as being the most pressure I've had on myself just because it was so expected that I would win.

Make sure you're having fun. Be around people who make it more fun and enjoyable. Try not to put too much pressure on yourself.

MARLA RUNYAN

Two-time Olympian; five-time Paralympics gold medalist; Pan-Am gold medalist

DATE OF BIRTH: January 4, 1969
CITIZENSHIP: USA
CURRENT RESIDENCE: Boston, MA
COLLEGE: San Diego State University

HIGH SCHOOL PRs:

100 METERS: 00:12.02
200 METERS: 00: 26.03
400 METERS: 00:59.2
HIGH JUMP: 5′7″

COLLEGE PRs:

400 METERS: 00:55.2
800 METERS: 2:15.78
HIGH JUMP: 5′10″
HEPTATHLON: 5,168

PRO PRs:

200 METERS: 00:24.2
400 METERS: 00:54.59
HIGH JUMP: 5′11″
LONG JUMP: 19′4½″
HEPTATHLON: 5,769
800 METERS: 2:03.18
1,500 METERS: 4:02.95
3,000 METERS: 8:39.36
5,000 METERS: 14:59.20
10K ROAD: 31:46
20K ROAD: 1:05:52
HALF MARATHON: 1:11:19
MARATHON: 2:27:10

MULTITALENTED FROM THE START

Growing up, I did gymnastics and soccer. When I was about 10, my parents signed me up for an after-school kids' track program. I did sprint events on a dirt 440-yard track. I also did the high jump. I loved the high jump. My dad built me a high jump pit in our backyard with scrap lumber, a PVC pipe, and old mattresses. I spent hours flopping over that bar until eventually I got too big for it and flew over the pit and landed on the grass.

In high school, I was on the JV soccer team as a freshman, but I started to lose my sight and could no longer see the soccer ball.* So I went out for track. I ran the sprints and the relays and did the high jump.

I also ran the 400 meters in high school and ran just under 60 seconds my junior year. I dreaded the 400 because it hurt so much, and once I graduated from high school and was recruited by San Diego State as a high jumper, I figured I was done with the running thing. My plan was to get my lawn chair and umbrella and sit on the high jump apron in sunny San Diego and watch those poor sprinters endure grueling interval sessions.

But it didn't last—I actually missed running. I asked my high jump coach if I could try a race. I borrowed a pair of running spikes and ran 00:59 in the 400. The sprint coach put me on the 4 x 400 relay. And that's how I became a runner again. I trained part-time with the sprinters and part-time with the jumpers.

BECOMING A DISTANCE RUNNER

In 1996, I moved to Eugene, Oregon, to train for the 800, or so I thought. I had knee surgery, foot surgery, plantar fasciitis, and hip bursitis—one injury right after the other. My coach and I parted ways, and the training group dissolved as athletes moved away or retired. In 1998, I was

---

* **MOLLY:** Marla has macular degeneration and—not that this stopped her in the slightest!—she did lose most of her sight.

injured once again, I had no coach, and spent my days on a stationary bike at the YMCA. I was almost 30. I could have just quit right then and there and got a real job, but I was not ready to give up yet.

I eventually found a new coach and a few girls to run with in Eugene. I also discovered a new event, the 1,500 meters. I ran my first 1,500 by accident at the Prefontaine Classic in 1999 because the race organizer said I was not fast enough for the 800. He offered me the opportunity to rabbit the 1,500, or just run it if I wanted to. I decided to just run it, and I finished fifth and found my new event. That was a breakthrough year, as I made the World Championship team in the 1,500, finished 10th in the final, and won gold in that event at the Pan-American Games. It was the beginning of my professional running career.

But I got injured again just eight weeks before the 2000 Olympic Trials with iliotibial band syndrome. I couldn't bend my knee. I saw several chiropractors and was finally able to run just a few intervals the week before the first round of the 1,500. I didn't even know if it was worth going to the Trials. But I did, and, miraculously, I made the team, even though I had missed five weeks of training.

MORE WASN'T NECESSARILY BETTER

Setbacks during my professional career stemmed from lack of recovery and/or lack of nourishment. I would push my training to such an extreme, believing that I needed to do more. I often ran more miles than I should have, or ran faster in a workout session than I should have. And I just wouldn't rest.

I also know now that I did not hydrate enough. I rarely felt thirsty, so I didn't drink enough. If only I had done some very simple things—rest, drink more, maintain a more nourished state—I believe I would have performed better. I do not believe I ever reached my true potential.

COMPLICATIONS AND COMEBACKS

With most of my injuries, time off was usually four to six weeks. I cross-trained when I was injured on various contraptions—elliptical, aerodyne bike, etc. I had soft tissue work and chiropractic work regularly. I also had a stretching routine and my foam roller. In the later years, gone were the days when I could just go out the door for a run. I had to stretch and roll before heading out for an easy run.

I had other memorable comebacks besides overcoming IT band syndrome to make the 2000 Olympic team. In 2002, I ran my PRs at 1,500 meters, 3,000 meters, and the marathon after a stress fracture in January. In 2006, I ran 15:14 for 5,000 meters seven months after giving birth, and 2:31 in the marathon 13 months after my daughter was born.

PROUD MOMENTS

There are two races that I am most proud of.

The first is the 2000 Olympic Trials 1,500, when I made my first Olympic team. I have no idea how I was able to run 4:06 when I had missed five weeks of training and could not run for more than 10 minutes before my knee shut me down. It challenged everything I thought I knew about training and racing. I couldn't even warm up normally for that race because jogging was worse than sprinting. I could get up on my toes and sprint, but I couldn't jog a simple warm-up.

The second race is the 2002 New York City Marathon. This was my marathon debut. My goal was to run 2:28 and, to my surprise, I ran 2:27:10 and finished fourth. I had so much fun preparing for this race. Because the marathon was such an unknown to me, I approached this more conservatively than other races, and taking the pressure off myself really helped me enjoy the experience.

LESSONS IN SPORT

I learned that distance running is a sport of faith. You have to have faith in the work you have done. You can't run the race before the race to prove to yourself that you can do it. Rather, you train for months, sometimes years, for a specific moment in time, and you have to have faith that all of that work that you have put in is going to pay off. What you do on race day, you can't do just any day of the week. A race performance is crafted for a specific moment in time.

Distance runners are typically high achievers, and we can do and overdo because we believe it is necessary to achieve the result we want. But sometimes our beliefs are off. We start believing things that are not entirely true, rather than trusting in ourselves. It is so easy to overtrain in order to align ourselves with our belief system, which is not always based on science or fact. Whether it is believing we must be a certain weight, or run certain times in a workout, or hit a weekly mileage number, we can become so fixated on what we believe we must do that we may overlook what our bodies are telling us.

Training, after all, is based on a theory or concept. We start to associate our best performances with a specific workout or body weight. We convince ourselves that we must meet those numbers in order to achieve the race result we are striving for. In reality, the race performance is the product of all that we do: months—and even years—of work, our state of recovery, state of hydration, and nourishment. It all plays a role in how we perform.

My best races were the races before the race, the tune-up races. Because I didn't put as much pressure on myself for these races, and because I allowed myself to be more rested and more nourished, I ran my PRs in the tune-up races. I then had to struggle to hold it all together for the real race.

You would think that I would have learned this lesson, but I kept repeating this same mistake over and over again. If I could go back in time, I would have rested more, abandoned some of my unsubstantiated beliefs, and allowed my body to properly recover. I would have had more faith in myself and in the work I had done.

MARLA'S MUSTS

It is important to have an unconditional support system. You need constants in your life, even if it's just one person. You need someone who is there no matter what. When you experience success, sometimes relationships with other people are conditional and short-lived. A person who genuinely cares about you and your goals, who is there through the ups and downs, is essential to long-term success.

Run for yourself. You should not feel as though you have to run well in order to be accepted or valued by others. People who genuinely care about you are there for you no matter what—and those are the only people who matter.

Be careful not to adopt unsubstantiated beliefs. Running is both a science and an art. Learn what works well for you and what does not. Be patient. There is no immediate return for distance runners. This is a sport of patience, a sport of maturity.

Remember that setbacks are temporary and are part of the sport. Learn from them. They will teach you something about yourself and, at the very least, instill you with gratitude on the day when you return to running.

Enjoy the process. You can't postpone your happiness for a single race result. Rather, you have to enjoy the journey to the starting line just as much as crossing the finish. When you look back on your days as a runner, you will be surprised at the moments that are most meaningful. Treasure every moment. Have faith in yourself and in the work you have done.

> " Run for yourself. You should not feel as though you have to run well in order to be accepted or valued by others. People who genuinely care about you are there for you no matter what—and those are the only people who matter. "

2010—2020

EMMA COBURN

Three-time Olympian; 2017 World Championship steeplechase champion; 2016 Olympic bronze medalist; 2019 World Championship steeplechase silver medalist

DATE OF BIRTH: October 19, 1990

CITIZENSHIP: USA

CURRENT RESIDENCE: Boulder, CO, and Crested Butte, CO

COLLEGE: University of Colorado

HIGH SCHOOL PRs:

800 METERS: 2:14

MILE: 5:08

COLLEGE PRs:

800 METERS: 2:09

1,500 METERS: 4:06

3,000-METER STEEPLECHASE: 9:23

PRO PRs:

800 METERS: 2:01

1,500 METERS: 4:03

3,000 METERS: 8:39

3,000-METER STEEPLECHASE: 9:02

A LEISURELY START

I signed up for track because my older brother and sister were on the track team. My family had a rule that to get your allowance money you had to participate in sports year-round during the school year. My school was so small that the only sport in the spring was track!

I immediately would win races, even as a sixth-grader against eighth-graders, which surprised me. My sister is a year older than me, and our first time racing each other, she said, "Whatever you do, do not beat me." So we ran side by side for a mile and then at the line I stopped and let her cross first. Afterward she said, "That's so embarrassing. Never do that again. Just run hard. Do your thing."

That was when I realized I'm kind of a good runner, but I didn't love it yet. I did other sports, and track was just like what the next sport was, but it wasn't my favorite of all. I did cross-country and volleyball at the same time. The night before the state cross-country meet, I would be across the state playing in a volleyball tournament, and then I'd drive overnight and race.

Compared to a lot of the greats, I was terrible in high school.* I came into college with the slowest PRs on my team. I remember looking at the résumé of my team and everyone had broken 5:00 for the mile, and my sea-level mile PR was 5:08. So I was different, but I was great at the

---

* **SARA:** I met Emma in high school. She came from a small town, and one of my teammates from college taught her and Joe. She was nervous that college would be too serious and the athletes would be too intense and it wouldn't be fun. I told her college is the next step and it can be intense and you want to strive to do things at a high level, but it is very important to have fun.

She is a great example of someone who has high expectations for herself and works very hard, but always enjoys the process! I love her story because it shows that you don't have to be a superstar in high school to become one of the best in the world. If you stick with it and you put the work in and you surround yourself with the right people, you can do things that you never imagined.

steeplechase. At the time, that was this obscure thing that high schoolers didn't really do.

I ran my high school mile PR at the Mt. SAC meet. That was a race
where I realized I am different from a lot of high school girls, because
I was running in a pack of tiny girls. I was the same size I am now,
5-foot-8, and maybe 10 pounds lighter than my current 125. All the girls
I was racing were like 5 feet tall, 80 pounds. That can be eye-opening
as a high school girl.

HURDLING INTO THE FUTURE

I did my first steeple my junior year after the regular high school season
in Colorado ended. There was a track meet in New Mexico where I was
going to run an 800 and a 4 x 800. My dad thought it was stupid to drive
to Albuquerque to only run an 800. So he looked at the schedule and
the only event to double-enter in was the 2K steeplechase. So I went
to Western State down the road and did a lap over hurdles with one of
their athletes and was like, *Oh, this is fun*.

I ended up running well enough to qualify for Nike Outdoor Nationals. I got fourth there. That's where University of Colorado coaches Mark
Wetmore and Heather Burroughs saw me and recruited me. I think he
saw that for a junior in high school I looked pretty good hurdling and
doing the steeplechase.

Later that summer, they called me, and I wasn't sure I wanted to
run in college. Running can be so hard and terrible. I had a lot of race
anxiety. I played basketball and volleyball, and I love team sports. The
fear of racing and being out there by yourself always freaked me out
and made running really not fun for me. So they stopped calling and
recruiting me.

A couple months later, I ran into Mark at Foot Locker Regionals and
eventually I decided I did want to run in college. Luckily, the steeplechase fell into my lap and I was good at it, because I didn't have many
credentials for being recruited to a big program apart from that.

OVERCOMING RACE ANXIETY

The physical pain of racing was really scary to me. I grew up in Crested Butte, which is a small town with so much snow that we really only had track season for about a month. I didn't run in the winter. I played basketball. I didn't run in the summer. I just hung out. I was always at a basketball camp or a volleyball camp. In cross-country season I'd go to practice and then I'd have volleyball immediately after, but our training was pretty chill.

So, basically, every time I lined up to race, that was the hardest effort I had ever done. I ran 15 miles a week and I was a fit person for my other sports, but physically I was a little unprepared for races. My body didn't know that it's OK to be in that much pain. As soon as I got in pain in a race, I would drop out or feel stressed. I only dropped out of a couple races, but that's where so much of that anxiety stemmed from, that fear of that pain.

Also, I felt this pressure, even though I was racing in the smallest division in Colorado. I was only competing against high schools that had 100 kids or less in the whole school. Before social media, before any of this, I found it scary that people had an expectation for me. I cried on the starting line of the state meet my junior year of cross-country, because I just didn't want to be there.

I met Joe Bosshard, now my coach/husband, my junior year. When I dropped out of a race, he'd say "Why? Why did you do that? What's wrong?" I'd say "My feet hurt, my plantar is really tight." He'd say, "It doesn't seem like you are in so much pain that you have to drop out of a race. Why did you do it?" And I'd say, "I don't know."

He was the first person I admired (and had a crush on) who thought

> **When I dropped out of a race, he'd say 'Why? Why did you do that? What's wrong?' I'd say 'My feet hurt, my plantar is really tight.' He'd say, 'It doesn't seem like you are in so much pain that you have to drop out of a race. Why did you do it?' And I'd say, 'I don't know.'**

running was cool and thought running had an upside to it. My high school experience was you all get in the warm-up tent, and some people are eating McDonald's and fried chicken, and you're all just waiting for your races to be over. He had serious goals on the track and said them out loud. He was extending himself physically and mentally to meet these goals. How cool is that? So Joe really helped breed that, and then I started working with a private coach, Trent Sanderson, and he was super positive. He was all about what upside I could have from running and really believing in me.

A bigger shift happened and I really started believing in myself and not being as nervous about racing when I started having the training needed to back up my races. I was less nervous when I stood on the starting line, knowing Mark and Heather at CU prepared me so well. They have always done a very good job of being able to predict what you can run. Through my freshman year, I really learned to trust in that and know they're not going to put me in this situation that I'm not ready for. Eventually, I learned to crave that competition, and even the pain of racing. I wasn't afraid anymore. I was much more anxious for a random high school race than I was for the Olympics, which is nuts!

> [My husband] had serious goals on the track and said them out loud. He was extending himself physically and mentally to meet these goals. How cool is that?

LEARNING FROM INJURY

I was healthy through college. My senior year, right before NCAAs, I started getting some pain in my glute. I went to NCAAs anyway and I raced the first round of the steeple, but my back really hurt. An MRI showed a stress reaction in my sacrum. I raced the final because I'm stubborn and managed to win, but it was so awful. I had to skip the US Championships a few weeks later and I didn't get to qualify for the 2013 World Championships team.

That was the first injury that I realized had a big repercussion: I'm not getting a shot at a US title. That was also a good lesson, removing myself from track. I went to Hawaii with Joe for three weeks and we just didn't pay attention to what was happening at Worlds. I told myself I'm just going to enjoy my life and find things outside of running that bring me joy and value and make me happy.

The next big injury I had was in 2016. I had Achilles tendinitis that bothered me all of 2015 and half of 2016. It caused a lot of sadness and anxiety. With tendon stuff, one day can be great and then some days I can't walk. Looking back in my training log, I was in a lot of pain most days, but it was leading up to the Olympics and I was stubborn and throwing everything at the wall so that I could get back healthy. Finally, I got it to be healthy in April 2016. My best race following my Achilles injury was winning the Olympic Trials and then winning the bronze medal in Rio.

I still do rehab to keep it healthy. I did a lot of eccentric loading exercises and progressed into heavy weighted eccentric loading exercises. I also did shock-wave therapy on my Achilles. I have to stay pretty diligent about my loading exercises or it will act up again.

GIVING BACK

Starting the Elk Run 5K in Crested Butte has been really rewarding and cool. We've been able to raise a lot of money and connect with my hometown. Sometimes we can get so focused on ourselves and our training, and we become horses with blinders on. It's good to be able to look out and look up and see the people who are helping you win and give back to them.

> "You need to have value and self-worth off the track."

You need to have value and self-worth off the track. However you want to find that is great. It could be academics, friendships, volunteering, or whatever. For me, in high school, it was other sports and academic clubs and having a social life. I saw myself as more than just this runner. I think that's where a lot of the anxiety with women in the sport comes from—they only know themselves as this type-A perfect runner who succeeds. When they have a setback or something isn't successful, they panic. It becomes like, *Who am I if I'm not the champion of this race?* It's important to fill your life with other things that bring you happiness besides the track.

ADVICE TO HER FORMER SELF

If I were to do anything differently, I wish early on I would have been less scared and would have enjoyed it more, especially in high school. I think I always loved, as an athlete, being a really competitive person. I've always loved competing in other sports and winning. If I am winning a race, that's always fun, but I wish I just would have enjoyed lining up on a Saturday in the middle of nowhere in Colorado and having the gun go off and seeing what happens. That was never a part of happiness for me. I was happy when the race was over.

If I could go back and talk to 16-year-old Emma, I would be like, "This isn't a big deal. Just do your best." And I'd trust that once the gun goes off, my race instincts will take over and my competitive side will take over and I'll work and I'll fight to do well, but I don't need to have it be this huge, stressful moment.

A CHAMPION'S SUPPORT SYSTEM

I have a lot of the same faces in my life from when I was a high schooler. My parents come to almost all of my track meets. My sister—other than that one race when she told me to not beat her—has been my biggest cheerleader, and my siblings have been great. I married my high school boyfriend, and he's been a consistent supporter and now coach, obviously, as well as his family.

I've had really great family support. But I do think a lot of it is choices that you have to make, choices to surround yourself with people who value and support you. Some of those choices were not being friends with some of the friends that I had in high school, because they weren't supportive of my goals as a college athlete.

I also set really good boundaries and communicate what my needs are as an athlete. People in my life know that at night I'm not going to be around. I'm going to be in bed. My friends know that on a Saturday night, I'm not going to be hanging out because I have a Sunday long run. I've made those choices to communicate that. Because of that, my support system is really on board. Even when I establish new friendships, I communicate what my job is and what my needs are, saying, "I can't do this because I have this workout or it's June and I have to race. I'll be a great friend in October." I like to set those boundaries and know what to be focused on. A lot of people struggle with that.

EMMA'S RULE BOOK

Eat well and enough!

Don't be afraid to push yourself in training. I think sometimes it can be a little scary to put yourself in discomfort. But if you're fueling your body well, you'll be able to handle it.

I also really believe in strength training, in the weight room. But everybody is different, so I understand that not every runner handles it OK.

Also, it's important to realize that nothing is given to you. You have to work and make choices and earn it. I think that's sometimes a misconception, that if you're not great right away, that it's just not for you. But you can work at it over time.

ELISE CRANNY

12-time NCAA All-American; 2021 Olympian 5,000 meters

DATE OF BIRTH: May 9, 1996
CITIZENSHIP: USA
CURRENT RESIDENCE: Portland, OR
COLLEGE: Stanford University

HIGH SCHOOL PRs:

1,500 METERS: 4:08
MILE: 4:40

COLLEGE PRs:

800 METERS: 2:04.53
1,500 METERS: 4:09
MILE: 4:31
3,000 METERS: 8:58
5,000 METERS: 15:20

PRO PRs:

1,500 METERS: 4:02
3,000 METERS: 8:30
5,000 METERS: 14:48
10,000 METERS: 30:47

HOW SHE STARTED

I really got my start in competitive running my freshman year of high school. Jason Hartmann* was the assistant cross-country coach at Niwot High School, and he completely opened my eyes to the world of competitive running. He introduced me to meets like the Nike Cross Nationals and the New Balance Indoor Nationals and expanded my expectations for what was possible in the sport, and to the opportunities that exist in the world of running. Before I had Jason as a coach, I thought the state championships were as high as you could go. He introduced me to the whole world of professional running.

TOUGH TRANSITION

I wasn't injured at all in high school. However, I had four different bone injuries in college and got stuck in an injury cycle. The next injury always seemed to come just as I was starting to gain footing again and feel like I was back to running like myself. I was off from running for about anywhere from 6 to 14 weeks, depending on which bone injury it was. The most difficult part wasn't a single injury, but the inconsistent training that I had over two and a half years. Just as you started to gain momentum, you lost it again with a new injury.

More than the running injuries themselves, the big challenges were the below-the-surface struggles. Entering freshman year, I was really afraid of gaining the freshman 15 and afraid of changes happening in my body. I was definitely trying to control what I was eating and halt my body from just normal development. When I started to get injured, that really brought that issue to a head. Looking back, I'm really grateful to those injuries for forcing me to work through these issues. I think this has allowed me to be able to run post-collegiately and be a much healthier and stronger athlete now. So I needed to change my eating

---

* **MOLLY:** Jason is an elite marathoner. He was fourth in the Boston Marathon in 2012 and 2013.

habits, eat more healthy fats, and get my period back. I wasn't getting my period on a regular basis before my first injuries, so that was impacting my bone density.

One of the toughest challenges is dealing with the mental battles that arise from injury—losing confidence in yourself as both a person and an athlete. I often questioned if I could be as good as I once was or if my body could handle training and running. When I first got to Stanford, I struggled to separate my running from my identity.

I had an injury in January 2020, which was my first as a pro. I learned with this injury that I still hadn't fully worked through that. I had to figure it out, because if I couldn't run, then that kind of leaves you feeling worthless and purposeless. I've had to focus on who I am as a person outside of just running.

HOW SHE OVERCAME IT

Relying on teammates and family was really important during these challenging times. Really opening up and being honest, identifying things that made me happy outside of running and taking the time to do those things throughout the day while I was at Stanford was really important. So whether that was getting a milkshake with a friend or volunteering, it allowed me to focus on other people and got me out of my own head. It got me away from the negative or unproductive thoughts that often come with injury or setbacks.

The other thing that helped me was taking the time to understand what led to the injury and how it can be avoided in the future. I always made goals throughout my recovery, just as I would throughout the season or when approaching competitions.

My sophomore year, my main goal had to be to get my period back regularly. When that was my goal, it allowed me to identify each decision I made throughout the day as either helping or hindering that goal. Framing it in that way allowed me to focus on it as a challenge when I wasn't competing and helped stress how crucial it was for me to start getting a regular cycle.

PROUD MOMENTS

One of the things I am most proud of is my junior year in high school when I won the New Balance Indoor Nationals mile. I hadn't broken 5:00 in the mile until two weeks before that. Jason had me go to the Air Force Academy at 7,000 feet above sea level to run a mile, and I ran 4:58, which was the first time I broke 5:00.

Jason had to convince the race director at New Balance to get me into the fast heat of the mile. He tried to explain the altitude conversion from 7,000 feet, and they were hesitant, thinking it was too big of a conversion for me to be in the fast heat. But they let me in and I ended up winning and running an 18-second PR. I ran 4:40, a new meet record. I had never been to New York before and had never run on a banked indoor track.

I am proud of that race because I wasn't thinking about what other people were doing when I lined up next to them, or the fact that one of the girls in the heat was the defending champ. I didn't overthink and I didn't allow myself to lose the race before it had begun. I just put myself in the race like I had nothing to lose. And it paid off! That's something that I still work on: to challenge each race and don't overthink and don't put competitors on a pedestal. You don't want to get beaten before you even start the race.

> "Challenge each race and don't overthink and don't put competitors on a pedestal. You don't want to get beaten before you even start the race."

WHAT SHE LEARNED

I wish I would have learned and understood the importance of getting a regular period earlier in my running career. I can't stress that enough. I've talked to a lot of teammates, younger teammates who came in after me at Stanford, about the importance of getting a regular period and allowing your body to change and develop. Especially during the later years of high school and most of the years of college, it's an important time for female development. You have to allow your body to grow and get stronger and change. If I were to go back in time I wouldn't have fought that change. I would have focused on getting healthy fats and fueling correctly and fueling for success. I wouldn't have been concerned about a changing or developing body, knowing that if I wanted to run and have a long career, that's what would need to happen.

I also would have been less caught up in the comparison game with accomplishments with peers, with body weight, and body shape. I wish sooner in my collegiate career I would have learned to own my own story and not compare it to others'. I would have focused on my own journey and the lessons that I was learning along the way. I would help others who may have been struggling or experiencing the same things. There is not just one body type, one recipe, or one approach to success. You have to find what works for you.

I also spent way too much energy at points in college comparing myself to my high school self instead of trying to move forward. It just wasn't healthy for me to be compared to what I looked like as a 15-year-old or how I was performing in high school. College is a completely different situation. You're living on your own. You're doing your own laundry. You're making a lot more of your own decisions. Your body's changing. It's not a fair comparison.

I am also working to not define myself by the times and outcomes, not tying my self-worth or even my fitness or how well my training is going to the performance of a race or the outcome. I think the race outcomes and performances don't need to be so black and white. There are so many things that we can learn and take away from each race and not allow ourselves to be defined by one race result or one workout or one outcome. That also makes it easier to find joy in the sport.

Another thing that I would have done differently in college is communicate better with my coaches. I didn't open up to them and let them know that I was struggling before an injury happened, or struggling during an injury. They're there to help you and help you develop as a person and as an athlete. The only way they can do that is if you're open and honest and vulnerable with them.

WIDESPREAD SUPPORT

My support machine is everything. My family has been the foundation. They kept me accountable and helped me to change the unproductive thoughts and habits I had. I can't explain how many times my mom kept telling me about the importance of eating healthy fats and getting my period back. In the moment, it would be irritating. She reminded me constantly. I think the more she continued to do it, the more ingrained it became. It helped to have her holding me accountable and reminding me of my long-term goals, and talking to me and supporting me in a way that allowed me to widen my vision instead of just being focused on what is right in front of me.

My teammates have also always been a crucial part of my support system. During college, it was really important to lean on teammates because we are all going through similar things. When you're connecting with teammates and you're sharing what you're going through, you're relating on that deep level of having both experienced something.

Friends are a big part of my support system as well. Especially my friends who are outside of the running world, because they've really helped me to focus on who I am outside of running and who I am as a person.

SECRETS OF SUCCESS

The biggest thing for me is being a part of something bigger than myself, like being a part of a team. It involves lifting those around you up and allowing those you're surrounded by to challenge and push you to new heights.

Being able to have trust in your training and your coach is imperative in this sport. You can be given the best training in the world, but if you don't believe in it on race day, you're not going to maximize your potential.

And gratitude! I am really grateful for the gift and the talent and opportunity to pursue this sport, and for people like my support system. It's what keeps me coming back day after day. I don't want the gift that God has given me to go to waste.

The biggest thing is to always place mental and physical health above outcomes or performances. I've learned that if you're not in a healthy mental and physical state, then you're probably not going to perform at your best. Or if you do, it's not going to be enjoyable or sustainable along the way.

> **Feel the strength, passion, joy, confidence that lives within you and hang on to that. Don't ever let anyone take that away.**

Be kind to yourself, because what you say to yourself about yourself becomes your narrative. I would encourage girls to pay attention to how they talk to themselves. Talk to yourself the way that you talk to your friends or you want your friends to talk to you. Feel the strength, passion, joy, confidence that lives within you and hang on to that. Don't ever let anyone take that away. Focus on cultivating that, because I think that is really, really most important for long-term success in the sport.

Celebrate progress along the way, no matter how small, because that also allows you to find success in the long term and gain that momentum and find that joy in reaching those little goals along the way.

Siri Lindley, a former pro triathlete I admire a lot, often talks about how we should love ourselves so much that we only allow ourselves to think happy, positive thoughts. So along the same lines, love yourself so much that you only talk to yourself with kind, caring, uplifting, productive thoughts. Because your confidence has to come from within. Appreciate yourself and love yourself.

COURTNEY FRERICHS

2021 Olympic steeplechase silver medalist; American steeplechase record-holder; 2017 World Championship steeplechase silver medalist; two-time Olympian; NCAA champion

DATE OF BIRTH: January 18, 1993
CITIZENSHIP: USA
CURRENT RESIDENCE: Portland, OR
COLLEGE: University of Missouri–Kansas City/University of New Mexico

HIGH SCHOOL PRs:

800 METERS: 2:24
5,000 METERS: 18:12

COLLEGE PRs:

1,500 METERS: 4:18
MILE: 4:55
5,000 METERS: 15:31

PRO PRs:

1,500 METERS: 4:07
3,000-METER STEEPLECHASE: 8:57 (American Record)

FROM GYMNAST TO TRACK STAR

Running was one of those things that, while growing up, I always knew I was pretty good at. I ran 7:10 for the mile in second grade. But for some reason, it never really stuck. I think it was because of gymnastics. That was where my passion really was. I started competing in gymnastics team training at age seven, so that was where most of my time went.

My parents were really big on participating in multiple sports and activities. In junior high, I played volleyball, I played softball, I ran on the track team. Gymnastics is definitely where I was spending most of my time. In high school, I committed to just doing gymnastics and playing soccer. I was really fortunate that the track team allowed me to just race for them without practicing. But it was mostly relays.

I don't think I really found my niche with distance running until my senior year of high school, when I decided to back off my training with gymnastics to run on the cross-country team. That was when I really fell in love with running and realized that I could shift the passion I had for gymnastics into it.

COLLEGE DAYS

I didn't completely focus on running until my freshman year of college. That first summer before college, solely focusing on running was challenging because I just didn't know what I was doing. I was sent a training plan that I couldn't complete. Freshman year was a really big learning year just because I was having to learn everything about the sport.

The University of Missouri–Kansas City was a really good place for me to start. I wasn't the best when I arrived. There were some good upperclassmen to learn from. One of the girls was kind of the mom of the team and wasn't afraid to let me follow her around, even though she was the senior and I was a little freshman.

With it being a smaller program, I was able to get a little bit more one-on-one attention. I had time to fully learn the sport.

I was committed to the four- or five-year plan. I started off at 35 miles a week. I think if I would have gone to a bigger program, it may have not been the best fit, since I would have been put into more mileage than I could wrap my head around. Physically, I wouldn't have been able to handle it.

Transferring schools is viewed in a variety of ways. But for me, doing my fifth year at New Mexico was like I got two families and two really great experiences. It was like the experience had allowed me to really develop and grow, and then also the experience of being on a powerhouse team.

> "I was used to being the best by like two minutes, and [at the University of Missouri] it was very one-on-one attention. Now I was going to a team where I was going to be number four on the descending order list for 5K."

I was so nervous arriving in New Mexico because I was used to being the best by like two minutes, and it was very one-on-one attention. Now I was going to a team where I was going to be number four on the descending order list for 5K. But I also knew training on my own was starting to get hard, and I knew if I was going to get pushed to the level that I really wanted to be, I needed to be pushed in those workouts.

I showed up and was immediately dropped in workouts. There were some tears. But I really had to remind myself that being pushed was going to be so much better, and I was going to find my limit that way.

GOING PRO

I think if I would have gone from UMKC straight to the Bowerman Track Club, it would have been a much harder transition. Anytime you transition up levels, there's a learning curve and a new environment. You get to find the balance between challenging yourself and respecting that these women have been doing this for a few years and they have all these experiences that maybe you don't. After graduating from the University of New Mexico, I think I was able to find that balance a little better.

But still, when I got there I had never really focused on speed before, and I'm trying to do speed with Shelby Houlihan and Colleen Quigley, who are so fast!

I was like, "OK, you'll get there one day. You just have to keep trying."

DECIDING NOT TO QUIT

I've really been fortunate in my running career so far to have stayed really healthy, which was a huge change from my time as a gymnast. I think that my time as a gymnast changed my outlook on taking care of myself. I was able to find some success pretty fast in running, I made the World Junior Championships my freshman year of college, and by the next year I'd finished All-American on the track and then made All-American in cross-country.

Then indoor season came along my junior year and I didn't even make Nationals. I went to my coach halfway through junior year and said, "I don't know if I want to do this anymore." It was all because I didn't make indoor NCAAs.

It was a really pivotal moment because I had to commit to doing it because I wanted to get the best out of myself. I was falling in love with results and not the process of running. I had to spend that whole second semester of my third year in school, realizing that it wasn't just about PRs and All-American finishes and awards. It was more about the process of pushing myself to become my best self. I think that was one of the biggest things I overcame: realizing there is the love for training and the love for being a runner versus the attention or the award. I still am always working on that.

TRUST IS KEY

Winning a medal at the World Championships is definitely, accomplishment-wise, the biggest thing so far. The biggest thing, regardless of the result, was my trust. Trusting my coach, Jerry Schumacher. Trusting the program, trusting everything that year because it was a very up-and-down year. I was transitioning to a new group, and transitioning to a new level.

I was also learning how to trust myself, how to put myself in the race, because I think you can get to a certain point where, as in high school, you know your competition and you feel really confident, you feel comfortable. Eventually, you feel that you belong. Then you go to college and you need to relearn that all over again. Then the same thing happened at the international level. That was a really big takeaway for me: Trust is key in any program.

Sometimes when you have success, you have to learn how to continue without expecting it. Every time you do a workout or a race, you might need to remind yourself that things don't have to be perfect to be able to get back to that point. I medaled because I stayed on the path and, no matter what bumps in the road came along, I trusted that I was going to be able to get to the other side of them and be ready.

LEAN ON THE TEAM

Shalane Flanagan and Amy Hastings Cragg collectively had over 20 years of experience running professionally. It was really neat that they weren't afraid to share the knowledge that they had obtained. I felt like I just tried to absorb as much of that as possible. It was the same way with Emily Infeld, who'd dealt with several injuries. I'm able to use things she had learned to try to avoid those.

In terms of the steeple, I remember watching teammate Evan Jager race in 2016 at the Olympics and watching him take control of the race. He went to the lead and made it the race he needed it to be to have the result he wanted.* I thought, *I want to have that in my career.* It's been great to be able to talk with him about how he got to that point.

It's been really fun to shift my role now with the younger athletes

---

* **SARA:** The result Evan wanted was a medal, and he ended up winning the silver medal!

   MOLLY: And this is very similar to how Courtney went to the lead of the 2021 Olympics and earned a silver medal!

we've been bringing in. For instance, Karissa Schweizer and I connected immediately when she came into the group, just from growing up in the Midwest. It was really neat being able to share some of the things I've learned now with the new incoming athletes in the group.

I was really lucky that I came to the group at the time I did, where all these women's training groups were really coming together. I had options to look at. And then with Shalane [Flanagan], she's always trying to bring us up with her success. I think back to 2018 being a year when I think I was my most confident self.

THE PATH LESS TRAVELED

Your path doesn't have to look like anybody else's. That's been key in my development as an athlete. I think that, especially with social media, it's great to see what other people are doing, but that doesn't mean you have to do it like them. Just be your own person and get there on your own time line.

MARIELLE HALL

Olympian; NCAA champion

DATE OF BIRTH: January 28, 1992
CITIZENSHIP: USA
CURRENT RESIDENCE: Providence, RI
COLLEGE: University of Texas at Austin

COLLEGE PRs:

3,000 METERS: 8:54
5,000 METERS: 15:12

PRO PRs:

5,000 METERS: 15:02
10,000 METERS: 31:05

FAST START

My mom signed me up for a youth track program. I was in fifth grade, I think. My first day I was able to keep up with one of the girls, whose dad ended up being my first coach and who is one of my best friends to this day. To be able to keep up with her just felt really natural. I enjoyed myself there. It was one of the first times that I remember forming friends that weren't my family.

I danced, I did ballet and jazz and tap when I was really young. I played soccer some. I did basketball. I did karate for a day. I just may have been an intense child. So as soon as I realized I liked running, I took it pretty seriously.

I was very opportunistic as a young athlete. I was able to get a scholarship to run because of my PRs in the 800. Coaches and people around me would say, "You're not really a middle-distance runner, you're gonna have a lot more success in some of the longer stuff."

I think early on, I had trouble expressing what I cared about. I kind of let other people dictate what they saw instead of being more in tune with myself and really standing up for where I felt I could excel. Everybody has their idea of who should fit where and what talents you have that will push you the furthest. As a young athlete, if it's all positive affirmations, that can be really important in shaping your competence and your identity. But if it's not in tune with what you believe, it can be really detrimental in how you see yourself in the sport and in the opportunities that you take. You want to have coaches and people around who have a vision for you, but it's always most important that you have your own vision of yourselves.

> " I danced, I did ballet and jazz and tap when I was really young. I played soccer some. I did basketball. I did karate for a day. I just may have been an intense child. So as soon as I realized I liked running, I took it pretty seriously. "

STANDING YOUR GROUND

I felt like I had a little bit of lag time in between trying new events or testing myself on the road or being open to doing longer events than just middle-distance. It's all about learning about yourself more. When I was younger, I was more keen to look to other people for how they saw me instead of saying to myself, *I'm the one who's doing all the running and spending all the time with myself. I should be able to identify where I think I'm good and where I can excel.*

I've definitely gotten better about saying, "This is what I want to do. How can you help me get there?" instead of "What do you think I should do?" Everyone really does just want to help. Sometimes not everyone knows the right way to approach things for each individual.

For example, I ran the 5K my last year of college. Prior to that, I did cross-country, and I would run one 5K a year and then focus on shorter events. All throughout college it was in the back of my mind how the mile and the 800 weren't really clicking for me or fun for me, but I wasn't ready to say, "Maybe I can use the skill sets that I have from shorter distances for the 5K or longer events because I think I have some promise in that."

> As soon as I articulated what I needed and the work I felt would benefit me, I was able to perform better.

It took me three years to do that. As soon as I articulated what I needed and the work I felt would benefit me, I was able to perform better. It was a confidence that this is the event that I chose for myself instead of flailing in between what I thought I should be doing or where I thought I fit. Once I was able to assert the 5K was the event I wanted to do, I was really excited about it. Some of the best athletes in the NCAA were in that event. That was in part why I wanted to be in that event; the challenge would be there. I worked really hard, but I also just had a voice in my running that I didn't have before. So I think that makes a big difference, and I ended up winning the 5,000 that year.

ON BEING A BLACK AMERICAN DISTANCE RUNNER

Some of those things, you do internalize: It's like, *I should be faster. Everyone who looks like me is a fast sprinter, so I should be fast.** It wasn't all the coaches' fault. I also was in that cycle of feeling like shorter events are what I should do or what I should be better at.

Texas was a school I really liked with the program I wanted to go into. Also, I could see myself enjoying being on campus even without running in the equation. I spent my visit with the whole track team, not just distance runners. I wanted a little bit more of that diverse experience.

And if I'm going to be honest, I wanted a Black roommate. I mostly looked at schools on the East Coast. I did look at Villanova and Georgetown, which are traditionally distance schools. But I was just excited about being a person outside of running. I grew into the idea of running being a career, but I wanted to have that twofold experience: I wanted to be on a good distance team that felt like it could grow, but I didn't want to sacrifice getting to see people on the track team or train and then hang out with different types of people. I wanted to try something new. "Do something different" was my mantra the last year of high school. Texas was that for me. Austin is an incredible city, and I loved it there.

Winning NCAAs in my senior year of college felt like a new beginning, in terms of making professional running a reality and accomplishing something that only really felt possible to me and a couple other people. I was really proud about my attitude. I have a lot of fond memories of feeling calm and confident and just sure of where I was in the world.

---

* **MOLLY:** While East African athletes dominate distance running at the world level, in the United States, distance running from the mile to the marathon at both elite and recreational levels is a largely white sport. Representation matters, and it's important for the distance running communities and industries to show that running is not just for certain kinds of people, but that it's for everyone.

COMMUNICATION IS KEY

One thing that I realize now is that you hear all of the same stories, whether it be feeling alienated, like there aren't people like you in your event, or sometimes it's about eating disorders, where it feels like all of these insular incidents. But everyone has felt that, or been on a team with someone who's felt that. I wish that I would have been more open with what I was experiencing. I think it could have helped other people grow around me. I feel like we're all quietly suffering instead of talking to one another a little bit more, being able to communicate a little bit better about how you're feeling. Realizing that there's a way bigger circle of support than you realized with whatever you're doing, and there are a lot more people rooting for you and who want to see you do well and understand you and your story. It doesn't have to be quite as isolating as it is, I think. And it's definitely getting better, for sure.

SARA HALL

Six-time national champion; second-fastest marathoner in US history

DATE OF BIRTH: April 15, 1983
CITIZENSHIP: USA
CURRENT RESIDENCE: Flagstaff, AZ
COLLEGE: Stanford University

HIGH SCHOOL PRs:

MILE: 4:47
3,200 METERS: 10:10

COLLEGE PRs:

1,500 METERS: 4:19
3,000 METERS: 9:05
5,000 METERS: 15:36

PRO PRs:

1,500 METERS: 4:08
3,000-METER STEEPLECHASE: 9:39
5,000 METERS: 15:20
10,000 METERS: 31:21
HALF MARATHON: 1:08:18
MARATHON: 2:20:32

HER START IN RUNNING

I grew up playing sports. I started playing soccer at age five and basketball at age eight. Through both of these sports I quickly found I had a lot of speed. I was nicknamed "Breakaway Bei"* because of my ability to open up and run away from the competition.

I also found I had a lot of natural endurance. My family did a lot of hiking and biking together. I was able to outride my older sister and found something I excelled at compared to my siblings.

I decided to go out for cross-country in seventh grade. I decided to train over the summer for the upcoming season. I ran most of the trails across from my house in Santa Rosa and loved exploring. I found running gave me a lot of independence. I was able to run places without having to rely on a ride.

I won my first race in seventh grade, beating the reigning league champion, which was a big upset. After that I was hooked on competing. This competitive side drove me to want to push myself and find my limits. I would often do hill sprints to failure, run to and from practice, none of which was driven by my parents or coaches. I just found a drive inside of me that wanted to keep finding my limits.

FEARING FAILURE

My first major setback was my junior year in high school. The previous year, I won the Foot Locker Cross-Country Western Regional as a sophomore and was third at Nationals. The next year my goal was to win the National Championship. It was supposed to be a showdown between myself and Shalane Flanagan.

---

* **MOLLY:** Bei is Sara's maiden name—Sara married Olympian and American record-holder in the marathon Ryan Hall in 2005. They are one of the fastest-running couples in American history!

This was the start of the website LetsRun.com.* I stumbled on the message boards and saw that people had expectations of me and were criticizing me. I started to feel more pressure from anonymous people judging me. In the Western Regional, I took off really hard, and halfway through the race doubts started creeping in. I ended up 10th and, at the time, only eight athletes went on to the National Championships.

It was heartbreaking for me because it was my first big failure in running. At that point in the sport, I had only experienced success. I began fearing failure a little more. That carried over into college, where the expectations ramped up—I was on scholarship, I was a Foot Locker champion. Stanford had several Foot Locker champions who didn't go on to get better as athletes. I felt a lot of pressure as a Foot Locker champion—that people were looking at me like I was going to end up like these other athletes. Would I continue to improve and win in college? I was focused on avoiding something instead of having a vision of what I wanted to become.

Fearing failure continued through 2010. What really changed that was my faith in God—realizing God's unconditional love for me as well as my family's and friends' unconditional love. I realized that I don't have to perform to earn anyone's love, that I'm loved for who I am no matter what I did in a race. It took me five years into my pro career to realize this. Once I did, I felt so much freedom. Realizing this allowed me to take more risks and run to my potential.

RESILIENCY AND REGRETS

I am most proud of my resiliency in the sport. I have been in the sport for over 15 years and experienced a lot of disappointment along the way. There were several points in my career where I thought it might be

---

* **SARA:** LetsRun.com is one of the first heavily trafficked running websites. It has a message board that is infamous in the running world because it's anonymous and often critical of athletes. It has a lot of up-to-date running articles, race results, and good information.

   MOLLY: Alongside some extremely harmful content.

time to move on. I didn't because I felt like God was telling me there was something more there and to persevere.

I am really happy I did. I have seen a lot of redemption and been able to enjoy the sport in the later part of my career more than I ever have. I found a love for road races and had a lot of improvement there.

If I were to do things over, one thing I would have done differently is develop my speed early on. In high school I did not do a lot of speed work. I did a lot of aerobic development. When I went to college, my coaches were afraid of doing too much speed because they were afraid of injury. I feel I never developed my top-end speed. I would have run less mileage and had more focus on speed.

I also would have focused on being stronger in the weight room. There was more focus on being lean and thin and not strength. I was afraid to put on muscle mass weight lifting. I wish I would have focused on muscle development. My coaches were afraid of injuries and neglected doing any leg work in the weight room. If I'd had better manual therapy, combined with lifting and speed development, I feel I would have thrived in the middle-distance races, which would have helped me in the longer races later in my career.

TURNING TO TEAMMATES

In high school I did a lot of training with the men. I was able to get pushed by them and found it very beneficial. However, in college I wanted to find a program where the women really worked well together and pushed each other in a healthy way. I wanted to avoid teams with a toxic feeling of competitiveness between them.

I really felt like I found that at Stanford. The athletes were very serious about running, but were there for each other. They had a healthy balance of school, life, and sport, and working together in training. I feel very lucky I had Alicia Shay and Lauren Fleshman to train with in college. We would often finish 1-2-3 in workouts and high-level races. I felt we were able to push each other and help each other to get better.

I also give a lot of credit to having a lot of friends outside of running.

Friends from church and school supported me no matter what and appreciated me outside of running. I felt it was always important to have things in my life outside of running to keep a good balance.

THE KEY TO LONGEVITY

Keep it fun! Find what makes you tick and make it fun. If there is too much pressure or you need to decompress, find ways to do it. If it is staying off social media or if there are people putting too many expectations on you, then address that and find ways to stay away or not let them bother you. Deal with race nerves so you enjoy racing and you aren't dreading it.

Also, make sure you are eating healthy and enough so you are building strong bones in the bone-building years of your life. I credit my healthy eating for my lack of stress fractures during my career. I have only had one, and it was when I was 34 years old. Taking care of your body and your nutrition is key to your health in the future.

EMILY INFELD

Olympian; 2015 World Championship 10,000-meter bronze medalist

DATE OF BIRTH: March 21, 1990
CITIZENSHIP: USA
CURRENT RESIDENCE: Portland, OR
COLLEGE: Georgetown University

HIGH SCHOOL PRs:

800 METERS: 2:08
1,600 METERS: 4:41
3,200 METERS: 10:28

COLLEGE PRs:

800 METERS: 2:06
1,500 METERS: 4:16
3,000 METERS: 9:00
5,000 METERS: 15:28

PRO PRs:

1,500 METERS: 4:05.6
3,000 METERS: 8:41
5,000 METERS: 14:51
10,000 METERS: 31:08

WILL RUN FOR PIZZA

I started running when I was around eight. In the summer, my dad and I would go from the local Pizza Hut, run down the street half a mile, then back. Then we had pizza and pop at 8:00 in the morning. I thought, *This is so fun*. My dad and I would do all the little races, like miles, 3Ks, 5Ks. It was bonding for us.

I did all sorts of sports growing up, but I was terrible at anything that involves coordination. I really just like the running aspect of other sports. Running with my dad and having bonding time is really what made me fall in love with it at first, and then trying to compete with my-self and better my times made me continue.

TRANSITIONS AND ADJUSTMENTS

Going from high school to college was pretty seamless for me. My col-lege coach, Chris Miltenberg, was amazing. He was super communica-tive, and definitely held everyone's hand a little bit.

I feel like we were a little bit undertrained, which is, I think, good as a college athlete. In high school I got up to 45 miles a week by senior year. At Georgetown we raised my mileage 5 miles every year or so, topping out around 65 miles a week. I had no serious injuries in college.

The transition from college to pro was hard. Jerry Schumacher is definitely a high-mileage coach, and I just hadn't done that many long workouts. I was running more like 80 miles a week now. And we just crushed it, doing like 10 miles worth of fast running in a workout. At Georgetown my long run was only 90 minutes, and I was nearly doing that every day now.

It was a huge adjustment. And I just wasn't listening. I wasn't as vocal with how I was feeling and how tired I was. I thought, *You should be exhausted all the time. That's what being a professional athlete is.*

Also, I was trying to control too much. In college, I would drink beer and eat unhealthy food. As a professional, I cut all that out. I mistakenly thought, *I can't eat any sweets, I can't ever drink alcohol. I need to be super diligent if this is what I want to be.* I was increasing the stressors too much and then restricting some of that stuff that I needed to keep my sanity.

I ran the 5K at the Olympic Trials in 2012, and then I didn't run a US championship until 2015 due to injury. I was digging myself in these holes and then getting injured. Even now, I have to check in to avoid that. In 2017, I was trying to run 100-mile weeks, and I just wasn't able to handle it. I just won't be able to get back up there, and that's OK. I know what I have to do now.

Shalane Flanagan was crucial for me during that time. She was helping guide me and steer me in the right direction. In this sport, everyone works so, so hard. It's easy to think, *Well, I can't let other people outwork me.* We're also all really talented. I'm trying to change that attitude of thinking I won't run well if I'm not working as hard as everyone who can do more, working as hard as possible. Shalane put it in perspective, reminding me that when she was competing on the track, she was running around 70 miles a week. She told me, "I worked my way up in different events. You have to just see what you need to do, and you need to be a little bit more vocal about what you can handle, what's pushing you over the edge."

> " I was crying to [Shalane Flanagan], thinking I'm never going to be good, I won't ever race. This was December 2014, when I got my second sacral stress fracture. She said, 'I'll come over and we can drink wine and just talk.' "

I was crying to her, thinking I'm never going to be good, I won't ever race. This was December 2014, when I got my second sacral stress fracture. She said, "I'll come over and we can drink wine and just talk." It felt normal and good. I realized that I don't want to cut out relaxing or enjoyable things like that; it keeps me sane.

It reminds me that we can give everything we have, but we don't have to be robots. Everyone's different. Just because someone can run

150 miles a week or 24 seconds in a 200m, that doesn't mean that I couldn't still get the most out of myself by honing my strengths. For me it's been a constant process to not play that comparison game. I need to do what my body needs to do.

FROM STRESS FRACTURE TO BRONZE MEDAL

After my first sacral stress fracture, I ended up taking six months off from running, and I got really out of shape. I started out doing a ton of cross-training right off the bat, and realized I was overdoing it and needed to take total rest. It took me six months to finally get back to running. That was the end of 2013. In the fall of 2014, I had gotten back to training and had some really good road races. Jerry said, "You can be a really good distance runner with how you're running these longer races."

As I mentioned, at the end of 2014, I got another sacral stress fracture, that one on the opposite side. At that time, too, I saw that I had a labral tear on my hip, which had never bothered me. I had a broken rib, too, because I'd fallen on a run.

I just had all this stuff going on. I felt like a hot mess of a human, like, *What is wrong with me?!*

I took a month completely off of activity and then another month of building up in the pool, starting slowly with arms-only swimming, then gradually adding kicking, and then aqua-jogging. From there I went to the AlterG treadmill and started doing a mix of run/walks while still keeping up all the pool stuff.

I was running on the ground by the end of February. I built up all of March to get to 65 miles a week, which I maintained the rest of 2015. Even though I was running less, I was doing everything of high quality. I started workouts again in April. In May I ran a 31:38 10,000m for my debut in the event. In June, I made my first US team, and then in August I got a bronze medal in the 10,000m at the World Championships!

THE SUPPORT SQUAD

I feel super lucky. My family is so supportive; my mom and dad are wonderful.

My sisters are really great. My older sister ran, but she's out of the running circuit now. She's my biggest fan and supporter. Same with my younger sister. They keep me in check and remind me that when I'm not running, there are other things in life. That's been really helpful for me because so much of my identity is running. It's important to have people around you saying, "There's so much else. You're so much more than just a runner."

> "So much of my identity is running. It's important to have people around you saying, 'There's so much else. You're so much more than just a runner.'

The Bowerman women are amazing. It's been awesome having the team grow and having lots of people who support you and understand your frustrations.

My coach doesn't sugarcoat anything. It can be hard with some things, but if he tells me, "No, you actually have a chance to do this," I know it's true. If I'm injured he'll tell me, "Yes, this sucks. You gotta take a lot of time off, and it's gonna be really hard. But you're talented. And I believe you can get there. You've done this before." Any small amount of belief just makes me feel more confident going forward that I can get back to that.

Our assistant coach, Pascal Dobert, is great. He's a good balance to Jerry because he's more of a softy and just wants to check in and see how everyone's doing. He even asks how my cat is doing!

LESSONS IN SPORT

Avoid the comparison game. It is a tough one. When I came out to the Bowerman Track Club, it was just Shalane [Flanagan] and Kara [Goucher], who were marathoners at the time. Seeing them and how successful they were at that stage of their careers was inspiring. I was trying to put myself in their phase of life, when they'd had years to build up to that strength. I lost a lot of confidence thinking I wasn't good because I was so far off their workload.

Reminding myself that I was only 22 and that I shouldn't be trying to do everything at their level was a big lesson. That would have saved me a lot of hardship and injuries.

I also would have tried to have more balance in life in those years. When I first came out of college, I thought, *If I want to be the best I can be and get the most out of myself, everything has to be about running.* I was, for sure, too anal, too type A. It was not a healthy or sustainable mind-set.

> " You should never feel like you can't breathe. You have to be happy in your life and have balance. It won't take anything away from your running. Having other parts of your life can enhance your running and make you a happy person. "

My first year as a pro, I lost a lot of weight. I wasn't running well. I was exhausted. I was super depressed. I remember thinking, *I'm giving it everything I have. This is just what it takes to be good.* Now I realize you should never feel like that. You should never feel like you can't breathe. You have to be happy in your life and have balance. It won't take anything away from your running. Having other parts of your life can enhance your running and make you a happy person.

There are times when, regardless of who you are, you're going to have a bad workout. And if all you are is running and you have a bad workout, it's so easy to spiral down. But if you have other things, it's easy to be like, *That's a bad workout. That's OK.* Not every workout is going to be great, not every workout is going to be terrible. Remind yourself that you're continuing to put in the work and know that the workout doesn't define you, the race doesn't define you, whatever it may be.

DES LINDEN

Two-time Olympian; 2018 Boston Marathon winner; 50K world record-holder

DATE OF BIRTH: July 26, 1983
CITIZENSHIP: USA
CURRENT RESIDENCE: Charlevoix, MI
COLLEGE: Arizona State University

HIGH SCHOOL PRs:

MILE: 4:56
2 MILES: 10:40

COLLEGE PR:

5,000 METERS: 16:17

PRO PRs:

5,000 METERS: 15:08
10,000 METERS: 31:37
MARATHON: 2:22:38
50K: 2:59:54

STARTING WITH SOCCER

I was a soccer player who was just too small. I had to be quickest to the ball and then have the fastest feet to get rid of it and survive. I realized that I was never going pro in soccer, but that I was pretty good at this other thing. I started soccer when I was five, and I fully transitioned into distance running my senior year of high school. I played three sports up until that point, but realized that I wasn't going to have a college career in soccer. It was going to be running.

GETTING THROUGH THE TOUGH PARTS

On an injury front, the biggest thing was the femoral stress fracture. That was in 2012, getting ready for the Olympics. That was definitely the biggest setback in my career.

I took almost three months off from running. I'm not a big cross-training person. I think it's OK to get out of shape. One of the big mistakes I see injured people make is they keep their cardiovascular fitness super high, and then they resume running and try to catch their body up to that cardiovascular engine when it's just not ready to get there. I would cross-train just to sweat and for mental sanity.

My outlook was, *You can do this comeback really slowly and patiently.* I looked back at college and the things that I did wrong, so I was using those lessons by trying to go one step at a time. Then you can celebrate your first long run and your first workout back. Don't compare to older times because that will just make you upset. You don't actually lose all fitness—you're not starting from the standpoint of a baby falling out of the womb! It's all in there. You just have to get it back. You're more likely to come back in a healthy fashion as opposed to having one system ahead of the other.

As far as feeling like myself again, I got to the Boston Marathon in 2014 and felt like I struggled through a lot of that buildup, and wasn't quite where I was before, but made progress. It was probably Boston

2015 where I felt I was ahead of where I'd been before. I was firing on all cylinders.

NON-INJURY STRUGGLES

Other than that actual injury, for me the struggle was not developing at the rate that I would like to. It felt like I was doing all this work and I didn't know where my results were. But that's a natural part of the sport.

In college I was trying to force results. I wondered, *If I can work out with these guys, why can't I race like them?* It was always a little bit over my head. The time line in college was four to five years and that's it. I was super fortunate to have the opportunity to continue developing as an athlete and run post-collegiately. I took off that hard deadline of thinking I have five years to get results and I felt I could slowly chip away at this, and naturally progressed. Once I took that pressure off myself and allowed myself to just develop at the right rate, I was really just soaking in the fitness and finally saw the results from that work paying off.

A LONG LOVE FOR THE BOSTON MARATHON

A cool part about the sport is that there's always a new thing to pick up. You go back and immediately analyze what you wish you did differently. Over 26.2 miles, there's so much real estate to figure out, all these little things that could go wrong, or I can fix and get better at, appear. On top of that, the Boston Marathon course is just so different from anything else that is out there.

I fell in love with that process. It's like putting together a puzzle. Maybe I always fall off in the Newton Hills or the Lower Falls, right before the right-hand turn at the fire station. Why does this happen to me? How can I push through there? If you fall off the pack, does that mean your day is over? How do you regroup?

I feel like it was a good course for my strengths. You can work on the little things that are to your advantage. If you're an intelligent runner, you could beat a really talented runner. Or you can use the course to balance out the field. For example, on a flat, fast Chicago course, world record-holder Brigid Kosgei is going to beat me every time. But, you know, in Boston, I've actually beaten her! That's crazy.

I debuted at Boston. It was 2007, and Deena Kastor was also running it, and it was like, *This is it. An American is going to win!* I saw that excitement around her immediately. I saw how the town is so passionate about it, but there was this nor'easter that came through and they almost canceled it because of the rain. The whole time it was cold. There was a headwind and there were no fans out there, really. And I thought, *This is awesome. This race is amazing.* I just fell in love with it right away, and I actually never thought I would be a marathoner.

WINNING BOSTON IN A DELUGE

I thought 2018 would be a rebuilding year. I had just come off a break from training. I got pretty fit, but I didn't think I had done anything that indicated a jump to another level. So my expectations weren't super high because I had gotten shellacked the year before. I felt like the weather for me was beneficial, because of where I train and weather and things I've run through before. It wasn't totally rattling to me. I thought, *OK, I can run in this. It's not pleasant.**

I thought that would play to my advantage. Although it didn't make it any easier the first 6, 10, 13 miles! I thought I might step off at any second because this weather is horrible. And not only is it not going to

---

* **MOLLY:** *Not pleasant* is an understatement—I was racing that day, too, so let me explain the weather: It was low 30s with freezing rain and a strong headwind for the entire race. A lot of the field ended up with hypothermia, myself included. This extreme weather shook up the race results, and took some athletes completely out of the race, depending on what they wore or how they handle the cold. It was a truly epic win for Des to conquer the other runners, the course, *and* Mother Nature.

go well, but how long is this going to take in the recovery process? Is it going to be detrimental to the rest of my year? I have only so many more years in sports. Analyzing a lot of long-term things on the course in the middle of something that you should be focused on short term is never good.

There were also these bonkers events that just don't typically happen, like Shalane [Flanagan] asking about a bathroom stop. I'm thinking, *I'm dropping out anyway, I do not feel good today.* So I slow up and wait for her. Then I was feeling good running a little bit harder and helping her get back.

I had few objectives. There was one where we were chasing the leader, Mamitu Daska, into the wind. That is like the worst spot to be in. But we had to close this gap. I thought, *I'll just go out in front and get us back to the leader, Mamitu Daska, and whatever happens after that, who cares? I'll drop out then.*

I looked back and I'd created some separation—I'd pulled away. Instead of focusing on how bad I felt, it was recognizing that actually everyone felt really bad. It was just a really tough day. I returned my attention forward. I know there's a body in front of me, so I worked on catching her. Creating objectives, moving forward. So there were definitely a lot of mind-set issues going on that day. Where is your attention? Is it too long term? Is there something that you can accomplish and feel like, *OK, I'm checking the box and getting closer to my bigger goal.*

It may sound weird, but not thinking about how you feel and just giving yourself goals helps. And if you do the next thing, then you move on and do the next thing.

> "It may sound weird, but not thinking about how you feel and just giving yourself goals helps. And if you do the next thing, then you move on and do the next thing."

PROUD MOMENTS

I'm proudest of the consistency of my performance in the marathon. I've made that my home.

When I started marathoning, if you could break 2:30, you were doing something special. That's not the case anymore—everyone is faster. But it's still a standard for me. The first time I broke 2:30 was in 2009 and I've been doing that since then. I am super proud of how long I've been able to compete at a respectably high level.

LESSONS IN SPORT

I'm pretty proud of most of my career, because I think even the things that go horribly wrong taught me a ton. I wish I had been a little more vocal in my London 2012 Olympic buildup about how I was feeling and expressing that to my coaches. We made some changes in that buildup, like trying to really mimic the London course. They were maybe an overstressor that on top of everything else contributed to my femur injury. I'd say having better communication with coaches when things aren't necessarily connecting is something I could have been better at.

PRIORITIZING PATIENCE

I think it's the advice we love to hate, but we need the most, and that's to stay patient. It's a sport that you can do for a really long time if you give yourself a long time to do it. If you're rushing things and you're forcing results, it's usually going to come at a price. In particular, in the marathon, it's a sport where age isn't necessarily a detriment. It comes with experience and strength in your body and your legs. So if you can get to the later parts of your career healthy and with a ton of miles, you can do this at a high level for a really long time. But you have to stay patient, and that's always hard.

A TRUE LOVE OF THE SPORT

Honestly, it's always been fun. When I started out as a pro, my high school coach said to do it until it's not fun anymore. Every time I'm going through something tough or having a setback, I realize that I would miss it so much because I do really enjoy it and it's been fun. That's surprising because it's also a job and it's a career and there's a lot of work involved that is not just the running parts. The joy of competing is still there.

BRENDA MARTINEZ

2013 World Championship 800-meter silver medalist; Olympian

DATE OF BIRTH: September 8, 1987
CITIZENSHIP: USA
CURRENT RESIDENCE: Big Bear, CA
COLLEGE: University of California, Riverside

HIGH SCHOOL PRs:

800 METERS: 2:16
MILE: 4:55
3,200 METERS: 11:16

COLLEGE PRs:

800 METERS: 2:00
1,500 METERS: 4:09

PRO PRs:

800 METERS: 1:57
1,500 METERS: 4:00
3,000 METERS: 8:57

HOW SHE STARTED

I was around five when I started running. I would wander off for a few hours and stress my mom out. She would get so mad at me and ask, "Where are you going?!" She just wanted me to have structure and discipline. One of her coworkers suggested that she put me in a track club.

I didn't know what track was, but I loved to run. I came in late in the season and I didn't even have a uniform. In my first meet, I wore a white undershirt and little jean shorts with flowers on them. I got my butt kicked at 100 meters. I thought that every practice we were racing—I was killing myself every day trying to hang on to the other kids.

Eventually, Coach Carlton said, "I think you're better at the middle distance," and he put me in the 800 and the 1,500. I've been doing the same events ever since. I'm thankful that I had a coach who was super careful with my development and who made it fun.

> I'm thankful that I had a coach who was super careful with my development and who made it fun.

When I was in high school, he put it in my head that school can be paid for if you run. I didn't know what a scholarship was. I knew I wanted to go to college. I would be the first in my family. Money was going to be a problem. I made an effort to do well in school, to be better at running. I hoped a school would be interested in picking me up on a full ride somewhere.

That ended up happening for me when I got a full ride to UC Riverside, which was 25 minutes away from my hometown. It was perfect. Coach Carlton helped me from the time that I was five all the way to me being a young adult.

STEPS TO SUCCESS

I was running around 5:00 for the mile my freshman year of high school, and then I just could not improve until my senior year. Then I finally ran

4:55. By that time, so many colleges had given their scholarships away, and there weren't as many resources on the internet as there are now to see what other programs were like. Mostly I wanted school paid for.

I didn't think about being a professional athlete. I took it one step at a time. I wanted to be a better runner in high school, then get a scholarship. Then once I got to college, I didn't know if I was going to be that good.

I remember seeing girls on TV racing at the famous Prefontaine meet. I thought, *Those girls are fast. I'm nowhere near that fast.* I would've never thought that I'd find myself in their shoes. It wasn't until my junior year of college that I was getting closer to 2:00 in the 800. My college coach said I should go to Europe and hopefully get some better marks, so that's what we did. There I ran 2:00 in the 800 and 4:09 in the 1,500. I kind of got my toes wet at the professional level, and I loved it. I realized this is something I want to do once I graduate. There wasn't much interest in me from sponsors or coaches because I was injured my senior year. New Balance was interested, and I went through that whole process of picking up an agent and getting started. It was always baby steps to get to that point.

HEALTH IN PERSPECTIVE

Athletes can be the most confident one day and feel that all slip away with an injury. In 2019, I had a nasty Achilles injury; it had been getting worse since 2016. I was really forcing it, thinking, *I have to go to Nationals.* I didn't know if I would make the World Championships team, but I just needed to be there. I wanted to be that type of athlete who wants to be out there and get to the starting line.

I wasn't having fun. I was dropping out of workouts because I was in so much pain, and every day was worse. Mentally, it was exhausting. A month before, my stomach started hurting. At 3:00 a.m. we had to go to the hospital, and I had to get my appendix removed. Honestly, it was a blessing. It forced me to slow it down mentally and physically. I had to take six weeks off. My Achilles injury ended up going away. I came back more motivated and injury-free. I won't ever take my health for granted.

MOTIVATION TO MEDAL

I'm proudest of the 2013 World Championship medal. Two and a half years before that, I had two training groups deny me. They said I wasn't good enough to be in their group and their athletes weren't worried about beating me when they stepped on the starting line. So, of course, that's a stab at my confidence, especially as I was coming off an injury in my senior year of college. As I got older, I started to tell myself, *Those are just opinions. They're not real.*

It wasn't until I started working with Coach Joe Vigil that I realized what matters is having a good support system and putting in the work. It took me about a year to adapt to coach Vigil's training. He kept saying, "It's going to happen—you're going to adapt." Two and a half years later, I was in Moscow for the World Championships. My husband, Carlos, couldn't go with me; Coach Vigil couldn't go. I had to be a grown woman and be independent, think for myself. They said, "We've trained you to the best of our ability. So go handle business." I was in a really good place.

> " I'm proudest of the 2013 World Championship medal. Two and a half years before that, I had two training groups deny me. "

I was happy to compete and promised myself that if I gave it my best effort I wouldn't be disappointed. Everything just went right. I thought I got fourth, and it wasn't until Ann Gaffigan threw a flag at me from the USATF section and said, "You got bronze!" that I realized it. I just started crying and did the podium victory lap.*

* **MOLLY:** Brenda originally finished third in this race, but a few years later the winner, Mariya Savinova, was retroactively disqualified for doping, so Brenda was upgraded to a silver medal, and Alysia Montaño (page 232) was upgraded from fourth to bronze!

Coach Vigil was giving a clinic in Morristown, New Jersey, with over 500 doctors. They ended up interrupting him and said, "Coach, we're going to put up this 20 x 20 screen and we're going to watch Brenda race!" He got to see it and then start his clinic super proud.

I'm grateful to have a coach like him. I just needed that one person to believe in me, even when I didn't even believe in myself. Working with him has allowed me to be in the sport for this long. So I don't ever want to give up on myself. I remind myself that I can be low and I can be really high, and just go along with it.

> "I just needed that one person to believe in me, even when I didn't even believe in myself."

LESSONS

There are moments in my career I would never take back, even the bad stuff, because, for example, then I would've never met Coach Vigil. Maybe I wish I would have been more willing to learn and educate myself when it comes to health, either mental or physical. I wish I would have had more bloodwork analyzed when I was younger and early in my career. I think that would have saved me a whole lot of time in training and adapting.

Also, I learned to make sure that I'm having fun with what I'm doing. I think that's part of how to have success. I also learned it's OK to mess up. I need to constantly tell myself it's OK, and to get back up.

BRENDA'S ADVICE

Don't compare yourself to anyone else. I think that's the biggest thing. Social media can be a good thing. You can use it as inspiration. But I think with these young girls, they start saying to themselves, *I have to look a certain way. I have to look like this professional athlete or this model*, and they start doing things in an unhealthy manner. We should tell our girls, "You're perfect as you are. You have to love yourself and be kind to yourself. Don't be mean to yourself. That's the worst thing that you can do in the world." We have to make sure that these girls are feeling loved.

If there's a moment in your career where you're not having fun, that's OK. Take a step back. Take a day off, explain it to your coach if you're not feeling yourself. Younger athletes are dealing with issues like depression and anxiety. So I think we need to be more careful with them because young athletes can be fragile. (I'm fragile, too, so I'm not afraid to admit that.)

CAMP BRENDA

It was Coach Vigil's idea to start a running camp [Big Bear]. I wanted to give back to my community and the running community. I would speak to campers who came to Big Bear, and Coach gave me the idea to have a girls' camp.

When I set it up I didn't want it to cost the girls money. I wanted anyone to be able to come experience it. That was my situation growing up, not having the money for that kind of thing. My coaches used to fundraise for me in high school. So there is a writing contest, and it's like a scholarship, so they don't break any NCAA rules. They can accept the free shoes and gear and things. They don't have to be fast runners to attend. I want to get to know them as people. I didn't realize how many kids need help. We have 10 to 12 girls come to the camp each summer. The first year was 5. I hope it can keep growing!

It's about more than just running. What helps me wake up in the morning and train is thinking there's a little girl out there looking up to me. When they see me on TV or come to my camp, it just makes me feel good. That's the woman that I want to be known for. That's me trying to leave my mark and giving back.

> "What helps me wake up in the morning and train is thinking there's a little girl out there looking up to me. When they see me on TV or come to my camp, it just makes me feel good. That's the woman that I want to be known for. That's me trying to leave my mark and giving back."

ALYSIA MONTAÑO

2011 and 2013 World Championship 800-meter bronze medalist; Olympian; two-time NCAA champion; seven-time USATF champion

DATE OF BIRTH: April 23, 1986
CITIZENSHIP: USA
CURRENT RESIDENCE: Berkeley, CA
COLLEGE: University of California, Berkeley

HIGH SCHOOL PRs:

400 METERS: 00:55.03
800 METERS: 2:08

COLLEGE PRs:

400 METERS: 00:53.01
800 METERS: 1:59

PRO PRs:

400 METERS: 00:52.09
800 METERS: 1:57

FROM FAMILY SPORTS TO OLYMPIC DREAMS

Getting into running was a very innate thing. I did sports across the board. I played soccer and basketball, but also my family made sports games. They were a part of every family function—a swim meet, family flag football, a family basketball game, or a family soccer game. That's how sports in general started for me. It was very much about play.

My high school coach talked me into cross-country. I was really good friends with his son Justin, who passed away the summer going into high school. He said, "Justin would have loved to run cross-country with you." I had a really good time with the cross-country team. I liked the camaraderie. Even though it wasn't my favorite sport, it reminded me of what I had with my family. I went straight to soccer after that. I loved keeping soccer in there because I just needed that. To this day I don't really identify solely as a runner—I like to call myself an athlete.

SMILING TO A STATE TITLE

In high school, I ended up at the state track meet freshman year. It was the first time I ran two rounds of the 800 and I was like, *Wait a minute. We've been running one race this entire season. I'm going to run again tomorrow?* I took on the challenge, but I didn't do that great. I think I was near last. The next year I finished higher up, like sixth or so, then fourth the next year.

I really wanted to win my senior year. I was doubting if I was ready. My coach said, "You can totally do this." Sensing my nerves, he told me, "When you come around in the first 100, look over at us and smile. We'll be there again on the backstretch. And if you need to do it again, smile again."

I was in second to last place. My coach said, "That's a fine spot. You can see everyone!" I slowly caught people, realized I was having fun out there, and then, with 100 meters to go, I found myself in the front by quite a bit and I ended up winning. All the things that I was worrying about had nothing to do with my physical ability.

BECOMING A FRONTRUNNER

One of the challenges I've overcome is not trying to fit in a box of what a runner should be and needed to be in order to be good. In college, I ended up specializing in the 800, and I didn't love how I was running the event. Tactically, everybody runs in a group together, and then everybody just kicks with 200 to go and it's a last-person-standing kind of deal. I felt like I had a ton of energy at the end.

I mentioned this to my cousin, and he said, "Well, why don't you go out faster?" I was like, *You don't understand the 800 . . . Wait. Why don't I?!*

I feel like I had to recognize and pull out my strengths. It was then I recognized I don't need to fit in a box. Maybe my strength in the 800 is going to be me changing the game on how to run the race so that I have the best possible chance at doing my very best.

I went back with my coach and asked if we could work toward going out hard in practice. I knew I could run a 50 in the 400. Can the other women? I feel good in 600-meter workouts where I go out hard. We went ahead and practiced for that tactic. Then I got to use it at NCAAs. Coach was terrified. He told me when I went out so fast at that meet he was worried I'd blow the whole thing. But I went out and I felt great. I just felt better in my body, letting my stride be open and free, and it gave me the win.

> My challenge was recognizing what my strength was and how it's individually different on purpose. I have the ability to write my own path in anything that I do.

My challenge was recognizing what my strength was and how it's individually different on purpose. I have the ability to write my own path in anything that I do. There's no one-size-fits-all. Certainly, in training, there are typical things that we do to make progress. But when it comes to your execution of craft, you get to write your story, you get to create and make changes that are necessary to make you feel more at ease and also hopefully get the best result.

DON'T BOX ME IN

I don't like using the word *regret*. I love evolving and just moving forward. But I think maybe I would have pressed more for my desire to do other events than my specialty, and not letting agents dictate doing the same thing over and over again. You don't have to do that. People might want to keep you in a box. Sometimes it works for a period of time, but you always have the opportunity to bust through. These walls are not permanent! There is a window or a door somewhere! You don't ever have to stay stagnant or in one place if you don't want to be.

INGREDIENTS FOR THRIVING IN SPORTS

I need happiness. I need to sometimes switch things up. I need a change of atmosphere regularly. I do not like doing the same thing over and over again. I'm not a stagnant being.

From a support standpoint, I need the ability to be flexible. I need women's health support that, from a professional standpoint, we can do a much better job of providing. We have physical therapists, but what about therapists specializing in women's health? I think that's what has been the game-changer for me from a mental and physical standpoint. I think that's why I even felt comfortable having kids and continuing running at a high level, because my coach didn't make me feel that I couldn't also have my family while pursuing my track career. I need people who are down with flexibility, down with change and encouragement and support where help is needed.

SEEING THE BIGGER PICTURE

This can become hard, but make sure that you keep it fun, don't take things too seriously. Obviously, become a beast and focus when it's time for the workout. But all the other things—they're not that serious.

I think the community is really important—embrace your friends even if they're not quite aiming for the same things you are, but also don't let the community dictate how well you do. What I mean is that sometimes your peers may not be as serious as you are; they may drag you into not doing a run or something. You are the author of your success. Don't forget that.

Think about this whole experience in sports as a book. Make sure you're writing in fun parts that make you laugh. There will be parts of it that you can't even control that will make you cry. But at the end of it, I want for young girls to think about, if they were writing this book, how it would make them feel when they were able to read it at the end of it all. Would they enjoy reading this book? Think of your life as a really good book that you'd want to read and you don't want to put down and also you're the author of it. Don't let anybody else do it. There are going to be ebbs and flows, but enjoy the process.

> **Think about this whole experience in sports as a book. Make sure you're writing in fun parts that make you laugh. There will be parts of it that you can't even control that will make you cry. But at the end of it, I want for young girls to think about, if they were writing this book, how it would make them feel when they were able to read it at the end of it all.**

BUILT BY ADVERSITY

This is such a cliché, but the hard parts are rewarding. Although I don't want any of the hard parts to happen, and it would be great for things to be easy all the time, it does always allow me to reset and have a little bit more clarity in thought after those challenges. The trials help me figure out what I didn't like about what was so hard and what I wanted to add to my journey to make sure that I can keep looking toward happiness.

My North Star is happiness. When hard things happen, I have been down in a funk, then later I'm better off because it leads me to implement something that's not only going to translate in my running and athleticism, but is also going to translate to how I operate in my daily life. That's rewarding to me, though at the time I don't want to go through the hard moments!

MOLLY SEIDEL

Four-time NCAA champion; 2021 Olympic Marathon bronze medalist

DATE OF BIRTH: July 12, 1994
CITIZENSHIP: USA
CURRENT RESIDENCE: Flagstaff, AZ
COLLEGE: University of Notre Dame

HIGH SCHOOL PRs:

MILE: 4:46
3,000 METERS: 9:43

COLLEGE PRs:

5,000 METERS: 15:15
10,000 METERS: 33:18

PRO PRs:

10,000 METERS: 32:02
HALF MARATHON: 1:08:29
MARATHON: 2:24:42

HOW SHE STARTED

I ran for my church when I was younger. We didn't have a track team at school. I grew up Irish Catholic, so my mom was big into making us go to Sunday school and getting confirmed. The church had a track team. I thought, *Well, this is fun!* I was more into the track team than the confirmation.

SETBACKS AND COMEBACKS

I've had a lot of injuries. The big one was breaking my hip and sacrum.

I broke my sacrum in 2016 right before the Olympic Track Trials. I was back running in eight weeks, but then broke my pelvis the next year and that was the really big one. It didn't fuse back together fully, so I ran on it not knowing it was broken for a year, then went back in the summer of 2018 and got it surgically repaired.

I couldn't walk for six weeks, I couldn't run for six months. Coming off that was the hardest. What caused it to happen was an eating disorder, and low bone density. I was just realizing that those kinds of things have long-lasting repercussions. I didn't realize at the time just how long it takes to get your bone density back.

HOW SHE STAYED IN THE GAME

I really love running, it's hard to explain because I love it so much, so I was always looking forward and thinking, *OK, how do I get back into it?* That was an especially big impetus for me to seek out eating disorder treatment. I was realizing if I kept going down that road, I wouldn't get to run anymore and I would absolutely destroy my body.

I think at the base of it, it is just a love of the sport, not even necessarily for competition. I like racing, but at the end of the day, I just really love running and training and doing that day after day. Those six months of recovery were really hard because you just can't do anything.

THE COMEBACK

My first race back after surgery was the B.A.A. 10K. It was a full year since I had raced. I actually set a road 10K PR, which I was super surprised by. Part of it was that I was finally running on a hip that worked correctly. That was a huge moment for me to see that I could do this again, because it wasn't a given that I'd still be able to run at a competitive level after I got that surgery. That was validation. I thought, *OK, I am really glad that I took all that time to get this figured out.*

PROUDEST MOMENTS

The Olympic Marathon Trials are a proud moment. Making that Olympic team in my first marathon was a big one. But even going pro was a really big moment for me. That was something that I always wanted to do. When I got hurt after 2016, the year I graduated from college, I didn't know whether or not I'd be able to get a contract. I was coming out of college injured. When I did get a contract, I felt like I was finally getting to live my dream, just by doing this.

LESSONS

I've learned not to be so much of a hammerhead with running. In college I would just run myself into the ground constantly, not even necessarily injury-wise. I would train so hard that I would completely exhaust my system. You hit a point where you literally can't run anymore. Your body's just fried. It really disrupts your hormones.

I think I'm much better now at taking time off and being OK with that. If something's hurting, I'm not afraid to take a day or two of no running. If I'm not feeling good in workouts, I'm not afraid to cut a workout or move things around because I realize it's not one workout that's going to make the difference. It's the consistency over time that's going to make the difference.

That's what has helped me stay healthier now that I've moved up to the marathon. Before I would barely be able to string training together because I would try to make up all this fitness at once.

STRONG SUPPORT SYSTEM, STRONG ATHLETE

I've got such a good squad around me of people who keep me going. I definitely wouldn't be able to do it alone. There's my coach, Jon Green, who's one of my best friends. We're constantly in contact anyway, and it's a very give-and-take relationship. Also, I'm still in contact with my college coach, Matt Sparks, who offers so much good advice and a lot of good perspective on my training. My physical therapists keep this hot mess together! They make sure that I'm doing the supplementary things that I need to do to keep running, even when I can't see them.

My family as well is a source of emotional support, and it's almost like an annoying amount of love sometimes. My mom is very into the idea of "We love you no matter how you do in a race." Whereas if I do badly, I tend to think, *I'm totally worthless.* They're so supportive, regardless of how I'm doing in running. Having that is why I've stayed in the sport so long, because, at the end of the day, I know they're going to love me regardless.

Also, they know nothing about running. So it's kind of nice.

STAY STEADY

Don't try to make it happen overnight. Don't be frustrated if it doesn't happen overnight.

At every point in my career when I've gone up a level, there was an adjustment period. When I came out of high school having won the Foot Locker Cross-Country Championships and then got to college, I was not successful. It was super disheartening. It's about putting in that time over and over and over, just getting out there and continuing to work.

As Des Linden says, "Keep showing up." I feel like it's the best piece of advice anyone can use, because you just need to keep putting in the effort. If you keep committing yourself like you're going to succeed, whether that means winning races or making a personal best, then it's going to show.

That's the nice thing about running—you get out what you put into it. Stay committed, even if it isn't going super well at the time or if you're struggling or not finding a lot of success. Put your head down and realize sometimes that you just have to work and keep loving it and keep enjoying what you're doing, and eventually you'll get where you need to be.

COMMUNITY CONNECTION

One of my favorite things about competing as a pro is getting to meet so many cool people all over the world. Growing up in a small town in Wisconsin, I never had any of that. It's been really cool to get the opportunity to travel around and to get to see so many things that I wouldn't get to if I wasn't in this line of work.

Having all these friends all over the world has been special. The running stuff is obviously very special, too, but I feel like it's almost more about the connections that you make while you're doing this. Running brings so many people together.

EMILY SISSON

Two-time NCAA champion; 2021 US 10,000-meter Olympian

DATE OF BIRTH: October 12, 1991
CITIZENSHIP: USA
CURRENT RESIDENCE: Phoenix, AZ
COLLEGE: Providence College

HIGH SCHOOL PRs:

MILE: 4:44
2 MILES: 9:53
5,000 METERS: 15:48

COLLEGE PRs:

5,000 METERS: 15:12
10,000 METERS: 31:38

PRO PRs:

5,000 METERS: 14:53
10,000 METERS: 30:49
HALF MARATHON: 1:07:26
MARATHON: 2:23:08

HER START IN SPORTS

I was 12 or so when I started running. I started playing soccer when I was maybe 6, so I've played sports my whole life. I have three younger sisters and we all played a bunch of different sports. My best friend and I would take turns picking what sport we were going to do because we always wanted to do something together. Usually we each hated the sport the other person picked. She would pick volleyball and then I'd pick soccer, and then she'd pick softball, I would do basketball, etc. We tried everything!

When I started running, I enjoyed the sport, but I was doing it to stay fit for soccer. I wanted to be the next Mia Hamm. I loved soccer, and I was obsessed with her. Eventually, I started to really like running. Soon enough, I just wanted to run. My dad encouraged me to keep doing team sports. He said, "You need to keep doing stuff with your friends. You're too young to focus on just running and be so serious about it at age 12."

It wasn't until high school that I quit the other sports and focused on track because we had to pick one sport.

My dad was also a runner in college at Wisconsin, and my mom was a college gymnast there. He was a miler. He ran low 4:00 in the mile. That's where I did my freshman year before transferring to Providence.

ADAPTING TO COLLEGE

I always wanted to go to Wisconsin because I loved the school and the campus from a young age. I didn't really take into account looking at teams and coaches. That's just where I'd wanted to go since I was 15 years old. When I went there as a freshman, I had a great experience with the team. My teammates were awesome, but the training didn't suit me at all. Over winter break my freshman year, I realized it wasn't working for me. I know I only gave it one semester, but I just didn't see this coaching style working for me. So I started looking to transfer. I think having had that one year to see what things didn't work for me led to knowing exactly what I wanted when I transferred, and it actually made it easier picking a school and a coach the second time around.

When you're 18, you may not know what you're looking for in a coach and a program.* I was confident when I did transfer to Providence College that this is what I wanted. This is the coaching style and workouts I think will really work for me. This team seems like a great support system. Even though it wasn't a great first year, it really helped me out, I think, in the long run.

MORE ADAPTING!

I kind of hit a performance plateau my sophomore through senior years of college. I wasn't even so sure then that I wanted to keep running after college, but then my fifth year was so good to me. Before that, I definitely had some setbacks and injuries and I had to figure out how to handle those without being miserable all the time.

For college kids, and even when you're older, injuries can really bring you down. That was something my teammates and I struggled with. I had tendinitis issues off and on in college. I think because I've had the same issues year after year, I learned from them. What do I need to strengthen? What do I need to get worked on? What stretches help me? Also, I learned how I can work on these things, still run, and not let it completely overwhelm me and get me down all the time. When I was younger, I struggled more with it.

When I'd plateaued for a few years, I kind of lost a little bit of interest

---

* **SARA:** As a former collegiate athlete and now coach, I agree that choosing your school and program is one of the toughest and biggest decisions you will make as a 17- or 18-year-old. There are so many factors that go into making your college choice (school, majors, team environment, training, weather, training environment, etc.). The one thing I ask recruits is this: Is this a place where you could be happy whether you're running or not? Can you see yourself here four or five years? If they aren't happy, they won't be as successful and won't run as well as they could. Most coaches will agree that your athletes perform much better when they have happy and balanced lives.

in the sport. Then when I started road racing right before my fifth year, some spark was reignited, and I started really enjoying running again. I decided I did want to do this professionally after college. That motivated me to have a really strong last year.

ONWARD AND UPWARD

Breaking through that plateau happened specifically after I did some road races in Ireland with Shane—who's now my husband—one summer. It was before my fifth year of college. We had tempo runs written down as workouts and we said, "Why don't we just jump in these road races instead?"

I'd never done a road race before. There was no pressure. That was something else I had to deal with in college—learning to manage pressure. I really enjoyed the road races as a whole new thing that I hadn't explored in the sport.

When I came back to school, I was like, I want to do more road races. I was really motivated. I didn't have a cross-country season that year, so my coach, Ray Treacy, threw me in road races I wanted to do for fun. I think the improvement came from a bit of an attitude change and a bit of just trying something new. For many years it was like, *OK, cross-country, indoor track, outdoor track, year after year for years.* I found this whole new road racing scene really fun and different.

KEEPING IT FUN

When I was younger, my parents were adamant about "You need to keep this fun" and would have to tell me not to take it so seriously. They would ask, "Are you doing things with your team or being a good teammate? Are you enjoying that aspect of this? How is soccer going?" A lot of runners are kind of type-A perfectionists, and I can definitely be that way when I'm running. That attitude from my parents helped dial things back a bit.

Through high school, we were so conservative with training. I had six different high school coaches, so my training was all over the place!

Each coach was very conservative with me because I was always new to the program. That helped me build things up slowly over time. In college, when I did hit that plateau, there definitely was a year or two where I didn't know if I wanted to keep doing this. Maybe I wanted to go back to school and get into teaching; I had all these other ideas.

But then I found that joy in the sport and I didn't want to step away from it. I really wanted to see what my potential is. So I think I've gotten enjoyment out of it, but I'm pretty motivated and I just want to see what I can get out of it, too.

MANAGING MIND-SET

I've learned to handle pressure. I've learned to manage it leading into races and how your mind-set before key events can really affect your performance and your enjoyment of it.

I was talking to Ro McGettigan, who does sports psych coaching with me, about the challenge-versus-threat mind-set. Some races I'm really excited to see what I can do. I'm curious what that's going to lead to. And there are some races I would go into where I'd be like, *Oh my god, just don't mess up.*

For example, I won the 5K at NCAA indoors and outdoors my fifth year of college. Going into the indoor one, I felt all this pressure. I felt like, *I need to win an NCAA championship.* I thought about how it's going to affect getting a contract, sponsorship opportunities . . . all this pressure. It was a relief when it was done. I didn't enjoy it that much.

Then going into the outdoors, I didn't feel all this pressure. I was just excited because it was my last NCAA performance. I was like, *Let's just see what you can do.* It was really fun. I won that one and I felt way better doing it. So I think the mind-set you have can really affect things. You can get away with the races as a threat mind-set, but it's just not quite as enjoyable and it's more anxiety-inducing. It still happens sometimes, but I'm getting better at handling it.

I used to be thinking, *Don't mess up* before any race. But now, it's only Olympic Trials–type races where I still struggle with it a little bit. But even then it's not as bad as it used to be. I used to be like, *I can't sleep. I'm so nervous.*

SUPPORT TEAM

In college, I was pretty lucky. We had a really, really good team environment. All of my really good friends today are from my team at Providence College. I moved around a ton growing up. I don't have as many friends from before college. My friends from the team are amazing. They are such confident, supportive people. Being around women like that, I gained a lot of confidence. I feel like it rubbed off on me a bit.

It's something I did look for when I was transferring. I wanted a good, positive environment. I went to one school on a recruiting visit and it was not a good team environment. There were just some toxic things I recognized I didn't want to be around.

I was lucky on our team. Even if we butted heads, some of that is normal and we still respected each other. I think that is so key. You don't always have to be best friends with everyone, but you need to respect them and know that sometimes what they're going through and what you're going through is similar.

EMILY'S ADVICE

Find ways to make it fun. It's my job now, so I do take it seriously. My husband, Shane, is great for reminding me to take a step back and gain perspective every once in a while. We're so used to working so hard. He reminds me to enjoy things I achieve, and to stop and enjoy those moments. Enjoyment in the sport will help longevity.

Taking care of your body is important, too. I never used to do muscle activation or mobility work or get worked on. Now it's helped me a lot. Investing in your body in that way is huge.

BODY POSITIVITY

I remember working out and this guy was walking around the track and he's like, "You're not a runner." I was as fit as I'd ever been in my entire life. He said, "You shouldn't run," based on how I looked! I get comments all the time because I'm short and I'm strong.

I was kind of insecure as a high school kid. I just wanted to look like everyone else. When I was at the World Junior Championships for track, my friend pointed out these message boards where everyone's making fun of my quads, and they're making fun of my friend's appearance, too. I just don't care anymore, but I did when I was younger. It really bothered me. It helped having confident, supportive friends and people I surrounded myself with.

> **I get told all the time, 'Oh, you're really strong.' I used to hate that. I was like, *No, I want you to tell me I look like a runner!* Now I think, *Yeah, strong. I like that.***

There was one thing Ray talked to me about in school—how when you look at the professional runners, you have to realize it's taken years and years for their body to mature into what it is now. I stopped caring so much about what other people thought of me and what I look like. I get told all the time, "Oh, you're really strong." I used to hate that. I was like, *No, I want you to tell me I look like a runner!* Now I think, *Yeah, strong. I like that.*

AJEÉ WILSON

2017 and 2019 World Championship 800-meter bronze medalist; 2012 800-meter World Junior champion; Olympian; former US 800-meter record-holder

DATE OF BIRTH: May 8, 1994
CITIZENSHIP: USA
CURRENT RESIDENCE: Philadelphia, PA

HIGH SCHOOL PR:

800 METERS: 2:00

PRO PRs:

400 METERS: 00:53.63
800 METERS: 1:55
1,500 METERS: 4:05

HOW SHE STARTED

I started in organized track when I was nine. I previously played soccer. My younger sister got into track first. She'd come home and say, "Oh, my gosh, it's so fun." She had so many stories. I wanted to join that! We were just running laps around the basketball gym, so it wasn't too serious.

I wouldn't say I got serious until my sophomore year of high school. I kept playing soccer and basketball for a while, but my parents were saying, "You have to pick one sport." So I stuck with track. I was definitely better at track than soccer. Also, I didn't like losing or being unable to control losing in soccer. I liked that track was more individual, but I still had the camaraderie.

I also ran cross-country in middle school all the way through high school. It wasn't really my best season. Cross was just something to keep in shape. I think at the Asbury Park 5K I ran 18:06 once.

IRON WOMAN

My most ongoing challenge with running has been maintaining my iron levels.

When I look back on my earlier career, I see how my iron levels affected me. Although I wasn't training as hard, if I felt bad I chalked it up to being busy. I thought, *Oh, it's because I'm in this club and I'm doing this and I'm doing that and I'm doing other sports.*

As I've gotten older, I realized that I had an actual low iron issue. My 2016 season was the first time I sensed something was wrong, that my performance was crashing. My ferritin level was 12 and I had zero energy. I had to be more mindful about what I ate and make sure that it was centered around keeping my levels up. That's something that I'm still not the greatest at.

My diet was a source of enjoyment for me. Growing up, food was a big part of our family life. Enjoying and not stressing over my food was my sweet spot. I normally don't want to be super strict or super meticulous about my eating. I still have to watch my iron levels to this day. Partnering workload with recovering with fueling right is the core of our sport.

I address the low iron now with supplements and diet. It's weird how, with the iron levels, for a stretch things will be going great—then all of a sudden it's not. Right now I take the iron dose every other day.

As far as the time line for feeling like myself again, it could be three weeks. The first time I had the issue diagnosed, it was more like five to six before I was back training well. I think now I come back quicker, just because I catch it earlier, and I know what symptoms look like. For example, I get little rashes or I feel like I can't breathe.

PROUDEST MOMENTS

It's a tie between the 2017 World Championship bronze medal and running the American record in 2017.

For me and my coach, the goal is to win—especially as I've gotten better. Those two races were the most competitive, most exhilarating, most fired up I've been competing. They were paired with great accomplishments, but more than anything, the way I felt after, like, *OK, cool, let's do this again!* was why they were special to me.

PRE-RACE VIBES

I don't like to be hyped up or too high-energy. My approach is, I just want to feel as confident as possible. Before that American record race, we'd just had a good run at Nationals. I'd done a time trial back at home and I actually ran 1:56, so in my head I knew what I was capable of.*

The main thing that I worry about before races is the question of

---

* **MOLLY:** To understate it, this is a very good time trial, as it was around the American record held by Jearl Miles-Clark (Hazel and Joetta's sister-in-law) at the time.

Can I do it? I feel a quiet, reserved confidence because I don't want to get overly antsy, which I feel like happened in 2017 before Worlds. I was talking to my coach and he's like, "You're ready. If you feel good with 300 meters to go, go for the win."

He's always saying, "You can do this better," even in my best races, even after an American record. So when he says, "You're ready to go," that gives me a huge confidence boost.

> In my best races, I kind of just go somewhere else and don't feel the pain. It's not until after that I'm like, *Oh my gosh, that hurt.*

At 2017 Worlds, at 300 to go I was a little too charged up and I went a little too early. So, especially since then, I've tried to keep it chill, because I know I have the tendency to overdo things when I get too hyped.

In my best races, I kind of just go somewhere else and don't feel the pain. It's not until after that I'm like, *Oh my gosh, that hurt.*

FAST FRIEND

I used to train with Olympic 10,000-meter runner Marielle Hall (pages 200–204) in high school and a little after college. She's the most intense person in the sense of doing crazy workouts and showing no pain. I've never seen her bend down on her knees after a rep. Meanwhile, the coach is yelling at me, "Will you please get up off the track?!"

SUPPORT NETWORK

My coach, Derek Thompson, is at the core, especially after all these years. He's definitely had the biggest impact on my career and my life in general.

He's kind of like the ringleader, and the supporting cast do equally as much in different ways. Those are my parents, my sisters, my brother, and my track family. My track family includes Miss Jackie (Derek's wife) and the Taylors, another local track family, and my teammates, who have changed over the years with people coming in and out, but we still keep a good bond and a good relationship. Having support off the track has made it easier to commit to what I have to do, because I know there's so much more on the other side that has nothing to do with track and how I perform.

MORE THAN A RUNNER

It's so important to have balance and perspective with where you are, what your goals are, and how long that will take. Be patient with yourself on that.

Also, do not be afraid to fail. That has been something I've had to work on throughout my career. There is a balance between pushing yourself and expecting more of yourself and training hard, then pairing it with balance. That stops you from overtraining or picking up bad habits that are actually hurting you in the long run.

Not having any other sense of self besides track used to terrify me. In high school, I quit track for maybe three weeks because I wanted to join an extracurricular club, the Character Committee. The mission was welcoming students and helping them feel comfortable in the new school. We'd host events for freshmen and other classes throughout the year to help them get to know each other. There was a pizza party and an ice cream party, so I was like, *I need to join this club.*

They met after school once a month or every two weeks. My mom said, "If you're doing this club, you're going to miss track, so you can't join." I didn't want to be 100 percent super-tunnel-vision focused on track. So I quit and I was like, "I'm not running if I can't join a club." After that stalemate, for a few weeks, she said, "All right, join the club."

Early on I realized that I knew how unhappy I'd be if track was a singular focus, and that was all I had and all I thought I was valuable for or

> **Early on I realized that I knew how unhappy I'd be if track was a singular focus, and that was all I had and all I thought I was valuable for or good at.**

good at. Most of the time I'm super focused. My mom will drive to visit me for an hour on a weekend, and it's just a short unplug, but it's refreshing. That's how it's sustainable.

I volunteer with an organization, Sankofa Healing Studio. It's therapy to people in the community who either were formerly incarcerated or for the families of people who were.

The opportunities and the position that track has put me in to be able to give back in ways that mean something has been the most rewarding part about all of this. Track is the biggest piece of my time, and I prioritize it, but my rule of thumb is this: If you ask for my help, if I can make it work, I'm going to show up for you as much as I can.

Things as simple as going to talk to a high school team or handing out medals at a local cross-country race matter to people. It takes me back to when I was in high school and kids would come back. I remember feeling so inspired by what they were doing with their life. I wanted to do something, too. That the high schoolers are looking up to me now is special and also a little weird to try to know what to say. All I can do is tell my truth, to tell my story, and hopefully it inspires you or you can take something away from it that helps you.

SARA VAUGHN

Member 2012 indoor and 2017 outdoor World Championship team

DATE OF BIRTH: May 16, 1986
CITIZENSHIP: USA
CURRENT RESIDENCE: Boulder, CO
COLLEGE: University of Colorado

HIGH SCHOOL PR:

1,600 METERS: 4:58

COLLEGE PR:

MILE: 4:47

PRO PRs:

800 METERS: 2:03
1,500 METERS: 4:04
MILE: 4:27
MARATHON: 2:26:53

PREGNANCY WHILE COMPETING IN UNIVERSITY

Having Kiki, my daughter, in college was a challenge and I didn't know what I was doing. I didn't realize the pure physical side of it; what's involved in having a baby and coming back from having a baby. I had no idea where to turn or what that was supposed to look like. I had my doctor giving me advice, but it wasn't necessarily advice for an elite runner. He had no running experience. So I was completely blind on that side of it.

The administration at the University of Colorado didn't know what to do, either. I think everybody involved was learning as we went. There was never an outline or a guide of what to do as a student, let alone an athlete. Professors didn't know how much time I was allowed to miss in class.

I was told to withdraw multiple times. I was told to drop out. I was told that would just be easier, to come back next semester. But I wanted to keep my scholarship. I wanted to keep moving forward. I found pretty quickly that I had to advocate for myself. Nobody was going to do it for me.

Kiki was born in 2006, and the NCAA passed that pregnancy redshirt bylaw in 2007.* I don't know if my particular case was the incentive for that. I had to really fight to get my redshirt eligibility. I applied for that paperwork and I told my coach and our compliance director that I filed. That person told me it wasn't worth their time filing the paperwork. She said anybody she's ever heard of getting pregnant just dropped out, and it wasn't even worth the conversation to do otherwise. I don't know to this day if it was ever filed. They told me that, statistically, I wouldn't graduate anyway, so why would it be worth trying?

---

* This bylaw states that a member institution may approve a one-year extension of the five-year period of eligibility for a female student-athlete for reasons of pregnancy.

POSTPARTUM RETURN

I didn't have any pressure athletically. I was told just to come back to practice when I felt like it, but no one actually expected me to come back to practice, either. I was told that I would be allowed to keep my scholarship for the next year, even if I didn't come back. There was no pressure and no expectations, but no guidance, either.

> " I decided that I didn't want my life to stop and I didn't want my running to stop. To stop school and stop running? I think that's a strange message to send to me. Just give up everything? I don't think it ever crossed my mind to drop out. With running, it never crossed my mind, either. "

I decided that I didn't want my life to stop and I didn't want my running to stop. To stop school and stop running? I think that's a strange message to send to me. Just give up everything? I don't think it ever crossed my mind to drop out. With running, it never crossed my mind, either.

My mom had me when she was really young. She didn't want me to drop out of school. Even if I had to withdraw, she wanted me to keep progressing forward toward the degree, because it is true statistically that if women take a semester off to have a baby, they have a really hard time finishing their degree in the traditional time frame, or at all. So I did have that in my ear.

As far as the running side of things, I wanted to keep running to keep my scholarship so that I could graduate. I would be the first person in my family to get a four-year degree, and I was getting it paid for. There was no way I would screw that up. So I thought, *OK, I gotta pass my 12 credits to retain minimum eligibility for my scholarship and then the next year just run well enough to stay on the team to keep getting my scholarship to graduate.*

GIVING BACK TO OTHER WOMEN

I now have a scholarship for undergraduate parents. They tend to drop out because of lack of resources, particularly child care. Even if they have a Pell Grant and they're getting a Fulbright scholarship, they're having a hard time making ends meet, especially in Boulder and other college towns where child care tends to be really expensive. So our scholarship is designed so that it doesn't take up any of their Pell Grants or take away from that. We pay directly to their child care provider, and hopefully it helps them stay in class.

We have had three recipients so far. The first one was an Army combat vet with twins. Her life was chaotic, and she is a super-hard worker. Our second one was a refugee with children. Again, a super-hard worker trying to start her own business, trying to get a business degree. They are a huge source of inspiration from the past few years.

SARA'S HARD-EARNED WISDOM

You don't always have to make choices of one or the other. I was told a lot that, if I wanted to go to college and have a career, having a family had to wait. While I respect that choice as making sense for most people, for me, that was never a choice. It just was my life and how it happened early on. I wanted to always show that you don't have to

> "If you have a big goal, it's OK to put other things on hold. You can't be all of the things all the time."

give up who you are as a person to be a mom. I actually feel like holding on to those dreams has made me a better mom. There's more than one way to do things.

The other thing I try to encourage in women is that, if you have a big goal, it's OK to put other things on hold. You can't be all of the things all the time. During competition season or when I start traveling or if I have a big race coming up, my house is a disaster. Other things slide to the back burner, and I'm OK with that.

GABRIELE GRUNEWALD

2014 USATF indoor 3,000-meter champion; indoor World Championships team member; fourth place at 2012 US Olympic Trials

JUNE 25, 1986–JUNE 11, 2019
CITIZENSHIP: USA
COLLEGE: University of Minnesota

HIGH SCHOOL PRs:

800 METERS: 2:14
1,600 METERS: 5:08

COLLEGE PRs:

800 METERS: 2:06
1,500 METERS: 4:13
5,000 METERS: 16:46

PRO PRs:

800 METERS: 2:01
1,500 METERS: 4:01
MILE: 4:27
3,000 METERS: 8:42
5,000 METERS: 15:19.01

COLLEGE CAREER AND DIAGNOSIS

DENNIS BARKER: In the spring of 2009, as a senior at the University of Minnesota, Gabriele was diagnosed with adenoid cystic carcinoma, a rare cancer, which ended her outdoor track season. A tumor was removed from her neck and she underwent radiation treatment. The NCAA granted her another year of eligibility and she made the most of it, finishing second in the 2010 NCAA 1,500 meters.

GARY WILSON: We were at Arizona State University for a meet. The day before Gabe was to run, she called me from her room and said, "I need to talk to you." Most of the distance kids were down by the pool when she came down. She told us all that the doctor had just called and that a biopsy of a lump in her neck had just come back and it was malignant cancer. The lump had to be removed immediately.

She asked the doctor if she could complete her season and of course the answer was, "No, this cannot wait."

> I told Gabe that she did not have to run the meet and that I could send her home on the next plane. She would have none of it. She said she was going to race the 1,500 the next day. Not only did she race, but she also set a new personal best of 4:23.

Her teammates were so upset. They all started to cry. I told Gabe that she did not have to run the meet and that I could send her home on the next plane. She would have none of it. She said she was going to race the 1,500 the next day. Not only did she race, but she also set a new personal best of 4:23.

After the operation, there was a long recovery. It was over two months before she started to train a little. Since she was a fifth-year senior, we had to apply to the NCAA for a sixth year of eligibility for another outdoor season. After the NCAA granted her that year, I saw the fire in her and a determination that was beyond anything I had ever seen. She was not about to waste any time.

She trained all the way through the late fall and winter, after which time we sat down to discuss her goals. She said, "I am going to set the school record in the 1,500 (which was 4:15 at the time), I'm going to win the Big Ten 1,500, and I'm going to be an All-American." I knew better than to doubt her to her face, but of course I had my doubts. That spring she set the school record and finished second in the NCAA meet. The only goal she missed was the Big Ten title, which she lost by 1/100th of a second.

RACING THROUGH MORE SETBACKS

DENNIS: In the fall of 2010, cancer was found in her thyroid. Her thyroid was removed. From 2011 to 2015, Gabriele trained and raced consistently, setting personal bests and placing high in US national races and on the European track circuit. In 2016, Gabriele qualified for the US Olympic Trials in both the 1,500- and 5,000-meter races but felt subpar at the Trials. Shortly after the Trials, a large tumor was found on her liver. The adenoid cystic carcinoma had spread to her liver. She underwent surgery in which over half of her liver was removed and she began immunotherapy treatment.

She began to train again during the winter of 2016–2017, and in the spring ran 4:12 for 1,500 meters and qualified for the USATF Championships. But shortly after running 4:12, several small tumors were found on her liver. These tumors were inoperable. Gabriele began chemotherapy. Even though she fought infections and fevers leading up to the USATF Championships, she ran her prelim in 4:31. It was her last professional race.

THE LEGACY SHE LEFT

DENNIS: Over the next two years, Gabriele continued training through her cancer treatments with the hope that a cure might be found and she could resume racing. But on June 11, 2019, she passed away with many family, friends, teammates, and competitors around her.

Throughout her career, Gabriele's best training partner was Justin Grunewald, her college boyfriend, whom she married in 2013. Justin was a very good runner at the University of Minnesota and continued to train and race after college as he worked his way through medical school. But the main focus of his running was doing what he could for Gabriele. There were very few runs or workouts Gabriele did as a pro when Justin wasn't with her.

Gabriele's entire professional running career took place during her 10-year battle with cancer. She faced many physical, psychological, and emotional challenges, and trained and raced hard, even when she knew she wouldn't be at her best. She overcame those challenges time and again to achieve success nationally and internationally. Near the end of her life, she established the Brave Like Gabe Foundation to raise money for rare cancers.

KIM CONLEY

Two-time Olympian

DATE OF BIRTH: March 14, 1986
CITIZENSHIP: USA
CURRENT RESIDENCE: Flagstaff, AZ
COLLEGE: University of California, Davis

HIGH SCHOOL PRs:

1,600 METERS: 4:52
3,200 METERS: 10:58
5K CROSS-COUNTRY: 17:47

COLLEGE PRs:

1,500 METERS: 4:22
5,000 METERS: 16:17

PRO PRs:

5,000 METERS: 15:05
10,000 METERS: 31:35
HALF MARATHON: 1:09:44

KEEPING HOPE ALIVE

I graduated from college without becoming an All-American or competing at the NCAA Championships. I harbored dreams of running as a post-collegiate athlete, but I thought that being an All-American was a prerequisite to that outcome. Ultimately, my coach and my family helped me see a path forward, even in the absence of joining a pro team.

I remained in Davis,* became an assistant coach in the program, and continued training in earnest. There were no magical breakthroughs, but I continued chipping away at my PRs, lowering my 5,000-meter best to 15:51 my first year out of college and to 15:38 my second year out of college.

BREAKTHROUGHS!

My third year out of college I opened my season by running the Olympic "B" standard in the 5,000. Suddenly, my PR was only five seconds away from being eligible for the Olympics, and that was the first time I considered the possibility that I could make an Olympic team.

Later that spring, at the 2012 Olympic Trials, I finished third in the 5,000 by 0.04 seconds and ran under the Olympic standard by 0.21 seconds. In that fraction of a second, I became an Olympian.

HOMETOWN PRIDE

In 2014, the US Track and Field Championships were held in Sacramento, California, which is just outside Davis, and only two hours from where I grew up. It felt like a home meet. The stands were full of family and friends from every stage of my life. In that setting, I won my first national title, outkicking Jordan Hasay in the final meters of a grueling 10,000.

---

* **SARA:** Kim was the most decorated distance runner to graduate from UC Davis.

LESSONS IN LOVE

I wouldn't change the path that led to where I am today. I wasn't recruited by major Division I programs when I graduated from high school, and I didn't have sponsorship options when I graduated from college, but I learned to focus on the process and seek steady improvement. This mind-set led to a 16-year PR streak, and eventually I became competitive on the national stage.

The foundation of success is rooted in love. Running at a high level takes discipline and commitment, but if you love what you are doing then you don't feel like you are forcing yourself to work hard or make sacrifices.

THE REWARDS OF INSPIRING OTHERS

In 2016, I bumped into a former college teammate after several years. He told me that he had always wanted to go to law school, but didn't initially apply out of college because he was unsure of himself and didn't think he had what it took to succeed. After watching my race at the Olympic Trials in 2012, he was inspired to chase his dream because he had seen me follow my own path and achieve success, even in the face of the obstacles that made becoming an Olympian seem unlikely.

When I saw him that day, he had just graduated from law school and was at the outset of the life he had always wanted. That story meant a lot to me, because on the surface sports can seem trivial. When I learn that any of my successes or failures have helped someone else feel inspired or grapple with a challenge, I am reminded that the Olympic pursuit is a worthy endeavor. I believe in the power of sport, and I am grateful to have been able to build a career around it.

> " The foundation of success is rooted in love. Running at a high level takes discipline and commitment, but if you love what you are doing then you don't feel like you are forcing yourself to work hard or make sacrifices. "

AMY HASTINGS CRAGG

Two-time Olympian; 2016 Olympic Marathon Trials champion; 2017 World Championship Marathon bronze medalist

DATE OF BIRTH: January 21, 1984
CITIZENSHIP: USA
CURRENT RESIDENCE: Chapel Hill, NC
COLLEGE: Arizona State University

HIGH SCHOOL PRs:

MILE: 5:06
1,600 METERS: 5:11
3,000 METERS: 9:53
3,200 METERS: 10:43

COLLEGE PRs:

1,500 METERS: 4:21
5K: 16:02
10K: 33:19

PRO PRs:

10,000 METERS: 31:10
HALF MARATHON: 1:08:27
MARATHON: 2:21:42

EMBRACING CHANGE

I became a professional in 2007, and my first year was terrible. I was running slower than I did in college. I just didn't know if I had what it took. I was really tired all the time and I was getting slower and slower. So I made this big change—I moved to Mammoth Lakes, California [to join the Mammoth Track Club, an elite training group]. It really was a struggle there for the first two years. The change in altitude is really hard.

I've faced a few times in my career that have been marked by big changes. I was always willing to get out of my comfort zone and move my situation, even when it was really tough. It's about making the decision about what is the best thing for my running, even though it's scary and really hard. I think I just had to shake things up in order to get moving again. There just have been a lot of highs and lows in my career.

By the time I had left Mammoth, I really wanted to make the Olympic Marathon team. I ended up being fourth at the Olympic Trials in 2012. That was another one of those moments where I thought I might be done or I just don't have what it takes. This is supposed to be my best event, and I was thinking there are just too many people who are better than me. That was a really tough one. But it was only like six months until the Olympic Trials on the track. I thought, *OK, double down. Just stick with it. Six more months' training; change up the training for the track.* All those tough times and going through all that struggle, it helped me reach a new level of focus and be able to train for that 10,000 and qualify for the Olympic team.*

ONWARD!

I think my biggest strength is being able to take a step back when things are really going wrong, looking at it and trying to figure out exactly why

---

* **MOLLY:** In the pouring rain, Amy won that 10,000m Trials race of redemption!

it's that way, and then reassessing and figuring out a way to get out of it and move forward. I think it comes from using those really tough times. It's not a skill I always had, especially when I started. It was slowly built throughout the years. I slowly developed the ability to use tough situations and tough times to my advantage later on.

PROUDEST MOMENT

I think it would have to be my 2017 World Championship medal. The last three miles I was in fourth place and kind of falling back. Then I made the decision that I was going to medal. It was just one of those moments. Coach Jerry Schumacher actually popped up on the side of the course as I was falling back. I felt like, *OK, it's too far now. There's no way I can catch her.* He was like, "Just like one more step. If you can just get a little bit closer, just a little bit closer, you'll be able to catch her with 800 meters to go!"

I switched that frame of mind, from *It's just too far* to *OK, just get one step closer.* As soon as I was able to do that, I was like, *OK, if I could do that, I can do another step and another, and maybe I'll catch you with 800 meters to go.*

It was one of those races where I know I left every ounce of myself out there. More than the medal itself, I'm proud of that. I haven't had that many races where I know I gave every little bit of me or there's nothing I could have done differently. That was one.

> It was one of those races where I know I left every ounce of myself out there. More than the medal itself, I'm proud of that. I haven't had that many races where I know I gave every little bit of me or there's nothing I could have done differently. That was one.

FORGED BY ADVERSITY

I don't think I'd be the runner I am without all the struggles and going through the tough times. I've gotten a lot better at, when something goes wrong, I don't let it really get to me as much. I'm able to look at it from a more logical perspective instead of getting very emotional about it. I think I'm able to look at it more from a coach's perspective now. What would I do with someone else? What would I tell them?

That just took a long time of seeing other people in situations and going through times and realizing it wasn't the end of the world. I believe that little bit of hope and holding on to that—that's all you really need. You'll be able to learn from it and use it. And it's going to lead to something better in the long run.

AN ENVIRONMENT FOR SUCCESS

The biggest thing is surrounding yourself with people who believe in you and can lift you up when you're going through those tough times and help you reasonably figure out how to get through them. As runners, and as females especially, if things are going wrong we tend to internalize it and blame it on ourselves. The reality is that sometimes it might just not be the right environment for you. And that's OK. We're all different. Before you just completely blame yourself or give up, reach out to those people who really care for you and talk to them and try to figure it out. Don't give up.

SALLY KIPYEGO

Two-time Olympian; 2011 World Championships 10,000-meter silver medalist; 2012 Olympic 10,000-meter silver medalist; college NCAA champion nine times (three in cross-country, 10,000m and 5,000m outdoor, and 3,000m, and three in 5,000m indoor)

DATE OF BIRTH: December 19, 1985
CITIZENSHIP: USA (originally Kenya)
CURRENT RESIDENCE: Eugene, OR
COLLEGE: South Plains College, then Texas Tech University

HIGH SCHOOL PR:

5,000 METERS: 16:35

COLLEGE PRs:

3,000 METERS: 8:46
5,000 METERS: 15:15
10,000 METERS: 31:25

PRO PRs:

3,000 METERS: 8:34
5,000 METERS: 14:30
10,000 METERS: 30:26
MARATHON: 2:25

SALLY'S START

I went to high school in Kenya. The first year of high school, all students are required to run at least 30 minutes every morning. Slowly, the teachers, coaches, and I realized that I was good at it.

PRIDE IN PERSISTENCE

I'm proud that I have been able to perform at a high level for a long time. I made my first national team running cross-country for Kenya in 2001, and 20 years later I ran at the 2021 Olympics on Team USA in the marathon.

LESSONS IN SPORT

At the beginning of my pro running career, I approached my running from a very serious, all-consuming kind of approach. But looking back I wish I could have relaxed a bit and enjoyed the places I was traveling to race. For example, I was in Paris for two weeks but hardly visited even the main attractions. In retrospect, I could have visited and enjoyed the city a lot more.

> " Running needs a very high level of discipline and commitment, and both of these qualities can be applied to almost any part of life outside of running. "

SALLY'S CREW

I believe that having a great support team is paramount. I have had great people around me, from my high school days, through my college years, and now in my pro life. My family have probably played the biggest role. My family is where I get my emotional stability, and when I'm emotionally together, all other aspects of my life seem to just thrive.

LESSONS TO TAKE HOME

Being able to surpass your goals is always rewarding. I always love what competitive running has added to my life. The qualities that you use in running pretty much translate to other aspects of your life. For instance, running needs a very high level of discipline and commitment, and both of these qualities can be applied to almost any part of life outside of running.

FIND JOY IN THE JOURNEY

Be committed, give 100 percent, and always bet on yourself. You should be your biggest cheerleader. I know that's easier said than done, but the beauty of it all is to one day look back and see how far you came. Don't forget to enjoy it while you are at it.

YOSHIKO SAKAMOTO

Zurich and Osaka Marathon winner

DATE OF BIRTH: March 27, 1979
CITIZENSHIP: Japan
CURRENT RESIDENCE: Yokkaichi, Japan

PRO PR:

MARATHON: 2:35:40

STARTING WITH SPRINTING

I actually ran the 100 meters and preferred sprinting. Someone suggested I try the 800. I wasn't excited about the long distance, but I ran it and let the other girl lead until the last 50 meters. I went around her to try to win and she came back to beat me. I remember crying to my dad about it; I was so upset. He said, "Of course you lost, you did no distance training!" After that I would go out in the mornings with my dad for his run.* I had success and eventually signed with a corporate team.

RUNNING CORPORATE IN JAPAN

A corporate team is a company team. You are hired by a company as an employee, and then you get to train on the team.

I was a top high school runner. My high school coach was a well-known and respected coach, and had a lot of connections with the corporate teams. So I had a lot of information about which was suitable for me, and went directly to one, for an insurance company, Mitsui Kaijo.

When I was on the corporate team, we had all day dedicated to training. The teammates were really strong. For example, one woman had the 10,000-meter national record and some others were Olympians. When I was training with them, I felt like I wasn't good enough. It was hard to deal with being second or third on the team. Now I think I was immature about dealing with those problems. Now that my mind is more mature I would be able to deal with it better. Now I would have kept on training, knowing I'd get better in the future.

But at the time I just couldn't deal with it. I quit the corporate team after three years, and after I quit I was really depressed. My high school

---

* **MOLLY:** Yoshiko became one of the best high school runners in Japan, winning the high school national ekiden championship in the 5K.

teacher, a coach, asked me to come and join her high school team to train with her because she was so good. I went, but I felt that this was not where I was supposed to be. After two months of that, I quit running altogether.

I had my three children during this long time away from running. After having my third baby, it was about five months until I started running again. I just kept jogging and also breastfeeding the baby. After six months, my body was feeling back to normal. During that time, I just kept jogging with a really slow pace for an hour. One day I tried a 1-kilometer time trial and it was 3:23, while kind of feeling good, considering all that had happened. I saw I could still tap into my speed. Next I ran an ekiden.* It had been nine years since I had raced!

YOSHIKO WANTS YOU TO KNOW

You will always face some difficulty or some problem; everybody has that kind of moment. It's important to stay calm in your mind and keep running. Take a broader view, rather than looking too narrowly at small things that may be going wrong or not perfectly. If things are not good, have a wider view of your environment. Consistency is important. Keep doing it!

> "Even if you're a true competitor, and very driven to win, you always have to keep the love of it and the joy of running in your mind. If you do that, you'll always be fine."

And enjoy running. Even if you're a true competitor, and very driven to win, you always have to keep the love of it and the joy of running in your mind. If you do that, you'll always be fine. I have made a lot of friends and I can communicate with many people through running. And now I'm teaching and coaching with some high school and junior high school kids and also running. Through running, I have a better life and I have more people in it!

---

* **SARA:** An ekiden is a long-distance road relay. It is the most popular style of racing in Japan.

JENNY SIMPSON

Three-time Olympian; 2011 World Championship 1,500-meter gold medalist; 2016 Olympic 1,500-meter bronze medalist; four-time NCAA champion; Bowerman Award winner; 1,500-meter NCAA record-holder

DATE OF BIRTH: August 23, 1986
CITIZENSHIP: USA
CURRENT RESIDENCE: Boulder, CO
COLLEGE: University of Colorado

COLLEGE PRs:

1,500 METERS: 3:59.90
3,000 METERS: 8:42.03
5,000 METERS: 15:01

PRO PRs:

1,500 METERS: 3:57
3,000 METERS: 8:29
5,000 METERS: 14:56

LESSONS FROM AVERAGE DAYS

Coming into my freshman year of college, I was highly recruited.* I was immediately on the varsity team, and so I had all these extra, personal expectations that I was going to contribute to the team and be really good. I ran really well in the early-season races and was on a trajectory to do really well. Coach Mark Wetmore was talking about what it takes to be an All-American. It's a big deal to be an All-American your freshman year. It was something that was absolutely within my ability. I went to Nationals and I did fine, but I didn't run great and I didn't take an All-American honor. I remember not understanding how I could run so well all year and, on the most important day, just have an average race.

It taught me that if you're going to develop as an athlete, there are going to be times where your upward trajectory takes a dip. It was humbling, and good to experience that on a really important day and learn from it. Life goes on. This is part of being a team. There are other people who ran better than expected, so my average race didn't ruin the score for the team. I had to take a humble step back and celebrate other people that day instead of myself.

MIXING UP THE TEAM POLITICS

I didn't have other elite-level women to train with in high school. My coaches had no problem sticking me in for a workout with some of the guys. Nobody got caught up, at least that I could tell, in some hierarchy of who belonged where. I really admire the way that they just never gave me the sense of feeling like I was supposed to belong in this certain category, and I shouldn't cross over.

---

* **SARA:** Jenny was one of the best distance athletes to ever come out of Florida. She won seven state championships and was a multiple-time Foot Locker finalist. We both graduated from Colorado, and she broke several of my school records! She really opened our eyes to what a special talent she was when she surprised everyone and won the NCAA steeple as a freshman!

When I came to college, I kind of lived that out, thinking that's just how it was. That's all I knew. Any type of competitiveness inside of a team or hierarchy, I just didn't know socially that that was even a thing. And so I wasn't even trying to navigate it or politically do or say the right thing. I look back and I'm sure people thought, *Wow, she totally has guts to do this or that or say this or that.* The truth is, I was just blissfully unaware. I just didn't know that you're not supposed to try to beat your senior teammates, because when I was a freshman in high school, there were seniors who were slower than I was. And so you tried to beat them!

PRACTICE MAKES PERFECT

I don't kill myself in workouts. I don't go out every single day and run as hard as I can. That's not the point of a workout. But I do intentionally try to do the scariest stuff at practice. And so if I ever want to be able to run a 1,500 and go out at a pace under 2:10 through 800 meters, then I'd better do it at practice first. I feel like that's a place where you can risk it a little. By the time I get to a race, I think, *They're not asking you to do anything I haven't already done. I just have to do it all without rest intervals this time!* I'm terrified of time trials, but I love them because I think they're a replacement for rust-buster races. Then I know I can do better when the pressure is on and the competition is there and it's a real race.

ON MAXIMIZING YOUR POTENTIAL IN RACES

During a race, it's not about finding out what you're capable of—it's *knowing* exactly what you're capable of.

The 1,500 meters is a good example. Sometimes the 1,500 goes out at a total jog and it's because everyone's sizing each other up and they're afraid of what other people are capable of. You're playing the chess match. But when people go out way too hard, I wonder, *Who told you you're capable of running five seconds faster than you've ever done anything in your life? What in practice told you you could do that?*

It's not that it's not good to dream and to try really hard, but I feel like in practice I find out exactly where the edge is. Then I go do that. If I can do better, I will find out in the last 200 meters. But I definitely don't try to find that out in the first 400 meters.

RUNNING RELATIONSHIPS

Being competitive with other women is OK. It does make your relationships harder. There are times where you have to take a step back and apologize, or you have to lean in to a friendship and say, "Hey, things feel weird. Why does it feel weird? You know, what have I done or what can I do better?" I think being a highly competitive, very ambitious, motivated woman makes relationships more difficult. But that's OK. You can navigate that and still have really healthy, fulfilling relationships and be competitive at the same time. It just takes some work.

It's really, really important who you surround yourself with. It's so important in your friendships, and the people who mentor you in your life, and eventually who you marry. All those big relationships in your life, the people you surround yourself with, end up either lifting you up or tearing you down.

> "I think if I could give one piece of advice to a young person, it would be: Look at the people you surround yourself with. Are they taking you in a direction you ultimately want to go? Are you lifting your friends up in the same way?"

The flip side of that coin is that you have to occasionally stop and consider what kind of friend you're being. I think if I could give one piece of advice to a young person, it would be: Look at the people you surround yourself with. Are they taking you in a direction you ultimately want to go? Are you lifting your friends up in the same way?

VIVIAN CHERUIYOT*

Four-time Olympic medalist; four-time world track champion; 2011 World Cross Country champion; London Marathon winner; 1997 World Junior Cross Country champion

DATE OF BIRTH: September 11, 1983
CITIZENSHIP: Kenya
CURRENT RESIDENCE: Eldoret, Kenya

HIGH SCHOOL PRs:

1,500 METERS: 4:23
3,000 METERS: 9:04
5,000 METERS: 15:42.79

PRO PRs:

5,000 METERS: 14:20
10,000 METERS: 29:32
MARATHON: 2:18:31

* Took a four-year break in 2000 to finish school, returning to competition in 2005.

A CHAMPION'S HUMBLE START

I started training in school. I would run to school each day, which was like two kilometers away. I would run home for lunch and run back for the afternoon session, and then run back home after school. I would end up running like eight kilometers a day. That was at age 14. Before that, from ages 6 to 14, I would just walk to school, often barefoot because my parents couldn't afford shoes for me.

I started competing in races at school and would often win. My parents supported me so much. They worked hard to help pay for my tracksuit, shoes, and travel. They saw my talent and that I worked hard. I started to have some big success. I got the silver medal at the 1999 World Junior Cross Country Championships in Belfast, Ireland. The next year I won. It was my first gold medal at a major championship.

From 2000 to 2005, I didn't do a lot of athletics because I was finishing school and preparing for final exams. I was not encouraged to run because my family wanted me to finish school. I didn't have enough time to go to do training and to do all of my academics. The school didn't allow me to run much and they didn't want me to travel to Europe because of my exams. They were strict, so I just concentrated on finishing school. The first summer I returned to racing was 2005.

THE COMEBACK QUEEN

I am proud of everything that I have done. But the thing I am most proud of is the 2016 Rio Olympics, when I won the gold in the 5,000 meters. The Olympic gold was missing in my medals.

That was a big goal for me. I had won the World Cross Country, the World Championships, and a World Marathon Major. I had a very disappointing 2008 Olympics. I got two medals in 2012, but they were silver and bronze. I was favored to win the 5K in 2012, but I was very sick. I really wanted to get it done in Rio.

I went into the 10K in great shape. I ran one of the fastest 10Ks ever at the Olympics and broke the world record, but I still got beat by Almaz Ayana. So going into the 5K, nobody in the world thought I had a chance of winning. If you go and watch that 5K in Rio, halfway through you would think I was out of the race.

YES TO PERSISTENCE, NO TO DRUGS

I'm proud of myself for only using my own energy and nothing else. I think that is why I've been doing this for 23 years. You're not going anywhere using drugs; you won't last. I want to encourage the young ones to work out, to train, and to be focused, smart, and prepared. You can't use drugs to help you succeed. At the end of the day, your career will be finished and your name will be tarnished. It's very important to be clean. It's important to me to know that I earned everything I have.

> I want to encourage the young ones to work out, to train, and to be focused, smart, and prepared. You can't use drugs to help you succeed.

I started from junior levels and went far. You have to go step-by-step; every one of them matters. It may not look like improvement immediately. You have to crawl fast to do a lot of things, and then suddenly you just stand.

HITOMI NIIYA

Japanese national record-holder at 10,000 meters and half marathon; Tokyo Marathon winner; two-time Olympian; fifth place 10,000 meters in 2013 World Championships

DATE OF BIRTH: February 26, 1988
CITIZENSHIP: Japan
CURRENT RESIDENCE: Tokyo, Japan

HIGH SCHOOL PR:

5,000 METERS: 15:28

PRO PRs:

5,000 METERS: 14:55
10,000 METERS: 30:20
HALF MARATHON: 1:06:38

INSPIRED BY A CHAMPION

I started running in 2004 at age 12 or so after watching the Sydney Olympics on TV. I saw Naoko Takahashi winning a gold medal in the Olympic Marathon, and I was impressed and wanted to start running track and field. Before that I did a lot of other sports in elementary school, like mini-basketball, soccer, swimming, and even baton twirling!

A CHALLENGING TIME

In 2013, I retired from track. The reason on the surface was an injury to my plantar. But, thinking back now, the real reason I had to retire was something else. I didn't have my period, and psychologically I was not in a good place. I had a severe mental breakdown. At the time I didn't know how to speak out to ask for some help. There was no one in my environment I felt I could go to for this.

There is a lot of research on the relationship between injury and the warning signs of low energy availability, like losing your period. In my case, I had an injury first and wanted to take care of it myself, so I researched it and somehow came to the conclusion that I had to lose weight to heal the injury.

> Really, the biggest problem at that time was that I didn't have anyone I could trust to help me. It's as if I thought that everyone else was the enemy. . . . I now know that was a huge mistake.

Really, the biggest problem at that time was that I didn't have anyone I could trust to help me. It's as if I thought that everyone else was the enemy. I was hiding. It was a problem mentally and physically. I now know that was a huge mistake. When I started running competitively again, I looked for someone I could really trust and work with on the mental side. In my case, it was the head coach and the team leader.

PROUDEST MOMENT

I'm proud of myself for being focused. I'm focused on certain records and times, and am proud that I reached them, but the attitude is what I value most.

A WORLDWIDE ISSUE

I'm not sure if this is a common problem worldwide, but when I'm looking at young Japanese athletes, some runners want to get faster, and they tend to have the wrong method. There are young athletes trying to get lighter and lose weight. I found this to be totally the wrong approach, and I really want to emphasize this!

RAEVYN ROGERS

2021 Olympic 800-meter bronze medalist; 2019 World Championship 800-meter silver medalist; five-time NCAA champion

DATE OF BIRTH: September 7, 1996
CITIZENSHIP: USA
CURRENT RESIDENCE: Portland, OR
COLLEGE: University of Oregon

HIGH SCHOOL PRs:

400 METERS: 00:53.02
800 METERS: 2:03

COLLEGE PRs:

400 METERS: 00:52.02
800 METERS: 1:59

PRO PRs:

400 METERS: 00:52.06
800 METERS: 1:56
1,500 METERS: 4:13

MULTI-SPORT START

I started running when I was five. I always ran summer track from elementary school to college. Once I got to middle school, I did volleyball, basketball, and track. I never did cross-country, just those three sports, and I feel like it helped bring some longevity to my career, because I wasn't solely focused on running all the time. That's where a lot of my skill comes from—by playing volleyball and basketball, I was getting quick and jumping, which is explosive. You have to be quick and very light on your feet and you have those fast-twitch muscles that get triggered in basketball. I didn't do a lot of miles, not even in college.

CHALLENGING TRANSITIONS

The biggest setbacks for me have been when I'm exposed to a new level in my career.

Going from high school to college, I was used to the way things were done in the South, in Texas, and how track was there. Going to the West Coast and starting over, that was hard. Everyone is as good as you, and it is hard to keep your confidence during that time. I was blessed to have done really well in my high school career and made the junior national teams, and that gave me confidence. Then you go to college and you have to reestablish yourself and prove to other people that you have that same confidence that you had prior to college.

When I was in high school, I had this confidence and this sense of who I was at the time. And then going to college, I didn't make it to the NCAA championships that first season. Not making that indoor team and having to watch the team go to nationals while I was at home in Oregon was hard. I had a moment to myself and knew that I wanted something different for next season. I had to check in and really rethink how I was doing things. My freshman year, setting that goal and rising to the occasion after that setback of not making the national team was an important lesson. I went from not qualifying for Nationals to wanting to win the National Championship as a freshman.

Being professional, I've kind of met with that same type of thing. You have a certain confidence from college, and you have to get uncomfortable again and rise to the occasion because you're on a different stage now. Now I know how to deal with it a little better.

LOGGING SUCCESS

What helped encourage the mental side and expectations that I had for myself was when our event coach gave us all these composition books. They wanted us to write our goals out. We also checked in on our diet and sleep and how we are feeling, and we had to turn them in weekly.

It was a good way of checking in and setting expectations I have for myself. I've carried that with me as an athlete to this day because I feel like it's different when you put the pen to the paper. You have to believe it in order to write it down. A lot of people have a lot of thoughts and genius ideas in their mind that never come to fruition because they never act on it. And I think that writing those goals down in that composition book really started the process, with me writing down the expectations that I had for myself.

I always write down my goals for myself. Not so much a vision board, but kind of. I do it around the same time every year. I write down the first thing that comes to mind. I feel like a lot of people pass up that first thought. But that's the one that you want to write down. Often, that thought came for a reason. Having those long-term goals has helped me stay in the sport.

So far, I've been able to check off the goals that I've written. That's encouraging to be able to accomplish, because usually it seemed crazy at the time I wrote it. Then you check it off and that's even more encouraging that you're progressing and thinking goals weren't so crazy. They're very much realistic.

REPLENISH YOUR MENTAL ENERGY

Being happy definitely goes a long way. I realize that more and more about myself, I can grow most when I am happy. In the past, when

I felt super overwhelmed I would go to the spa and get a massage. That massages your spirit. It's an area dedicated to relaxing. And that's where I used to gravitate to. I also love eating by myself. I love eating really great food and having that time alone. Being able to enjoy a nice meal or doing something that makes you feel at peace. The sport is so demanding—mentally and emotionally. With everything going on in the world, there's a lot of things that can be overwhelming, if you take them in all at one time. You need to be able to take that time to find out what helps you relax.

In the past, when I've been so overwhelmed, it's usually followed by an injury. When you aren't happy and you are too stressed, it can cause your immune system to suppress and trigger illness and injury. There are so many things that fall under the umbrella of being happy. You can appreciate things a lot more when you're happier.

At the same time, you are not going to be happy all the time. I try to do little mental check-ins if I'm feeling very overwhelmed. For example, I've definitely felt more happiness being in Oregon where I can go outside hiking or something like that.

ALIPHINE TULIAMUK

Olympian; 2020 Olympic Marathon Trials champion

DATE OF BIRTH: April 5, 1989
CITIZENSHIP: USA (formerly Kenya)
CURRENT RESIDENCE: Flagstaff, AZ
COLLEGE: Wichita State University

COLLEGE PRs:

3,000 METERS: 9:07.21
5,000 METERS: 15:18

PRO PRs:

HALF MARATHON: 1:09:16
MARATHON: 2:26:50

HOW SHE STARTED

I grew up in a very small village in rural Kenya, at an altitude of 10,000 feet. We ran everywhere. We had to run to go get water because no one had tap water. As soon as you could walk, you would want to follow the older kids to go get water or firewood, or to take care of the animals in the evening. Our school was built about two miles away from where my parents live. We had to run to school because walking two miles to school as a kid, that would take forever. It was never training as a kid, it was just my way of life.

In third grade, I started competing against my peers. We used to have a track season around summertime. My sister was training in track, too, and she was doing well and leading races, so my mom was OK with her competing. At first my mom said to me, "You're too young and you have to do chores." Eventually, I got to go run and I came in second behind my sister.

When I was about 10 years old, in 2000, I went to a cross-country race. I won a blanket as a prize, and that really inspired me. I took that blanket and I gave it to my grandpa. He was very happy and pleased, and he held on to the gift for a very long time.

That year I went as far as the equivalent of a state meet, and I really enjoyed it. I liked the aspect of traveling and how my parents and a lot of people from our village came to watch me. I realized I have a talent for this, and I was able to run with other kids who were older than me and often beat them. People even decided to contribute money to me because I was such a little girl, and I was running barefoot and still beating these other kids who were way older than me. After that I was hooked.

SETBACKS

Throughout college, I was very durable. But as a pro athlete I've had injuries, including a herniated disc in my lower back and in 2019 a stress fracture. It was definitely challenging for somebody who is used to running every day. You see somebody posting online about their runs and you think, *Oh my goodness, I'm losing a lot of time and fitness.* Once I came back to running, it took 16 or so weeks before I started feeling like myself again.

PROUD MOMENTS

Winning the Olympic Marathon Trials is my proudest moment. I always felt like I had a lot of potential in me, and my training over the years has shown that I have so much in me, but I often went to competitions and never really produced races that were as good as my training.

I feel like the Trials were the first time where I really felt like I could do it. I wasn't afraid to take charge when the opportunity presented itself. That race was on a very challenging course. The field was very strong, and there were a lot of women ahead of me on paper. It would have been easy for me to be afraid, but I'm proud of seeing that opportunity and running with it.

Aside from that, I'm proud to have discovered a new life and big goals after coming from the village where I grew up. There've been a lot of improvements there now, but when I was growing up education wasn't something that we thought we could have. For example, my older sister got pregnant when she was in seventh grade and she got married off. Growing up, I always thought the path was get married young, have kids, and you have your own family and that's everything. It was through running that I was on a path to a new life, basically skipping teen pregnancies and moving away from home and living here in America and getting a college degree. I think that's a huge accomplishment for me.

I never thought that I would be able to live on my own independently and do things for myself and have a college degree and have a mind of my own and not have anyone control me or control my decisions. That, to me, is huge, and it's something that not a lot of women in my village, even today, have the opportunity to do.

LESSONS

I've learned to be open-minded and go after opportunities when they present themselves.

You have to have goals. You have to know, "This is how I want my life to unfold," and look out for those opportunities. For example, I transferred from Iowa State to Wichita State, and then graduated and moved to Santa Fe to train, and then from Santa Fe I moved to Flagstaff. You can look at that and think, *Wow, do you not like being in one place?* But I look at the opportunities that I went after, and I know now more than ever that if I hadn't gone after those opportunities, I wouldn't be the person that I am today.

Leaving my family behind and leaving Kenya wasn't easy. The night before I left, we all cried, and I cried the whole day traveling from my village to Nairobi. You go into this new country, you don't know anyone. You don't know what it is all about. On the other hand, that is the greatest opportunity that you've been given, so you can't really turn it down.

PEOPLE IN YOUR CORNER

You need to have people in your corner who care about you no matter what happens. For example, having a partner who cares about what I am doing with running but also cares about me as a person has definitely contributed a lot to my success, especially these last few years.

If I don't have people to share success with, then that success has no value. As a pro athlete, I think my teammates have played a very big role in my success, because I see them juggling lives. They have kids, they have families, they are wives, and they have extended families. Yet they still show up at practice and give everything they have for these two hours. Then they leave and they go do their own thing.

Being able to have those people to push you along and inspire you is awesome. My coach, Ben Rosario, has played a very big role, too. When I was diagnosed with my stress fracture, I talked to him and was almost ready to move on and have a family. He said, "I believe in you. I know that you need eight weeks off, but I think that you have a chance of making that Olympic team." I think that having people who not only believe in you but actually tell you that they believe in you goes a long way.

WINNING WISDOM

Be coachable. I know this is kind of tricky, because we read about coaches who want to win at all costs. And that's really sad. But I think a majority of the coaches are good people. And so if you listen to the instructions that your coach gives to you and stop competing with your teammates, I think you can have a long career.

Listen to your body. Take advantage of the resources that your school gives you. I think strength training is very important. I mean, it doesn't have to be like going to the gym and lifting full-on weights. But I think strength training is very important so you can prevent injuries. Take care of your body and fuel your body properly.

Be aware of the relationships, the people who care about you, for who you are, for when you're running well or when you're not running well. Keep those relationships closer, because the older you get, you're going to need them.

Find yourself a good team. When you find yourself that team, believe in what that could give you. There's no one magic way of training to achieve success. You just have to buy into the philosophy of that training, believe in yourself, and that you're going to be successful.

A REWARDING JOURNEY

Being able to use this gift that I was given to inspire other people to believe in themselves has been very rewarding. Being able to go back to my village and talk to kids and have them listen to me and dream of doing this someday makes me very happy. I feel like, as a person, I could stop running today and I would be totally OK. But when I think about a generation of athletes that I can inspire, that always gets me going.

NIKKI HILTZ

2015 Team USA member; World Championship finalist

DATE OF BIRTH: October 23, 1994
CITIZENSHIP: USA
CURRENT RESIDENCE: San Diego, CA
COLLEGE: University of Oregon/
University of Arkansas

HIGH SCHOOL PRs:

800 METERS: 2:09
1,600 METERS: 4:42

COLLEGE PRs:

800 METERS: 2:05
1,500 METERS: 4:09
MILE: 4:32

PRO PRs:

800 METERS: 2:01
1,500 METERS: 4:01

DISCOVERING THE SPORT

Growing up in the central California beach town of Santa Cruz, I spent all of my summers on the beach doing a program called junior lifeguards. Guards was a summer program that taught children ages 6 to 17 how to be ocean lifeguards and was held on beaches all along the California coast. Twice a summer the local beaches would have mini competitions against each other. I fell in love with the competition aspect of guards very early on, and my favorite event to compete in at these competitions was the distance run. At the age of seven I fell head over heels in love with running. I loved running barefoot on the hard sand next to the low tide, I loved pushing my body and seeing how far I could go, I loved saving a tiny bit of energy for the very end to see how fast I could go once the finish line was in sight, and I loved running for something bigger than just me. It gave me so much pride to represent my hometown beach in those races.

I also loved the distance run because that was one of the only events in these lifeguard competitions where they would start the boys and the girls at the same time. The little competitor in me loved that gender wasn't a part of it—it was just about beating the people around you. But at the same time, when the race would end and we were all funneled into the finish chutes separated by boys and girls, it was so satisfying to win, even against all the boys. At seven years old it's safe to say I was hooked on distance running.

NAVICULAR STRUGGLES

Like any athlete, I've had to face and battle through my fair share of injuries. My senior year of high school right before cross-country season started, I found out I had a stress fracture in a bone called the tarsal navicular in my right foot. After getting an MRI, I was informed by my doctor that my fracture was indeed a pretty bad break and if I ever wanted to run pain-free again, I'd need surgery to put a small screw through the fracture.

A couple months earlier, during my junior track season, I had won the 1,600 meters at the California state meet, and in a few months I was planning to go to universities around the country on recruiting visits to run in college. I was 17 years old and I felt like my running career was just getting started, so when the doctor proposed that ultimatum, the decision was an easy one: I scheduled the surgery for the next day. After surgery, I was in a cast and on crutches for 2 weeks, then in a walking boot for 10 weeks. It was 12 weeks total of no running. During this time I was also going on my college recruiting visits and deciding where I wanted to run and go to school for the next four years. I remember being on crutches on all my visits but still having a blast! Having a big decision to make and college just around the corner really gave me perspective and something to look forward to during my injury.

One of my favorite parts about this sport is that there will always be another race or another season on the horizon to set big goals for and come back even stronger. I remember really gaining perspective during this time. Of course injury really sucks in the moment, but at the same time setbacks always show me just how much I love this sport. I think sometimes we don't know how badly we love or want something until it is taken away from us. There's also nothing like a setback to get your motivation back.

A BRIDGE ACROSS COMMUNITIES

The most rewarding part of my career has been putting on a virtual Pride 5K where all the proceeds go to the Trevor Project, a national organization providing crisis and suicide prevention services to LGBTQ young people. As a member of the LGBTQ community, I felt it was important to find a way to unite these communities that mean so much to me. For me, running was something I could always turn to when I felt alone and lost, when I was coming to terms with my gender identity and sexuality. Bringing my two communities together (my

LGBTQ one and my running one) through the Pride 5K has been just as, if not more, rewarding than any state title, All-American honor, or medal I have ever won. Plus, the Pride 5K has raised more than $75,000 for the Trevor Project—such an important and incredible life-saving organization!

STEPHANIE GARCIA

Team USA member; World Championship steeplechase finalist

DATE OF BIRTH: May 3, 1988
CITIZENSHIP: USA
CURRENT RESIDENCE: Phoenix, AZ
COLLEGE: University of Virginia

HIGH SCHOOL PRs:

1 MILE: 5:09
2 MILE: 11:10

COLLEGE PRs:

1,500 METERS: 4:13
3,000-METER STEEPLECHASE: 9:47

PRO PRs:

1,500 METERS: 4:04.63
3,000-METER STEEPLECHASE: 9:19.48
FLAT 3,000 METERS: 8:52
5K: 15:16

THE STARTING LINE

I started running in elementary school when my mom would take me and my brothers to a local track to wear us out—I would run laps behind her while my brothers would totally ignore the track and play in the infield. I really had no idea that running could be a competitive pursuit, as the sports I was used to were the big ones on TV: football, basketball, baseball. In middle school, the school would take those who ran the top 5-mile times during PE and have us race at the end of the year, and that really opened my eyes to the idea of "racing"—in sixth grade, I fell (ha, foreshadowing!) and came in third; in seventh grade, I won; and in eighth grade, I came in second. From there, I decided to ditch my dream of being a cheerleader and join the cross-country team in high school with some friends, where I became the fastest freshman. That trend of jumping into a new challenge without any expectation and finding success continued into my college and professional career!

BARRIERS TO SUCCESS

The biggest setback I faced was in 2016, when I was contending for a spot on the Olympic team in the steeplechase and fell on the very last barrier of the race. My immediate reaction was to use it as fuel, to power me through the rest of the summer and to run a PR at the Paris Diamond League meeting after the Olympic Games. That PR made me the fourth American woman ever to break 9:20 in the event, which was kind of seen as a goal, like breaking 4:00 in the mile for men. But after that success, I struggled to find my stride again in the steeple. As we prepared for the 2017 season, I put a lot of pressure on myself to perfect my barriers, since that was the thing that prevented me from achieving my Olympic dream, but the harder I focused, the more I struggled. I ended up falling again during the 2017 US Outdoor Championship and taking a big step back from the event. I did end up running PRs in the 1,500m and mile in 2017, so I was proud to be a well-rounded athlete who could compete in multiple events!

LESSONS LEARNED AND POINTS OF PRIDE

I learned so much during the height of my track career—the biggest lesson is that *elite* is a mind-set and a lifestyle; sure, your talent is important, but so much can be gained from embracing a committed, healthy lifestyle and from having ultimate belief in yourself and your plan. I would have leaned in to the lifestyle much earlier. I really didn't have any idea what being a pro runner actually looked like when I left college—simple things like getting eight to nine hours of sleep minimum; investing in good, consistent physio; rolling out consistently; doing prehab/rehab drills to keep my body healthy; even just drinking more water throughout the day! As for mind-set, I would have been smarter with how I talked to myself—what you think during training is where your mind goes during racing, so I would have been careful to not give in to negative thoughts when I was feeling tired and to be my biggest hype man!

I'm really proud to help move the steeplechase forward for American women. I was part of the first group of six men and women from Team USA to make the final in the event at the 2015 World Championships in Beijing, showing that we had some of the top steeplechasers in the world. I was also one of the first American women to break 9:20 in the event, which is still a challenging milestone (but probably won't be for much longer!). I'm also so proud to represent the Latino community in American track, as there still is an underrepresentation of BIPOC in distance running!

STEPHANIE'S ADVICE

Keep it simple—you don't need to live a monk's life, but it will help you to prioritize good sleep, great hydration and nutrition, and physio. Surround yourself with teammates, coaches, friends, and family who share your champion mind-set. Stay hungry and humble, because an injury can take away whole seasons from your journey, but one great race can set you off on a new trajectory. Believe in yourself more than anything, because you're the only one out there on the starting line—it's always going to be you against you.

LAUGHS ALONG THE WAY

Sometimes you look back on your time in the sport and remember the moments that will always make you laugh. We wanted to hear about some funny running stories, and we hope they make you LOL, too.

DEENA KASTOR

PORT-A-POTTY PROBLEMS

During the 2003 London Marathon, I felt well-prepared to attempt Joan Benoit Samuelson's American record. Unfortunately, I couldn't poop before the race. Three miles in, the urge came and I fought with it the remainder of the race.* I'd always talk myself into continuing to run: *I'm chasing down a pack of women. Don't stop now.* The next set of port-a-johns, I negotiated again: *You're shoulder to shoulder with the Olympic champion, don't lose this opportunity.* The negotiating was as exhausting as the pace and distance. I fulfilled my goal that day, but it was a bigger battle than anyone could actually see!

AJEÉ WILSON

FAKE SPLITS, REAL DIAMONDS!

At the very end of my first professional track season, I heard there's this 1,000m race in Brussels at the Diamond League. The meet asked if I could run it and said that I may want to go after the world junior record. I was initially thinking I'm tired, as I had never run this long into the season in my life. Then I was talking to another athlete about it. They said Brussels is such a fun meet, you get a little diamond as a gift, there's a Jamaican afterparty, and Usain Bolt is the DJ. I was like, "Oh, OK, cool!" So I told them I'd do it. I went to Leuven, Belgium, for a week to train before the race. I had a pre-meet workout of 10 x 400, and I was at least 20 seconds off-pace every lap! I was so worn out and so tired. But I knew if I told my coach these times, he was gonna send me home and I wouldn't get to go to Brussels. So I sent him fake times! I didn't make them too good or too bad. Then I went to Brussels and I ran. In the first 700, I was thinking, *Cool, I don't feel as bad as I thought I would,*

---

* **MOLLY:** If this has happened to you on a long run, you know this makes Deena's record that much more impressive! The mental strength to hold it for 23 miles is on par with running 2:19 in my book!

this is all right. We came through the 800 in 2:04, and then I just tanked. By the time I get to the last 100, they're like clapping me in—one of the only times I've been pity-clapped home. It was a terrible race, but once I finished, I got my diamond, I went to the party—it was the funnest meet I've ever been to!

MARLA RUNYAN
FINDING HER FLUIDS

When I ran the New York City Marathon in 2002, I did not know how I was going to see my water bottle at the elite fluid stations, as I am legally blind in both eyes. There was no way I would be able to see it. I couldn't even see the table until I had passed it. I don't have any distance vision, so I don't know what is up ahead. I really can't run tangents in a road race or anticipate which side of the road to be on in order to retrieve fluids.

In New York, the elite athlete coordinator came up with a solution. He had a volunteer ride her bike to each fluid station, get off her bike, and then stand behind my bottle at the fluid stations and shout, "Marla, over here, over here! Your bottle is over here!" So every 5K, I heard her voice, and she would be waving her arms over her head trying to flag me down. It was an unbelievably kind gesture, but it didn't really work. It was just too difficult for me to find something I simply couldn't see.

EDNA KIPLAGAT
WINNER OF BOSTON, NEW YORK CITY, AND LONDON MARATHONS; WORLD CHAMPION IN THE MARATHON

RACING HER HUSBAND

The funniest race was the 2010 Los Angeles Marathon. I ran with my husband in the same race, and the race has a gender challenge, so whoever crosses the finish first between the male and female winner earns a bonus. The stagger was about 16 minutes, so the women started first, then men and all competitors went in the next wave. I told my husband if he won, I would pay for dinner, but if I won, he would pay for a vacation! I was so nervous, because when I was at 41km, the motorcycle for elite men approached. I had only 1kM to go and was able to fend the men off and win the challenge. I finished the race and waited for my husband at the finish line—he didn't even realize until he got there that I won. He paid my vacation as promised!

AISHA PRAUGHT-LEER

COMMONWEALTH GAMES
STEEPLECHASE CHAMPION;
TWO-TIME OLYMPIAN

STEEPLE BELLY FLOP

At the Oslo Diamond League in 2018, one of the steeple barriers was stuck at the men's height during our race and it was a disaster. I was in good shape and my goal was to go out toward the back of the field, around eighth, and work up the field. I did a good job of getting on the rail—then there was a lot of commotion and I heard people yelling, and a big scuffle. It wasn't until I was 10 meters away from the barrier that I realized the barrier was at the wrong height—it was so much taller than the women's height! I ended up stopping right before the barrier and I just took it to the gut and then rag-dolled over it. I thought maybe they would restart the race because that was all within the first lap, but they didn't. Our coach, Joe Bosshard, jumped out of the crowd onto the track because nobody else was fixing the barrier. Emma [Coburn, training partner] was in third place in the race, running, waving her arms at the officials, waving her arms at Joe, trying to get someone to fix the barrier. And at one point on the third lap, they got

only half of it down, so the barrier was at an angle. Everyone was now trying to jump the barrier on the one side where it was lower at the correct height, but some people were still going over the higher side. It was actually my highest finish at a Diamond League—I got fifth that day. When we were traveling out the next day, we were in the Oslo airport and saw on the TVs that it was on the news ticker as one of the top five news stories of the day. It was in Norwegian, but the footage was Joe banging the top of the barrier, trying to fix it. We could only imagine what the Norwegians were saying about this crazy coach.

MOLLY SEIDEL

SUPPORT FROM THE WHOLE SQUAD

On my trip to Ethiopia, I was working out at the dirt track in town with a friend. When I was at the far side with her, a guy came and stole all of our stuff from the opposite side of the track. But it's such a small town that everybody knows everybody else. The entire town rallied behind me, and over the course of the next two days, it was like a hunt around town to find my phone.

Amazingly, we got the phone back. It was me being really stupid by leaving my phone in my bag at the track while we were working out. But then it was just so funny to see 200 people in the street all being like, "We've got to find this guy! I know where he is. Let's go to his house!" and the squad is all walking down the street. The police officers were so into it. It has a happy ending, and I took all the police officers out for dinner.

CARRIE TOLLEFSON

2004 OLYMPIAN

A PROPOSED PIT STOP

Charlie proposed to me on a run. I had been hurt with a heel injury and this was one of my first weeks back running. I was 4 miles in and we were going to flip around at Minnehaha Creek, which is a beautiful spot in Minneapolis. Charlie said he sprained his ankle and wanted to ice it in the creek. I got kind of ticked off because I was finally having a decent run. I was trying to get back in shape for the season. I told him, "I'm not going to stop and wait for you to ice your foot." He pretended to go down and ice his foot, and then he came up with the engagement ring. So needless to say, we sprinted the last four miles home and I didn't feel my heel!

COLLEEN DE REUCK

FOUR-TIME OLYMPIAN; WORLD CROSS-COUNTRY MEDALIST; BERLIN MARATHON CHAMPION

WHEN MOTHERHOOD MEETS RACE DAY

Six weeks after having my daughter Tara, I did the Falmouth road race. I was nursing at the time, and Tara did not like the bottle. My husband, Darren, went halfway along the course with her in case she needed to be fed, and I would have stopped to do it! Luckily she didn't, so I was able to finish the race without having to nurse halfway. That was one of my first runs back after pregnancy.

ALIPHINE TULIAMUK

THE WRONG SHAMROCK

In college I was so used to being taken care of for every race, I never paid attention to where we would go. When I graduated, I signed up for a Shamrock Race on Saint Patrick's Day. In my mind, I was signing up for a race in New Orleans, the 8K. I ended up actually signing up for a race in Virginia Beach! The day before the race I ran into this manager for some of these athletes and he was like, "What are you doing here? You should be in New Orleans because

New Orleans is a bigger race and actually it pays more than this." I was like, "Wait a minute, are you telling me that I'm actually not at the right race?" I realized I have to be independent and wind up where I'm supposed to go without depending on people. But I did end up winning the race and actually running a pretty fast time.

THE LATE GRETE WAITZ

1984 OLYMPIC MARATHON SILVER MEDALIST; SIX-TIME WORLD CROSS-COUNTRY CHAMPION

AS TOLD BY HER HUSBAND, JACK:

Before Grete was going to retire from running, it was suggested she go for some Norwegian records in longer distances, like the 10,000 meters and the marathon.

So I contacted the New York City marathon and asked if she could come to run the race. I didn't hear back for a while, and then the week before the race, the organizer of the race saw her name and said maybe she would be a good rabbit. She hadn't even thought about the race. She hadn't prepared. Her longest run was about 11 miles. To her it was just a chance to go to New York and see it before she retired. Well, she won the race and she broke the rec-

ord with a couple of minutes, but her legs were so badly hurt and she was so angry at me that I had talked her into doing this painful race. She said never again to anything like this!

We returned to Norway and she retired again.

But then in early December, she was invited to California to do a midnight race for New Year's and have a seminar.

I said, I'm sorry. She has retired and we have plans to go to the mountains to ski with her family. He asked, If you bring the family to California and you can stay as long as you want, will you do it then? She actually enjoyed that race because road running is different than track racing, and she hadn't had a chance to do it much. So while she had been going to retire that year, instead she ran forty-seven races!

SARA SLATTERY

PAN AM GOLD MEDALIST (AND COAUTHOR OF THIS BOOK!)

I met Steve, my future husband, at the Foot Locker National Cross Country Championships during my sophomore year of high school. Later that spring, we were both invited to run the Golden West Track and Field Invitational in Sacramento. The meet hosted all the athletes in dorms near the track. I ran into Steve in the lobby and he came over to say hi and talk. Coach Klecka immediately teased me about it. I was super embarrassed and insisted he was just my friend. Coach Klecka kept teasing me and said, "Just watch, one day you will end up marrying this guy and I will tell you I told you so." Coach Klecka was right, and we have now been married for 17 years!

FAVORITE WORKOUTS

Although we've heard many times in this book that it takes a long time to build up to this level of workout, it's impressive and inspiring to see what these women do in practice in order to crush it on race day. Some of these workouts may sound familiar, and some may be a structure you've never tried before. A workout is just part of a larger system of training, so it doesn't tell the whole story, but we hope these give you some ideas and inspiration as you tackle your own training.

GRETE WAITZ

AS TOLD BY HER HUSBAND, JACK:

Cross country was her favorite. A favorite training session was running about three and a half miles into the woods, then she would run as hard as she could back again.

She hated going to the track. Every time she was going to do a track workout, she was nervous the whole day. She actually ran faster once in an 800-meter repeat than her PR. She concentrated very hard for those.

It was a challenge to train in Norway sometimes. She was running in these rubber boots, sometimes, in the winter when the snow was so high.

In winter, she also did 10-mile runs back and forth on the quarter mile of clean road that the buses traveled on.

We always worked out at 5:00 in the morning because of work, and she continued that even when she didn't have to do it. She always said, If you and I are as tired as we are now in two or three miles, we will turn around—but we never did, of course. You know that as soon as you get out, you're finishing the run!

ANNA WILLARD GRENIER
2008 OLYMPIAN

I loved all the speed stuff. That was by far my favorite. I got through all the endurance stuff just so that I would be strong enough to start going to speed stuff. Any time we did all-out 200s, all-out 300s, 150s, that was my favorite. I coach the sprinters at Boston College, and I'll threaten the guys that they need to at least beat my times [*laughs*].

The only "punishment" workout I was ever made to do was pretty good. I'm super proud of this workout. I totally sandbagged an 800 at Prefontaine, and Terrence [Coach Terrence Mahon] was so mad at me.

He was like, "You're in phenomenal shape. What the hell's wrong with you?

If you're afraid to go out fast, we're going to do 2 x 500m. All out." It was either the next day or two days later, it was really soon after. He said, "You're really strong right now." I ran I think a 67, and a 68. We went through in 55 on the first one and 54 on the second one.

After that I thought, *All right. I can handle any pace that we go out in.*

BRENDA MARTINEZ
2012, 2016 OYMPIAN

I love mile repeats when I'm fit. Before 2013, we worked up to 5x/mile at altitude, and I think I averaged sub 4:50 with around 3 or 3.5 minutes rest. It was windy and cold, around 35 degrees. I was throwing on my jacket on the recovery, and my hands were hurting, mucus was running from my nose, it was just that cold. That workout was tough, and the conditions weren't great. I just held on to Carlos, who was on the bike pacing me, and visualized it as a race! That strength led to a great year in 2013.

JULIE CULLEY
2012 OLYMPIAN

I did a memorable time trial before the 2012 Olympic Trials.* Coach Gags [Frank Gagliano] had me run 3,200m. I ran 9:48, which isn't anything to write home about when you're trying to make an Olympic team, but it was a crazy workout.

I had a pacer, and at each quarter the pace was going to change, but I didn't know what the pace would be for any lap. As I would come through the 400, my coach would yell out the next split. It was teaching me how to race championship-style, where you often don't know what's gonna happen next and your body has to figure out how to get from a 75-second lap to 67 in a heartbeat. You've got to be ready for what's happening next. I remember coming off that workout knowing I was in really good shape and that my mind was sharp. I knew I would be able to adjust to anything.

AISHA PRAUGHT-LEER
COMMONWEALTH GAMES STEEPLECHASE CHAMPION; TWO-TIME OLMYPIAN

One of my favorite workouts is actually long runs.

As Sara knows, in Boulder, you don't do easy, long runs! It's not a thing. They don't exist. Sometimes we'll just do a steady, long run or sometimes we'll have a structure built in.

* **MOLLY:** Which she won!

My favorite structure is a 15-mile long run with a hard 10 miles in the middle. We warm up 3 miles moderate, about a 6:40 pace. Then we aim for about 10 miles in 60 minutes. Then you jog or run moderate the rest of the way to hit 15 miles.

When I first moved to Boulder, I couldn't do it. Emma [Coburn, training partner] would just murder me in these sessions. But I got so much better at them over the years, and it's one of my favorites now. I know that if I can run 10 miles in 60 minutes at altitude, I'm in a good spot. One of my best long runs ever was when I ran 15 miles at something like 5:51 average. I was like, "I am the best!"

CARRIE TOLLEFSON
2004 OLYMPIAN

My favorite workout is a ladder down: 1,600, 1,200, 800, 400, 4 x 200. I think the fastest I've ever done it was 4:46 for the mile, and then got faster as I progressed down. I also liked 8 x 1K at 3:00 or faster.

COLLEEN QUIGLEY
2016 OLYMPIAN

Speed Day is my favorite. You run as fast as you can, no holding back.

We don't do it very often. It's a warmup of 4 x 200m with a 30-second jog as our first set to get the legs moving. So I might do 32- to 33-second 200s there. Then you get a full rest, around 5 minutes. Then we might do 2 x 300m, which for example I might do at around 43 to 44 seconds. Then you get maximum rest again, as much as needed. Then we may do 8 x 150m, where you do a 50m build, getting faster every 50m from 3,000m pace to 800m pace. We walk back to the start for the rest period. For the end of the workout, you have 2 x 300 again and try to run equal to or faster than your first set of 300s.

It's not much mileage for the day, but it's super fun, and you're so lactic. You don't think you can physically do the 300s by the end. But then, somehow, you do!

COLLEEN DE REUCK
FOUR-TIME OLYMPIAN; WORLD CROSS-COUNTRY MEDALIST; BERLIN MARATHON CHAMPION

My favorite workouts are hill repeats. I don't go too far because I think if your form breaks down, then you lose some benefits. About the longest I would go would be 3 minutes. I like to do workouts like that, which are more on feel.

JACQUELINE HANSEN

WOMEN'S RUNNING PIONEER; TWO-TIME WORLD BEST MARATHON

I was raised on Laszlo Tabori's interval training. A favorite workout has been "25-lappers." These were solo workouts on the track. I absolutely loved them. Often they were my morning workout, and they served me well when traveling. No coach, no watch needed. Five laps warmup, followed by 5 sets of 4 laps each in this order:

- Lap 1 – 2 x 100 medium + jog the curves (100m)
- Lap 2 – 2 x 150 buildup + jog half of each curve (50m)
- Lap 3 – 2 x 100 medium + jog the curves
- Lap 4 – 2 x 100 all-out effort + jog the curves

This was a nonstop running effort throughout, just changing gears accordingly. No walk recovery, just jogging in between.

MOLLY HUDDLE

AMERICAN RECORD-HOLDER; TWO-TIME OLYMPIAN (AND COAUTHOR OF THIS BOOK!)

The workout that gets me fittest is the one I like the least: 2-mile repeats at just under threshold pace. It tests my ability to focus and be patient while in discomfort.

Example for a marathon buildup: 4 to 5 x 2 miles at 5:10 with 2.5 minutes rest. If I can do that, I know I'm ready!

HOW SHE STARTED

Here are some snapshots early in their careers of the runners you read about. See if you can guess who is who—and then flip back to their profile to see how much they've transformed since these early days! Answers on page 325.

1

2

14

15

16

17

18

19

20

21

22

23

24

25

26

27

KEY: 1) Amy Rudolph; 2) Elise Cranny;
3) Alie Wilson; 4) Molly Huddle;
5) Emily Sisson, 6) Marielle Hall;
7) Courtney Frerichs; 8) Hazel Clark;
9) Aliphine Tuliamuk; 10) Sara Slattery;
11) Jenny Simpson; 12) Emma Coburn;
13) Joan Benoit Samuelson; 14) Joetta
Clark Diggs; 15) Kara Goucher;
16) Jo Pavey; 17) Kathrine Switzer;
18) Kim Conley; 19) Lisa Aguilera;
20) Lynn Jennings; 21) Molly Seidel;
22) Nikki Hiltz; 23) Deena Kastor;
24) Raevyn Rogers; 25) Sara Hall;
26) Sonia O'Sullivan; 27) Des Linden

ACKNOWLEDGMENTS

MOLLY

This book was the ultimate collaboration, and we want to thank everyone involved.

Thank you to the women in the book for sitting down to talk with us, sometimes for hours at a time. Thank you to our experts who were happy to help guide young athletes toward their potential: Dr. John Ball, Dr. Randy Wilber, Dr. Trent Stellingwerff, Dr. Holly Thorpe, Ro McGettigan LMHC, Meg Waldron MS, Laura Moretti-Reece RD, Dr. Stacy Sims, and Dr. Adam Tenforde. Thank you to our agent, Danielle Svetcov, for connecting our idea to the people who could turn it into pages and for giving us great advice and pep talks. Thanks to Danielle Curtis, our editor, and the crew at Rodale and Penguin Random House for pulling it all together. Thank you, Scott Douglas, not only for helping us edit the interviews but also for the early advice about publishing. Thanks also to Cheryl Bridges Flanagan Treworgy and Victor Sailor for help collecting photos, and to Annika Sisson for helping us organize the early book stats and photos.

And thank you to our friends in the business who helped us interview women in other countries and in other languages: agents Ricky Simms and Brendan Reilly and Brett Larner of Japan Running News and the gracious Mika Tokairin for translating between myself and the Japanese athletes during our calls.

And finally, thank you to my husband, Kurt, for always being my best teammate as we focused on my running career and learned all these lessons together. Thank you to my coach, Ray Treacy, for steering me toward my potential on the track. And to the ladies I've trained with who showed me how to thrive in the sport: Kim Smith, Amy Rudolph, Roisin McGettigan, Mary Cullen, Amy Mortimer, Amy Hastings Cragg, and Emily Sisson—thanks for sweating alongside me and showing me the way!

SARA

First, I want to thank my family: my husband, Steve, who has been my biggest supporter, cheerleader, and motivater in whatever I pursue. I couldn't have done this without you. To Stevie and Cali, I love you more than I can ever explain. My parents, Terry and Helen Gorton, who have given me unconditional love, shown me how to work hard, and to always put family first. My sister, Lindsey, who is always there to listen and support me no matter how crazy my ideas are.

To the coaches I have worked with: Glen Coy, Steve Schafer, Sabrina Robinson, David Klecka, Mark Wetmore, Jason Drake, and Ricky Simms. You have made me a better person, athlete, and coach. I am so lucky to have your guidance and support.

Thank you to all my training partners and teammates throughout my career. Especially: Sally Meyerhoff, Maria and Anna Rodriguez, Jenny Doyle, Jorge and Ed Torres, Dathan Ritzenhein, Renee Metivier, Kara Goucher, Kendall Schoolmeester, Christine Bolf, Molly Londo, Natalie Severy, Jodie Hughes, Shayne Culpepper, Sara Hall, Jen Rhines, and Amy Cragg. You inspired me and taught me so much as an athlete.

My GCU family (my amazing athletes, colleagues, and administration). Especially my fellow track coaches: Tom Flood, Todd Lehman, Chris Riggs, Kenia Sinclair, Mary Duerbeck, Jonny Holsten, and Kayla Ferron—you make me truly love my job!

This book would not have come together without the efforts of so many people. A huge thank-you to all the support from all of the athletes and experts involved! So many women sacrificed their time and shared their stories, and I am so grateful!

Our experts were also so humble in sharing their wealth of knowledge to guide the next generation: Dr. John Ball, Dr. Randy Wilber, Dr. Trent Stellingwerff, Dr. Holly Thorpe, Ro McGettigan LMHC, Meg Waldron MS, Laura Moretti-Reece RD, Dr. Stacy Sims, and Dr. Adam Tenforde.

Thank you to our amazing agent Danielle Svetcov, who understood our vision and connected us with the right people to allow this book to come together; to Danielle Curtis and the Penguin Random House publishing team for making this book a reality; and to Scott Douglas for editing our interviews and making it all flow so well. We could not have done this without you!

ABOUT THE AUTHORS

MOLLY HUDDLE is a two-time Olympian for Team USA in the 5,000 meters and 10,000 meters, a six-time American record-holder, and a twenty-eight-time USA champion across road and track events. She lives between and trains in Providence, Rhode Island, and Scottsdale, Arizona, alongside her husband, Kurt Benninger, and her Yorkie mix named Rusty.

HIGH SCHOOL PRs:

MILE: 4:46
2 MILE: 10:01

COLLEGE PRs:

1,500 METERS: 4:22
3,000 METERS: 9:08
5,000 METERS: 15:32

PRO PRs:

1,500 METERS: 4:08
5,000 METERS: 14:42
10,000 METERS: 30:13
HALF MARATHON: 1:07:25
MARATHON: 2:26

SARA SLATTERY is an American middle- and long-distance runner who competed in track, cross-country, and road races. Slattery has represented the United States at the IAAF World Cross-Country Championships both at the junior and senior level and was a four-time NCAA champion. She is currently the head cross-country coach for men and women at Grand Canyon University and is one of the few women coaching both teams.

HIGH SCHOOL PRs:

800 METERS: 2:10
MILE: 4:47
3,200 METERS: 10:12
5K: 16:50

COLLEGE PRs:

800 METERS: 2:08
MILE: 4:40
1,500 METERS: 4:14
3K: 9:07
5K: 15:24

PRO PRs:

MILE: 4:32
3K: 8:57
5K: 15:08
10K: 31:57